CISTERCIAN STUDIES SERIES: NUMBER ONE-HUNDRED FIFTEEN

Sighard Kleiner

In the Unity of the Holy Spirit

By the same author:
Serving God First
Spiritual Conferences on the Rule of St Benedict

CISTERCIAN STUDIES SERIES: NUMBER ONE-HUNDRED FIFTEEN

IN THE UNITY OF THE HOLY SPIRIT

Spiritual Talks on the Rule of Saint Benedict

Sighard Kleiner, O.Cist.

Translated by
James Scharinger

Cistercian Publications
Kalamazoo, Michigan
1989

© Translation copyright,
Cistercian Publications Inc., 1989

Translated from the French: *Dans l'Unité du Saint-Ésprit. Entretiens spirituels sur la Règle de St Benoît.*
Paris: Librairie Pierre Téqui, 1980.

The editors express their appreciation to Peter Joyce for his help in preparing this manuscript for publication.

The work of Cistercian Publications is made possible in part by support from Western Michigan University to the Institute of Cistercian Studies.

Available in Britain and Europe through
A. R. Mowbray & Co Ltd
St Thomas House   Becket Street
Oxford   OX1 1SJ   England

Available elsewhere from the publisher:

Cistercian Publications Inc.
Editorial Offices:
Institute of Cistercian Studies
Western Michigan University
Kalamazoo, Michigan 49009

Distribution:
Cistercian Publications
St Joseph's Abbey
Spencer, MA 01562

Printed in the United States of America

Library of Congress Cataloguing-in-Publication Data
Kleiner, Sighard.
    [Dans l'unité du Saint-Ésprit. English]
    In the unity of the Holy Spirit : spiritual talks on the rule of Saint Benedict / Sighard Kleiner ; translated by James Scharinger.
        p.   cm. — (Cistercian studies series ; no. 115)
    Translation of: Dans l'unité du Saint-Ésprit.
    ISBN 0-87907-415-9. — ISBN 0-87907-715-8 (pbk.)
    1. Benedict, Saint, Abbot of Monte Cassino. Regula.
2. Benedictines—Rules. I. title. II Series.
BX3004.A2   1989
255₉.106—dc19   88-34190
                                                              CIP

TABLE OF CONTENTS

v

To my brothers and sisters
of the Order of Cîteaux

Frère Sighard Kleiner

The year 1980, which begins today, will remind us of the figure of St Benedict, whom Paul VI has proclaimed patron of Europe.... This date and this figure have such an eloquence, that a simple commemoration will not be enough; rather, it will be necessary to reread and to interpret the contemporary world in their light.

Of what does Saint Benedict of Nursia speak? *He speaks of the beginning of that gigantic work from which Europe was born.... The Benedictine spirit is the direct opposite of any program of destruction.* It is a spirit of saving and promoting. It is born of the consciousness of the divine plan of salvation, and trained in the daily union of prayer and labor.

...He also embraces the Europe of the future with his spirit.

Pope John Paul II
Homily of 1 January 1980

TRANSLATOR'S NOTE

We believe, of course, that everything is a matter of divine providence, but some things are more noticeably so than others. This translation strikes me particularly as a product of divine providence. I had just been promised a year of sick-leave from my parish work when Mother Paula of the Valley of Our Lady cistercian monastery told me about Dom Sighard Kleiner's second book. Knowing that I had translated his first book, *Serving God First*, Mother Paula wrote: 'So if you are someday in need of a worthwhile project, you could put it into English also'. Since I was about to begin a year of leisure (so I thought) I accepted, thinking to translate the work for the sisters and not knowing at first that it would be published.

I worked on the translation during the months that I was resting at Our Lady of the Prairies cistercian abbey at Holland, Manitoba. I had barely finished the next to the final draft when my bishop asked me to cut short my rest in order to take over a mission area which had become vacant. It seems that the Lord gave me just enough time off to be able to complete this work.

My enthusiasm for the present work might well be expressed in the very words of Mother Paula: '...it is indeed a wonderful book, worth many times more than much of the stuff published today'. I am grateful for her encouragement. Another big source of encouragement has been the community at Our Lady of the Prairies where most of my work on this translation took place. I thank the monks of this monastery as well as the sisters of Valley of Our Lady for having the manuscript read in their refectories and for offering their corrections and suggestions which were incorporated into the final draft.

A special thanks is due to Brother Bernard, keeper of the gatehouse where I stayed while translating. How many times I interrupted his work to ask his opinion on this or that turn of phrase, always to find him both helpful and interested. It was no doubt also by divine providence that I should find myself in this bilingual monastery with a bilingual gatekeeper, but then, everything occurs by divine providence, including the publication of this book.

Advent, 1984

James G. Scharinger
Oblate of Hauterive

PREFACE

History shows us that the Rule of St Benedict, in spite of its antiquity, has lost none of its relevance. And why? Observing due proportion, one might apply to it these words of Our Lord: 'My words are spirit and life' (cf. Jn 6:63). Many passages, it is true, and even entire chapters of the Rule have fallen into disuse, the letter no longer responding to contemporary needs or practices. Some have gone so far as to make abridged editions of the Rule. For all of that, the spirit has not abandoned the Rule, which is what explains that continuance upon which time wreaks no havoc. It is one of those rare human documents in which a mind close to God expresses itself with liberty, charity, and firmness, and does not fetter the spirit which, on the contrary, it aids in developing and in lifting toward the eternal destinies. This combination of qualities is at the root of the vitality of the Rule. It has permitted generations of monks who were afire seeking God to omit this or that secondary prescription of the Rule which would have impeded their journey toward the Lord, while leaving the way open to other generations, in the name of reform, to reinstate the Rule with greater fidelity where human misunderstanding or laxity had betrayed the spirit incarnate in its text.

Some have held that the Rule was written under a sort of inspiration. Why not? That inspiration which animates the Holy Scripture and makes of it the Word of God is not in question. But has the Church not recieved the promise of the special aid of the Holy Spirit? If pastors receive it in a special way, then surely the holy animators of the great renewal movements in the Church were led by the Holy Spirit in a very special way. St Benedict was one of them, and the authority of his Rule over 1500 years is an indirect proof that successive generations have recognized in it a privileged expression of the Holy Spirit. Certainly, each prescription or counsel is not thereby sanctioned in its practical usefulness, and every age recognizes what is suitable for itself. It is also necessary to take into account the literary *genre*, that is to say, the character proper to a monastic rule. Nevertheless, nothing prevents us from thinking that God has given in the Rule of St Benedict a document of great

3

religious value, capable of leading generations of monks, and even Christians in general, to familiarize themselves with the Word of the Lord and to sanctify themselves.

It is, therefore, the seal of the Spirit which distinguishes this little book, without, however, conferring divine authority on it. The author of the Rule was a man. Its validity is measured by its conformity with the Word of God, the Holy Scriptures, which are its source and touchstone. Whereas the Holy Scriptures judge the Church, the Rule is judged by the Church from which it receives its authority. It is not an absolute, but it should be interpreted and applied according to the criteria to which all human authority should be submitted: the Spirit of God who speaks to the Churches (cf. Rv 2:7) and through the Church. Certainly, the Holy Spirit speaks in very different ways to the Church for the building up of the Body of Christ (cf. Eph 4:16). But the duty of determining where there is a manifestation of the Holy Spirit or of the spirit of man falls to the Church.

In order to pass judgment, the Church has received from the Lord the gift of the discernment of spirits, which she exercises according to the criterion which he confided to her: 'You will know them by their fruits' (cf. Mt 7:16). The Rule of St Benedict has often been praised by the voice of supreme pontiffs. Let us mention only the encyclical *Fulgens Radiatur*, where Pius XII affirms that Benedict 'was led not by human, but by divine counsel' because Providence had imparted to him a word which was entirely special and important. In this way the Church recognizes implicitly that the Holy Spirit who governs her was not a stranger to the composition of the Rule, the work of St Benedict. As a matter of fact, the *magisterium* of the Church cannot recommend a work in which the mark of the Holy Spirit is not found. The fact that the Rule of St Benedict has attracted and sanctified hundreds of thousands of men and women is already a sign of consensus of the People of God in union with their pastors. The Holy Spirit, by means of this Rule, has given a priceless gift to his Church.

Undoubtedly, he teaches his Church (cf. Jn 14:26) in a mysterious way and unceasingly distributes his charisms for the common good (1 Co 12:7). In the same way as the *Imitation of Christ* of Thomas à Kempis can be considered one of these gifts of the Spirit for building up the Body of Christ, so also, St Benedict is one of the great charismatics of the Church whose work carries with it the savor of the Spirit.

But it is necessary to know how to read his language throughout his works. And if the Rule is one of his manifestations (cf. 1 Co 12:7), and if, on the other hand, no one can affirm that each and every detail can be accepted as such, we propose to point out the marks of the Spirit in the Rule, insofar as that is possible. Is it pretentious to wish to attempt such a task? We will carry this out very modestly by seeking to find, all through the text and between the lines, the signs which respond to the characteristic traits of the Spirit, as he has revealed himself throughout the Sacred Books. Our work will be like that of a son seeking to discover the spiritual countenance of his revered father, whom he has not known, and whose character traits he collects: his tendencies and his ideas, in the work which he has left and in which he lives on.

Seeking and discovering the manifestations of the Spirit in the Rule will at the same time make us discover the spiritual personality of St Benedict, who is a veritable Spirit-bearer, and will, we hope, permit us to win new admirers over to that Rule. Certain people, in fact, may have been put off until now by the concrete wording of a work linked to a past age and masking the full effectiveness which the Rule can contribute to the spiritual person of our times.

We will leave in the background the question concerning the author of these texts. As the basis of our conferences, we will take the Rule as it is read in our monasteries and considered to be an authentic text. St Benedict is an historical person, clearly portrayed in what St Gregory the Great has told us about him, and in the characteristic modifications he made to the text of the *Rule of the Master*. In attributing the Rule to him, we do no injury to other authors from whom St Benedict has generously drawn, in the very first place to the 'Master', because the typical modifications he made on the pre-existent texts show that he made them his own and covered them with his full spiritual authority. Some people have thought that several chapters should be attributed to different authors coming after St Benedict. Let us repeat here that for us the problem consists not in knowing who the first authors of these passages were, but in how the action of the Holy Spirit appears and manifests itself through the Rule attributed to St Benedict.

As we have written in publishing the book, *Serving God First*, we wish to repeat here all our thanks to the Mother Prioress and the

6

nuns of the Cistercian Monastery of Sainte-Marie de Boulaur dans le Gers, for the precious help of a technical nature which has greatly facilitated the publication of this book. May the Holy Spirit reward them by realizing in them the promise made by the prophet Joel: '…upon my servants I will pour out my Spirit' (Ac 2:18), and may he make their community grow 'in number and in virtue' (from the Missal).

Quotations from the Rule refer to the edition of Rudolphus Hanslik, *Benedicti Regula*. Editio altera emendata. Corpus scriptorum ecclesiasticorum latinorum, 75. Vindobonae, 1977.

INTRODUCTION

IN THE UNITY OF THE HOLY SPIRIT

THE MONK, BY DEFINITION, is a man (or woman!) of one sole purpose: God. By vocation he undertakes to fight against dissipation. The Holy Spirit is divine Love, Love which embraces the whole universe in one bound and leads all things back to the Father, that God may be all in all. The monk desires to let himself be carried away by Love, by the Spirit, so that his love may be ever purer, ever more united, and that its dynamics of unity may embrace the whole world, and in particular, those who are near him, his brothers in religion, arriving thus at the union and the love of the Father, his rallying-place, his peace, his life.

With its many counsels and prescriptions, a Rule written for monks and monasteries, as also the various commentaries on that Rule, offers numerous subjects of interest, and is addressed to each person according to his (or her) particular character, aptitudes, and basic education, as well as according to his personal way of living or of dealing with problems. Everything is aimed at seeking God in the monastic way of life. This way should not alienate, but rather, give each person the means of fulfilling himself so as to arrive at a maximum of serenity and peace. These are the effects of divine grace, which is received with eagerness, and of the instruction of the Rule, which is the teacher of life.

Now this delicate work can be accomplished only beneath the infinitely tender and unifying touch of the Spirit of God, who is Harmony personified and Love, without which no work above the powers of nature can be accomplished. The Holy Spirit will bring about unity in the soul of each monk who becomes tractable beneath his pacifying action. He alone is able to succeed in co-ordinating the individuals in the monastic community with their personal attributes, and in making of them a constructive force of present and eternal life.

A monastery ought to be under the influence and the guidance of the Spirit; otherwise it will find itself faced with insoluble problems,

7

8

both community and individual. May these conferences, modest collection of considerations that they are, help those responsible for the monastic life orientate themselves toward the Holy Spirit, who is always ready to come to the help of those who call upon him with faith! Come, Holy Spirit!

Beyond this Introduction, no attempts have been made at 'inclusive language' in the translation of pronouns which, in French, refer to women as well as men. 'Monk' should be taken as a person vowed to observe the Rule of St Benedict — ed.

THE IMPRINT
OF THE HOLY SPIRIT
IN THE RULE

WE CALL IT THE 'HOLY Rule'. Now, all holiness comes from the
Holy Spirit who, with the Father and the Son, is alone Holy by
essence. Yet we should not be surprised that we do not find the Holy
Spirit explicitly named more than four times in the Rule, and then
only in passing. St Benedict did not choose to bolster the merits of
his prescriptions with theology; moreover, he did not wish to write
a treatise on theology. He has given us a theology which has been
lived, when he teaches us the instruments of the theological life.
Knowing the Spirit is not, for him, having a treatise on the ways of
the Holy Spirit, but finding himself under the influence of the Spirit
by following the Rule and by its power. As a matter of fact, the Spirit
is so far from being a stranger to this venerable work that the very
letter of the Rule exercises a great influence on our souls. This is
the concrete fruit of the profound imprints of the operation of the
Holy Spirit.

It is for us, then, to follow these imprints, to adore and to admire
the sweet force of the Spirit, who, by means of the Rule, purifies,
enlightens, and sanctifies many souls.

In wishing to analyse the work of the Holy Spirit in the Rule, let
us not fall into the error of letting ourselves be impressed by certain
phrases or prescriptions which, from our point of view, seem due
more to the human spirit than to the Divine. We know that the Holy
Spirit breathes where he wills and operates as he wishes. The channels of his grace can be the work of man and even show in a glaring
manner the imperfections of the human co-operation. They serve
none the less as vehicles of the Spirit to give us his grace or to touch
us inwardly. The literary *genre* of many passages of the Rule may
seem to us too closely connected with historical circumstances, with
narrow views, with a state of science now obsolete. The Holy Spirit

is free in his action. He is not prisoner of the human word, even if its expression appears beautiful or true to us. He passes through the words, between the words, outside the words. He expresses himself perfectly where the words stammer. He touches the heart where the Rule frightens or shocks us.

By what right do we say this? Is this a lot of pretension? If we listen to the Rule with the ear of the heart (RB prol. 1.9) in its substance, its marrow, its characteristic doctrine, we will perceive there the pure breath of the Spirit.

Let us make a little digression here. The temptation may arise to proceed by cutting the Rule up into little pieces, relegating chapters or sentences which no longer square with our twentieth-century views to the category of outdated ideas, thus reducing the Rule to whatever is left after that. If that is done *ad usum Delphini*, for people in the world, let it pass. It would be hard for them to understand why St Benedict speaks of using the rod, should the need arise. But the Holy Spirit—who is not afraid to threaten us with the eternal punishment of the damned whose lot is to be the 'weeping and gnashing of teeth' (Mt 8:12 etc.)—can make us understand the seriousness of our commitments by means of the sharp admonitions stated by the Rule, even though we know that today these warnings are not literally carried out. The monk learns to read the Rule as he should likewise learn to read the books of the Old Testament. He knows that the Rule of St Benedict should not be read like a modern book on ascetic doctrine. He also knows that people's manners and customs have changed considerably since the sixth century and that St Benedict had to treat people in line with the attitudes they had acquired during the course of their education at that period and according to contemporary ways of thinking.

We might also fall into another trap: That is to say, we might attribute what concerns monastic discipline, observances, structures, the institution, exclusively to St Benedict's spirit of organization and limit the Spirit's action to the spiritual part of the Rule. Some go farther still and retain only the purely spiritual doctrine of the Rule as a value which transcends times and places. In other words, the imprints of the operation of the Holy Spirit should be sought not in the institution, but only in the ascetic doctrine. The truth is somewhere in between. To attribute to the Holy Spirit the details of the monastic discipline proposed by the Rule would be to make him responsible for trifles of passing worth. To exclude from his action all that pertains to the institution would be to exclude from the Rule the Breath which gives the structures their superior authority and all the sanctifying power that dwells in them. As a matter of fact, it is not for us to try to limit the action of the Spirit. He breathes where he wills, inside and outside human frameworks, and he transcends them infinitely. To wish to limit his action to what is purely spiritual would be to end up in a dichotomy contrary to the great mystery of the Incarnation, through which God has deigned to identify himself with all that is truly human, and to open to all that is human the door of the Most Blessed Trinity.

The present book proposes to try to discover the sanctifying action of the Holy Spirit throughout the monastic institution of the Rule of St Benedict, and to make known how the whole theology of that life is manifested in his fundamental marks. The Spirit introduces us to knowledge of the Father with the figure of the abbot, and through his teaching reveals to us the action of the divine Word. It is also the Spirit who speaks to the heart by means of *lectio divina* and the entire liturgy, and unites the brethren inasmuch as he is the bond of charity and peace that makes of them the Body of Christ. It is he who operates in their hearts by means of *conversatio morum*, conversion as a continual excelling in charity. Through his gifts he enlightens and deepens the faith of the monk and helps him, little by little, by climbing the ladder of humility, to lift the too-fine screen which his attachments and desires oppose to the manifestations of God's love. He introduces him little by little into the school of prayer of which He is the Master, in order to awaken and deepen in him the awareness that he is, in very truth, a son adopted by the Father.

The monk is a person like others. On the level of perfection, nothing distinguishes him from his fellows, except that he has been admitted into an 'institutional intimacy' with the Spirit, the Director of souls. His condition is a privileged one, thanks to the Rule of St Benedict who, as long as he remains his faithful disciple, guides him along the paths of the Spirit.

The Rule is not, in fact, a book inspired in the same way as the Holy Scriptures, the Word of God, but it is nevertheless true that the light and the grace of the Spirit operate mysteriously within the Rule. The fruits of holiness and the beneficial effects that it has produced in the Church throughout the ages proves this. Without the Spirit, the Rule would have remained a dead letter. Thanks to the Spirit, it has become the 'Holy Rule'.

THE CALL
OF THE SPIRIT

'VOCATION' is a burning issue. If it is so much discussed today, it is under the heading of goods from which we suffer by default.

'Vocation'. The word itself means call—*vocatus*, 'vocation'. The Lord has come to call each and every one of us to the Kingdom of Heaven. Let us recall the parable of the wedding feast: *vocatus ad nuptias*. The wedding feast is the Kingdom of Heaven. It is the Lord's place to call those who have been given him by the Father. He tells us this during the final high-priestly prayer: The Father has given him a certain number of persons—it seems that there is already a restriction in the very phrase 'those whom you have given me'. It expresses a selection, a choice, a preference for some, a refusal of others. Yet, our faith in the infinite love of God makes us add here that the disfavor for those who are not called to salvation cannot have its reason for being in God, and is explained by the refusal which some oppose to the universal choice of God.

It is a matter, then, of a call. Think of the call Christ made to the apostles: to Peter, to Andrew, to John, and to James. The Gospel is extremely laconic on this matter: *vocavit eos*, he called them, and they followed him. Afterwards he loved to repeat to them, 'I myself have chosen you; I am sending you'. He wanted to make a sort of ceremony of choosing them; with the disciples and apostles assembled before him, he called the twelve one by one 'to himself' (Mk 3:13). It is, therefore, Jesus who chooses. The apostles themselves do not choose: 'It is not you who have chosen me; it is I who have chosen you' (Jn 15:16).

There is essentially in every vocation, then, the call of Christ, or, to put it another way, the call of grace, of the Holy Spirit. Thus we are all called to baptism to live in Christ, to be incorporated into the Church and into the Kingdom of Heaven; and we know that this is a grace, the grace of vocation. The Lord has called us to his Kingdom; (RB prol. 21), says St Benedict, making his Rule begin with a call, an echo of the divine call: 'Listen, my Son' (RB prol. 1).

13

Is it not simply St Benedict who is calling there? Now, the question is: who is calling? The apostles, Christ in person called. But Christ is no longer here; he no longer calls as he once did. So, who calls? We are not deceiving ourselves if, in the last analysis, we decide that through the Holy Spirit, the Lord is always calling us to follow him along extraordinary paths, for example, those of the priesthood or the religious life. But his voice makes itself heard ordinarily through the Church to which he has given the power to call men to the Kingdom of Heaven, to baptism, to life in Christ. It is the Church which calls to the apostolate, to commit oneself to the salvation of others, to ministries, and especially, to the priesthood. It is also the Church that calls to the religious life. It is always the Church that calls. When a call comes to a special task in the life of the Church, which is the mystical Christ, it is always for the Church to invite. It is she who urges and calls, and the more special a vocation is, so much more is special the call. The Pope names the bishop; it is for him to choose, and not for the bishop to present himself saying: 'I feel that I have the right qualifications for being a bishop'. The Pope calls in the name of the Holy Spirit, for 'the Holy Spirit has appointed you as guardians to shepherd the Church of God', as St Paul reminds the 'elders' of the church of Ephesus (cf. Ac 20:17,28). Likewise, the bishop calls to the priesthood. The candidate does not approach on his own initiative; the Epistle to the Hebrews makes this very clear (Heb 5:4): 'No one takes this honor upon himself; he must be called to it by God, just as Aaron was.' The candidate may reveal that he possesses the qualities to be a priest, but the call itself must come from the Church. It is up to the bishop to call or to refuse him, for it is his ministry and his charism to judge the signs of vocation.

As regards the religious life, admitting to the novitiate and to profession, according to Canon Law, the Rule, and the Constitutions, belongs to the superior who, with the consent of his council, calls the candidates or refuses them according to the signs of their vocation. The candidate, for all that, does not remain entirely passive. St Benedict, after having subjected him to probation (cf. RB 58:1-8), puts this question to him: 'Behold the law under which you wish to fight. If you can observe it, enter; if not, you are free to leave' (RB 58:10). In other words, he is asked whether he feels called to that life. Nevertheless, even according to Canon Law, it is up to the superior to make the final judgment and to 'call' in the name of God.

It is necessary to notice two reactions in this matter: firstly, that of the one called; secondly, that of the one calling. The final judgment belongs to the latter. But how shall I undertake the necessary steps to realize my vocation unless I know, at least generally, that I have been called?

All things considered, the answer to this problem is simple. Neither the superior nor the candidate can count on inspiration to determine the reality of the candidate's vocation. The superior should, therefore, form his judgment from what we usually call the signs of the vocation. The candidate is also able to recognize these signs and to quiz himself on them.

We have said that one should not count on inspirations or on an express call from the Lord—'Come, follow me', like the call addressed to Peter, Andrew, and the other apostles: yet, we are not by any means to exclude the possibility of such an intervention, and there are extraordinary cases of it happening. Many of us have, in a wider sense, heard some sort of secret call, some invitation, have felt an impulse capable of transforming into certitude our attraction to follow the Lord more closely. At the moment, we did not have a clear consciousness of it, but it did not occur to us to doubt. Grace strengthened us in our choice and established us in our path. Yet, even there, mistakes are possible. Where do those inspirations come from anyway? They may come from grace, as they may also come from the voice of nature. Hidden there may be a too natural attraction, an unconscious seeking of human advantages, an unexpressed need for being settled, or even for fleeing certain efforts. In brief, someone who feels called should ask if he finds in himself the signs of a priestly, religious, or monastic vocation. Anyone can be mistaken; therefore, in order to avoid missteps, it is advisable to ask the opinion of a man of God, a director of souls, or a competent confessor. With the support of such a favourable judgment, the candidate can then address himself with more certainty to the person who has to make the final judgment.

One more remark: in principle, the invitation of the Church to a ministry or to the religious life, does not necessarily have to be preceded by a desire on the part of the person called, or by a feeling that he has a call. God is sovereign in his will, and the competent authority of the Church can make a call of that sort in his name by recognizing in the subject the objective signs of a vocation, which he can then freely accept or refuse. St Ambrose was postulated for the See of Milan by the throng of Christians without having thought about it in advance.

In sum, it is always the Lord who calls, first by putting the desire for a vocation into the chosen soul, or again by making him hear a mysterious voice, or more simply by addressing that invitation to him in a family setting or in the course of an event which is in itself unimportant. But in any case, the Lord will verify that vocation through the competent advice of a representative of the Church.

We have alluded to the signs of a vocation which, in lieu of a special inspiration, enable us to discern divine grace working in a soul to guide it toward the monastic life, and then, in the name of the Lord, to make a decision for admission to the novitiate and to profession. St Benedict requires that the candidate be tested in order to know if his intentions come from God (cf. RB 58:1f). The fifty-eighth chapter of the Rule makes this clearly understood, for the master of novices ought to 'watch over them very attentively in order to discern if each of them truly seeks God, if he has zeal for the Work of God, for obedience, and for humiliations' (RB 58:7). These are the most important objective signs which serve as criteria for the abbot and for those responsible for discerning a monastic vocation.

The first sign given by St Benedict, 'if the novice truly seeks God', is absolutely fundamental, and one could write a book on the subject. Let us limit ourselves to the essential. In a human soul, orientation toward God can be dominant and theological, or accessory and utilitarian, or finally, non-existent. There is no need to speak of the third case. In the second case, the cares and pleasures of the world suffocate and choke the faith which exists in the soul; it seeks God not for his own sake, but to escape misfortune. To become a monk under such circumstances is to risk wasting one's life, for God is not the first one served and is not really the most loved. It is a matter here of an indispensable sign of the monastic vocation. The postulant should therefore examine the deep motivations which led him to knock at the monastery door: whether he truly seeks God, or whether, in fact, that quest is rather a pretext for finding something else.

The three other signs: zeal for the *Opus Dei*, for obedience, and for humiliations, are dependent on the first condition, adding to it a community dimension. A cenobitic monastic life does not exist without prayer in common, without a regime governed by obedience, and without a readiness to overcome pride and points of honor. St Benedict requires of the beginner a zeal which is entire and which does not count the cost, because he knows that a monk does not truly seek God if he does not direct all his fervor toward arriving at the love of God. Now, he will attain it by these means, which are efficacious *par excellence*; the recognition of the living sovereignty of God, divine praise in common, and loving submission to what comes from God and is made visible in his representative. The beginner will learn respect and mutual love of the brethren and the joyous acceptance of all the renunciations of those things to which he may think he has a right.

But the young person who has within himself the desire to turn toward the monastic life and knock at the door of the monastery, has not yet arrived there. He must have the signs of a vocation *before* he presents himself at the monastery. And, to be more exact, he must have *perceptible* signs in order to begin his project. These signs come in an unlimited variety, and we must add to them those favourable dispositions which are capable of preparing one for a call from the Lord. We will list some of them here without distinguishing them from things which are signs in the strict sense of the word. They are graces, not of nature, but of divine election, beginning with baptism, a Christian education, an orientation toward the service of God since childhood and youth, a precocious piety toward Christ and the Eucharist, and finally, a devotion to the Blessed Virgin. Those are some of the privileged dispositions. But more and more the call of God is making itself heard to men and women whose youth was not spent in a Christian environment, who, spiritually speaking, come from afar off. The Lord has met them at a turning point of their life and has desired to enroll them in his personal service. He wants to show toward them the abundance of his grace and the power of the Spirit that animates them (cf. Rm 8:14).

To these signs of divine grace it is proper to add natural predispositions: the healthy environment where vocations develop more easily, like plants in good soil. A great part of the success of a vocation comes from parents, ancestors, and family with all its store of good physical and mental dispositions, its strong and wise traditions concerning material, religious, and moral life where the principles of the faith dominate. All this may be decisive for the natural equilibrium and for the openness of the soul to grace and to good influences. On the other hand, anomalies in the family life often mark the child deeply and make it less easy for him to integrate himself into common life and social life, and may even disturb his normal progress in a life lived according to the faith. Where a father or mother has left a painful memory in the child, he may be traumatized and may later risk having difficulties in developing normal relationships with his superiors.

Grace presupposes nature. What pertains to the moral character of a man improves with time for the one who co-operates with patience and humility. But we must not expect miracles, and grace rarely corrects serious tendencies of a psychosomatic origin; they revive periodically. Those superiors who confuse them with faults of the moral order and accept such subjects—however out of place in a religious community—and who believe that they will be able to convert them, do an injustice to their community and to the candidates themselves by exposing them to situations which they are not able to confront without harming themselves. For example, a person so lacking in judgment that he can see faults only in others and who reacts to any kind of correction by making a scene, would always be a cross for the common life.

It is true that St Benedict seems to have been very generous in admitting subjects, for he counted among his monks the indocile, the turbulent, the negligent, the rebellious, the bad-natured, the disobedient, the stubborn, and the proud (ch. RB 2:25, 28). It is not impossible that there were among them men who were unsound, for in those days people were much more tempted to call a moral fault what would today be classified as an unfortunate psychosomatic disposition rendered incorrigible by habit. On the other hand, the methods of correction were rude, and St Benedict used them, calling for corporal chastisement (cf. RB 2:28; see the chapters on the penitential code). The practices of the time also explain the existence of prisons in medieval monasteries.

Let us return to more pleasant things. A vast range of possibilities, of professions, or activities opens before the young person looking for his final vocation. Little by little the choice narrows down, becoming more definite until it finally stops at the monastic vocation. The sweet and infinitely loving work of the Holy Spirit can be seen in that inclination which takes form and asserts itself, and if that good desire is confirmed by joy and ardor in the service of God, by the need to discipline oneself and to sanctify oneself by dedicating oneself to the will of the Lord out of love for the Church and its interests, and especially by a disposition full of charity towards one's neighbor, then the call of the Lord is certain, and the young person would let pass an exceptional opportunity for making his life a success if he resisted the Spirit's overtures (cf. Mt 19:22f).

The monastic vocation has, indeed, special signs. A certain natural attraction for solitude and silence can be a positive sign, but if there is a need to run away from difficulties, to flee before the struggle of life, or a certain inability to overcome the problems of the social order, then it would be negative. Negative also would be an excessive timidity accompanied by the fear of facing others. On the other hand, the attraction for solitude is a precious trump if it is balanced by a good measure of spontaneous sociability and of the spirit of commitment. The attraction for solitude is indispensable in a vocation where the hours of silent occupation, of common and private prayer, of meditation and study of the Sacred Scriptures are many and leave the monk face to face with himself. It is clear that a disposition to purity of heart is necessary from the very beginning in order to find one's happiness in solitude with the Lord. The restless person, subject to superficial agitation, will have many obstacles to overcome, but he can learn to calm his life in the sweet and serene heart of the Lord.

As a general rule, one must remember before committing oneself that theological adage that grace presupposes the nature which it perfects. It would, therefore, be false, through a spirit of sacrifice or humility, to wish to hide or stifle those abilities which would not find their full development in the monastery. On the other hand, the Benedictine life, as history shows us, offers an extraordinary adaptability, and, provided it can be integrated into the monastic society, almost every talent can be developed there. Impressive lists of men of worth: philosophers, theologians, astronomers, biologists, mathematicians, poets, painters, technicians, and architects, as well as every kind of craftsman, prove this. On the other hand, the Benedictine life shows us the ease with which it permits the development of the handicapped, the blind, the crippled, the seriously ill who have left to the world the memory of their works and to the monastery the memory of their holy life.

A hearty, growing concern for the interests of the monastic community is a general sign of a vocation. A natural affection for the life and for the persons in that community prepares the heart to docility and to the acceptance of the renunciations which always crop up in the details of daily life. It sensitizes the heart to the spirit of fraternal charity and mutual assistance which supports each person, while still allowing it freedom of judgment and decision. The human person has a natural intuition for discerning means which favor his growth, progress, physical and moral health. He can prudently let himself be guided by this gift of God.

Certain aspirants to the monastic life hesitate to get started, although realizing that they are called, or they search indefinitely, running from monastery to monastery to find their ideal. Such intemperance has nothing spiritual about it and leads to indecision and to the failure of vocation. If the Lord guides us along the path and leads us to this or that community, we must have confidence in him and accept the risk. And then, once profession has been made and the alliance concluded with him, we must not look back again, neither to one side nor to the other.

In conclusion: if God calls us to the religious life, guided by human beings who are, it is true, fallible, we must have confidence in the Lord—a prayerful confidence. He will support the humble efforts to be faithful of those he has accepted into his special service: 'to stand in your presence and serve you' (Eucharistic Prayer II). The Spirit is not deceived and does not deceive. 'It is by the grace of God that I am what I am' (cf. 1 Co 15:10).

BECOMING HUMAN

GOD BECOME HUMAN

BECOMING HUMAN—are we not that already? So why speak this way? The Son of God becomes human—an unfathomable mystery. He becomes what he was not. An infant, he enters into life, he grows, he becomes an adult. Should we dare pretend that we have no need to become human, that is to say, to grow with age in wisdom and in the grace of God, as well as in the perfection of human nature?

We might assert that, to be human, it is enough to be an adopted child of God. The grace of divine filiation, does it not include, does it not transcend all that nature can offer us in the line of fulfillment?

Now, the Son of God has become human 'like unto man' (Ph 2:7), our brother, in taking upon himself individualization and all the limits which go along with human nature, except sin. He became human, too, with all the potentialities for perfecting the human moral personality, having immense riches to begin with, of course, but also having the possibility of developing his human character.

From whom did Jesus receive his admirable individuality, his manly and generous character, entirely dedicated to his human brothers? The answer to that question was given to Mary: 'The Holy Spirit will come upon you' (Lk 1:35). It is the Spirit who formed the man Jesus in the womb of the Virgin. It is he who made him grow in wisdom and in grace and who, throughout his whole life, formed the human heart of Jesus, so united to himself that he can be called the Spirit of Jesus.

THE HOLY SPIRIT AT WORK

Certainly, the work of the Spirit is above all a work of grace which transcends the formation of nature. But the Spirit Creator formed and forms man in his entirety. Adam was his work. He is the Former and the Educator of the whole person, and fashions persons in the order of nature as well as in the order of grace. For him there are no limits; the entire person is the work of his love.

21

Let us note, this work of the Spirit forming the heart of man in the area of grace has some repercussions, some wonderful consequences from which the whole man benefits. Jesus grew in divine grace, and the fact that he grew in grace before men in the human arena was simply a consequence of this. In spite of the essential distinction between the two orders of nature and of grace, the unity of the human personality requires that as grace presupposes nature, so nature profits from the work of grace.

The monk, if he has the required dispositions, finds himself in blessed possession of the grace of the monastic vocation, a special grace of the Spirit, about which the prologue of the Rule speaks to us in enthusiastic terms. Within his reach, wonderful opportunities for human growth under the operation of grace are available. Silence of passions and thoughts, calm attention to the divine presence, simple and confident prayer prepare the soul to receive the delicate touches of the divine artist who works in our souls and forms there the image of Christ, the most beautiful of the sons of man. He works there, sometimes by arousing sad experiences to purify the soul, sometimes by encouraging it to acts of generosity and to victorious renunciations. He also enlightens it so it can arrive at a deeper knowledge of its good qualities and of its faults, so as to correct its deficiencies and its infidelities. Thus, thanks to the gentle and powerful work of the Holy Spirit, the human person is formed in us, revealing little by little his true identity, that is to say, the idea God had of us in his eternal foreknowledge.

The monk ought, therefore, on his part, to welcome the formative action of the Spirit of God with complete receptiveness. From the moment he realizes that the Spirit is offering to take his education in hand, he ought to prepare himself to receive, with joy in his heart, his admonitions and his inspirations with complete docilty. Let him repeat with his whole soul the words of the Virgin Mary: 'Be it done unto me according to your word' (Lk 1:38). Knowing that the work of his perfection in grace and his sanctification depend entirely on the Holy Spirit and that he cannot add a thing to it, he should submit himself, in imitation of Jesus, by a joyous and unconditional obedience, to the action of the Spirit. Yet this is not a matter of passive attitude. He should co-operate with that action of the Spirit by removing the obstacles which oppose His work, so as to prepare for Him a virgin land, cleared of dross and inordinate attachments, that is to say, of the desires of the triple concupiscence.

In the very work of purification, the monk has great need of the help of the Spirit who alone is pure and capable of ridding his creature of sin and its consequences.

In the course of this work of interior purification, the monk should avoid the danger of counting on only his own strength like the ancient pagan philosophers or according to the methods used by the non-christian monks for whom asceticism found its end in itself or in man as such. The Spirit cannot work in a person who is sure of himself and of his personal effectiveness. The purification of the soul and the formation of the character cannot, it is true, take place without asceticism, but asceticism nourishes pride if the Holy Spirit is not its ally. See why, from the very prologue of his Rule, St Benedict invites the monk to prayer: 'Above all, ask him by fervent prayer to lead to a good conclusion every good work that you begin' (RB prol. 4). Now, what good work is he talking about? St Benedict invites him to traverse, in reverse order, the path travelled by Adam from the time he was obedient until he became disobedient; in other words, to tend to the state of the former Adam, to become again the person that Adam was, and this by obedience, following him who through obedience has restored the state of justice in sinful humanity (cf. Rm 5:19).

WHAT THE RULE SAYS ABOUT THIS

Was it St Benedict's concern to make the monk a new person, a new Adam? Practically speaking, he does not make a distinction between the person who is good by nature and the person who is restored by grace. For him, to become a child of God, given the consequences of the action of grace on nature, is the same as to become a true human being. And, as a matter of fact, a person living in the grace of the Spirit, penetrated by his charity, possesses all the conditions for becoming man according to the image of the perfect Man, the second Adam. St Benedict's counsels, the exhortations, the instruments of good works (cf. RB 4), in short, all that concerns the formation of the monk, finds its meaning in the area of the moral virtues as in the framework of the life of grace. Although St Benedict is conscious of the limited powers of nature (cf. RB prol. 41), he feels no necessity of drawing a line of demarcation between the two orders.

Today, modern man sees the task of his humanization, of his fulfillment in his human qualities, as a personal duty imposed on him by the Creator. The Holy Spirit has formed him in the image of God in his psychological and physiological being, in his sociological condition. With God's help, he follows his vocation as one predestined, by reproducing in himself the image of the Son of God (cf. Rm 8:29). If he perfects himself as a human person, he will be more in accordance with the image of God and consequently will offer to grace a terrain better prepared to receive the likeness of Christ. Grace supposes, then, the use of the powers of nature. Man is called to co-operate with the Holy Spirit whose love urges him to reproduce in himself the image of the Son of God. The anthropological turn taken by the attitude of man over several centuries requires that we take into account the proper value of human dignity and the dimensions of its potentialities.

Monastic life contains stimulants which are very simple, but which concur powerfully in human development 'Seeking God' (cf. RB 58:7) keeps a person continually alert and makes him conscious that he is a pilgrim on a journey. Striving for the virtues (cf. RB 4), enlistment in an army (cf. RB prol. 3, ch. 2:20), the idea of a school (cf. RB prol. 45), suggest a state of continual growth. Certain monks respond better than others to the Lord's call, run faster, and progress more actively (cf. RB prol.). But above all, charity is vigorously stimulated. All this presupposes a development in the monk and a perfecting of his knowledge and his energies.

On the other hand, St Benedict is rather sober on the subject of institutions apt for the promotion of human qualities. It is principally in working that a man perfects himself. He learns, develops his faculties, goes out of himself, and outdoes himself (cf. the Pastoral Constitution *Gaudium et Spes*, 35). The possibility of cultivating himself stimulates him to do it—St Benedict does not speak of this in an explicit way, but the monastic day as he conceives it—*lectio divina*, the organization of work and the conventual life, the fact that the monastery is economically independent with the repercussions of this on activities, the desire to organize the industries necessary for the life on the spot, such as bakery, mill, etc., instruction to be given to young people, the employments to be carried out intelligently — are so many stimulants for acquiring new knowledge, for making discoveries and inventions, in a word, for bringing about an improvement in the quality of life of the brethren and, as a consequence, a better quality of life in the community. The history of Benedictine monasticism in this area is a good witness to the dynamics of the Rule.

THE CONTRIBUTION OF THE CENOBITIC LIFE

Finally, the life of the community is itself extremely formative. Does the Rule furnish directives of a socio-psychological type? The abbot is the educator of his monks; the Rule does not, therefore, explicitly envisage a community, or interpersonal formative action of brother upon brother, but leaves to the abbot the task of developing himself through exercising his function and of becoming psychologist and teacher. Like all social life, community life nevertheless exercises a profound influence on those who live it. There is no need to enter into details here, for every page of the Rule contains that marrow which strengthens the character of those who open themselves to the influence of the common life, of which we shall speak separately. To comment on the chapter about good zeal (cf. RB 72) would be enough to underline the refinement with which it forms obliging and generous persons, persons deeply committed to the fraternal life: communicative, open, and peaceable.

And then, 'where the Spirit of God is, there is liberty' (2 Co 3:17). The monastic life, rightly lived, sets free in man very great forces of personalization: chastity enlarges the capacity for charity and gives it a great intensity capable of going beyond the walls of the monastery. Obedience liberates forces of initiative for the Kingdom of God and apostolic projects. Poverty becomes service for society. The monk, freed from every attachment, becomes a truly free person. Asceticism, self-discipline, far from making him withdraw into himself, sets him free and gives him an enlightened confidence in his own abilities. Prayer opens horizons as vast as the world. Reading the Scriptures sheds the brightness of light and the calm of security over the monk's footsteps. In short, the monastic life offers the monk a set of qualities which little by little make him a man of moderation, of orderliness, of calm, and of peace. He recognizes more and more his innate weaknesses, and that knowledge makes him humble, wise, and indulgent toward his brethren. That clear knowledge of himself gives him serenity, the natural companion of wisdom and maturity.

The Benedictine cenobitic life has the dynamics needed to form strong personalities. However, like every institution, it must avoid certain dangers. The monastic community lives apart from the world, separated by an enclosure. This system carries within itself the danger of withdrawal, a tendency which can recoil on individuals and create in them a petty, aggressive, restless spirit, lacking understanding for everything which exists outside the monastery walls. Perhaps it was to avoid this danger that St Benedict seems to have conceived his community as more numerous than that envisaged by the *Rule of the Master*, and that the monastic tradition has considered the number twelve as the minimum necessary to assure any new foundation. Thus, in the community, the possibilities of communication are more diversified and commit the monk to nourish a spirit of co-responsibility as regards his brethren, as regards all of humanity, for the construction of the Kingdom of God upon the earth. This enlargement of the community forces him to forget petty things, little physical and moral worries, and obliges him to lift his sights beyond the limits of his little self. Everything incites him to share in the preoccupations of those who are in charge of public life. Far from being petty in judging his superiors, he 'loves his abbot with a sincere and humble love' (RB 72:10) and makes human problems his own. He suffers with those who are hurt, the victims of war and violence, with the poor and the hungry. Peace in the world, the promotion of justice among men, the frustrations suffered by the young, those without work, the marginal, the Calvary of the physically or mentally handicapped, are not questions that touch him only from afar while he feels himself protected in his ivory tower. Fully human, the monk realizes that he is in solidarity with his brethren; he is conscious of his duty to serve the common good.

In fact, liberated from the many attachments of the world by dint of the fully-accepted structures of the monastic life, he should be a liberator for his brethren, if it were only by the testimony of his own liberty. This, indeed, should be real, deeply felt, shining out in his face and in his gestures. His renunciations ought to radiate the joy, the eagerness of his service, his generosity. His human formation must not be selfish or withdrawn, nor narrow and morbid, for that would be to imprison the dynamics of his vocation in a sterile and petty attitude instead of stimulating and liberating the great powers of creativity which the consecration of his life to the service of God and humankind contains within itself.

Let us mention also another danger which arises from experience in community and which can paralyse a good formation. The common life, and the monastic life in particular, imposes a certain uniformity of gesture, a participation in the actions of the community. Over-accommodating personalities adapt themselves easily without, however, putting enough of their heart into it. It is a matter of true and sincere obedience which walks hand in hand with exterior conformity. There is a real danger of manipulating a person, of imposing on him, by a gentle yet continual and decisive pressure, a set of attitudes, and even a spirituality, without bringing him to a convinced and fully experienced conversion. Instead of mobilizing his personal powers of integration, this risks imposing on the young person such a constraint that if he one day breaks it, there would be nothing left but a frustrated and unhappy individual. Not only should the common life not reduce persons to a common denominator by creating a sort of personality-type, but, on the contrary, it should awaken and set free the powers hidden in each individual, because each is a creature loved by the Holy Spirit. He is the Creator of individuals. How can we dare to want to constrain them or to put them into a mold which is foreign to their special value? Obviously, one cannot allow to develop in the monastery eccentricities, caprices, illusions of a right to be recognized in exorbitant personal demands. The intelligent person feels the need to be formed more and more and to cultivate dispositions which express his personal individuality. In this spirit and with gratitude, he receives the enlightened counsels of the elder (cf. RB 58:6) who has the gift of winning hearts and who is in charge of guiding him and watching over him in the love of the Lord with an attentive vigilance in order to help him in his development, in his crises of growth, and in his doubts and discouragements.

The Holy Spirit is love. He could create only in love and disseminate love. The law of love is the law of creation. It is in the warmth of that love that everything grows, increases, and develops. Man is not exempt from that law. More than any other creature, he needs love to become human and to be able to develop normally according to the conditions willed for him by the Holy Spirit and by nature. As flowers need the sun in order to unfold their beauty, so the human person needs genuine love in order to develop and become that which God expects him to be.

THE GATES OF
THE MONASTERY

THE SECOND VATICAN COUNCIL insisted on underlining forcibly the solidarity of the Church with the whole of humanity, for the Church is made up of persons united in Christ by the Holy Spirit in order to be a visible sign, lighting the pathway for all of humankind who, whether they actually like it or not, are journeying toward eternal goals (cf. *Gaudium et Spes*). The Word of God is the light offered to humanity to brighten the way. The Church is the agent, the guardian, the bearer of that light.

THE MONK IN SOLIDARITY
WITH HIS BRETHREN

Not only as a community does the Church have the task of orientating humankind along the path of salvation—especially if one identifies the Church with the hierarchy and their immediate collaborators. No. Every person is responsible for his brother. Only a Cain can object: 'Am I my brother's keeper?' (Gn 4:9). The human person is created in the image of God, an indelible likeness which fixes his destiny and his solidarity with his companions. The Holy Spirit delineates his countenance and makes him everyone's brother. Even those who deny the Spirit cannot deny this activity within them.

Siblings in a large family, not by the will of the flesh, but, from the beginning, by the will of the Spirit, cannot be disinterested in each other. They cannot escape the interdependence by which their life is woven. They share joy and sorrow, freedom and anguish, peace and wars, doldrums and natural disasters, economic ups and downs, and the more technology joins them, the more their destinies are bound together. Their life is necessarily either one of co-operation or one of continual conflict.

In no way do monasteries have as their aim offering people an excuse for avoiding fulfilling their duties toward their neighbor, or a

29

refuge permitting them to flee from distress or responsibilities. St Anthony penetrated ever further into solitude, not in order to avoid men, but to seek God and to remove far from himself everything that could turn him away from that search. The great exodus of monks into the desert did not aim at fleeing men—they found them again in the desert—but at fleeing from all that was seductive in the human world.

There is, therefore, a very penetrating logic in that requirement: 'to be in the world' without 'being of the world' (cf. Jn 17), and the problem presents itself in a very vivid way to monks and nuns. On the one hand they cannot and should not break solidarity with their brethren in the world, children of God like themselves, often their equals in their sincere quest for the Lord. On the other hand, it is precisely the thirst for God which makes them follow his invitation to the apostles: 'Come aside to a solitary spot' (Mk 6:31), not so as to live a peaceful life there, but so as to bear with Jesus the opprobrium outside the gate of the city (cf. Heb 13:13).

Let us pause first of all at a monk's duty to share the life of his brethren. Not to do this would be to refuse the appeals manifested in the mystery of the Incarnation of the Son of God, who came into this world to share with us our entire life, except sin, including death itself. If the Father has so loved the world that he gave his only Son for its salvation (cf. Jn 3:16), how could we remain aloof from this emulation of the love of the Father and the Son for the world by abandoning humankind, our brothers and sisters, to their lot? Could our withdrawing from men 'in order to serve God better', please the Lord who mingled with humankind, to whom we also belong, in order to save all? It would be an aberration to want to retire to a monastery or into solitude in order to withdraw from the cares, from the anguish, the problems, the privations which man undergoes in this world, in order to be sheltered from the injustices, the struggles, the disappointments, and the risks of life. And even if that withdrawal was made with the intention of living for God alone, but without carrying in one's heart, and even in one's body, the sufferings of humankind as Jesus did, that would be a spirituality of base quality or, quite simply, an evasion. It is not even enough to take their problems to the Lord in a platonic fashion; it is necessary to know our brothers' sufferings. It is necessary to experience them in a concrete way and to carry with them the cross of humanity without letting the heaviest of them fall.

The monk should be sensitized to human problems. This is the first condition of his presence in the world. If a monastic community, whether because of the old age of its members, or because of a lack of concrete contact with the realities of the world, little by little loses that sensitivity and, too withdrawn into its own little problems, limits itself to deploring the crimes and excesses it hears about, such a community no longer has the vitality to face the future. As it is of primary importance to enlighten the great movements of life by the light of the Word of God, so it is indispensable for a monastery 'to have an adequate knowledge of conditions, of the times, and of men' (Decree *Perfectae Caritatis*, 2). Let us add that these change quickly and often unexpectedly.

To be sensitized to the difficulties of the person of today is not enough; it is necessary to experience his problems with him. Monks cannot content themselves with knowledge that is abstract and disincarnate from the realities of the world. Such an abstention would end up by creating in them an attitude of complacency allowing them — since they find themselves sheltered from difficulties — to bless the Lord, in a rather equivocal manner, for having chosen the better part.

But in a monastery, how can one live the life of a person living in the world? Is it therefore necessary to leave the convents in order to mingle in concrete daily life? Is it necessary to become a laborer in a factory? Is it necessary to take training in various places in order to grasp their psychology and their needs? Not to mention those who claim that in order to understand the sinner, it is necessary to have experienced sin. This would be to fall from an esoteric theorist to a pragmatic existentialist. Each of us has received his own gift from God. If the Lord has called a monk to the monastery, it is there that he will find the 'workshop' for his labor, along with the 'tools of the spiritual art' (RB 4:78, 75), for his salvation and for that of humankind, his brothers, under the direction of the Holy Spirit.

No, the monk has no need to look outside the monastery for solidarity with his brethren. He is a man among his fellows. Monks have always chosen the monastic state to experience, often with emphasis, the want, the insecurity, the sufferings, and the needs of man. By his poverty he experiences human poverty. How careful he ought to be not to give in to the pressures of the consumer society and not allow himself to become middle-class! Obedience properly lived puts him into the situation of the poverty of the person who is dependent on circumstances and on his superiors. In the face of the lack of justice, of peace, charity, and sincerity among nations, in society, and in the family, how can a community give witness to justice, peace, and supernatural charity if there are injustices in its own bosom, a hypocritical peace, a charity without generosity, and a superficial sincerity? How could such a community be a cell of ideal social life (c. Paul VI at Monte Cassino) if it were not able to resolve, by means of repeated sincere community *examens*, its own social problems? How could the monks and the nuns bring the world to the Lord in their prayer without themselves experiencing, in an appropriate way, the problems of the people of our times? Their prayer will be truly ecclesial if the needs of the Church and of mankind re-echo in them. The monk should be able to say with St Paul: 'I die daily' (1 Co 15:31) by the labors of the monastic life which is, by definition, a life of asceticism. And it is in this way that he accompanies mankind, his brethren, by a daily dying as he journeys toward the resurrection.

Thus the monk is in solidarity with humankind, his brethren, in their distress, but also in their efforts to build a better world. He even finds himself in a privileged situation. His monastic life, orientated toward the transcendent God, helps him to make allowances for things, to maintain a serene judgment concerning events, to see them in the light of the Word of God and even to become the interpreter of this world which is unfolding before the Lord. Far from living behind doors hermetically sealed to the anguish of mankind, he often experiences these griefs more deeply than many of his contemporaries who perceive only the fleeting image offered by the communications media, or who grasp only the phenomenon without being able to integrate it into the plan of the history of salvation.

THE THOUGHT OF ST BENEDICT

St Benedict does not speak expressly of this dimension of the monastic life, and seems, relative to his ideal, to give a questionable meaning to the 'world' (cf. RB 53:4f, 23f, 66:7, 67). He insists, then, on separation from the world, while yet making it clear by his own life, as told by St Gregory, that the world ought to be saved, and that, in this work of salvation, the monastic life has its special and important, although seemingly modest, role to play. Besides, we must not forget that the idea of the mutual human co-responsibility for salvation, strongly anchored theologically in the Scriptures, was at that time in practice more presupposed than expressed. If St Benedict does not speak of it explicitly, this does not mean that the point of doctrine was unknown to him. His language on this subject is, at any rate, closer to that of the Lord himself who reminds each person, before all else, to be faithful to his duty in order to assure his personal salvation—a duty which he will not fulfill, however, without the fervent practice of effective charity: of the *New Commandment*, 'Love one another as I have loved you' (Jn 13:34), and give your life for your brethren (cf. 1 Jn 3:16)

That the monastic life has a deep salvific orientation could not have escaped the theological thought of St Benedict. Because, for the little world which the community represents, this truth is strongly insinuated in the Rule. The whole penitential code supposes the supernatural solidarity of the monks. Community prayer is used at the most important moments in its life (cf. RB 27:4, 67:1f). Mutual obedience (cf. RB 71) is quite another thing than a mere organization rule. And if St Benedict hesitates to let a monk go out from the 'ranks of the brethren' to 'single-handed combat' (cf. RB 1:5), it is without doubt because he enjoys in the cenobitic life the many kinds of help and the support of the prayer and encouragement of his brothers. If he presents these considerations more under an ascetic than a theological light, it would be erroneous to conclude from this that he was ignorant of the propitious truth of the Communion of Saints, which for monks is more immediately communion with their brethren, communion of life and of death, communion of will and of spirit in the Holy Spirit.

But there is more. Not being able and not wanting to entrust his monks with direct pastoral activity among their kindred in the world, he assigned them works of charity appropriate to their style of life: someone who comes to the monastery will find at the gate an hospitable monk, a messenger of the 'fervor of charity' (cf. RB 66:4) of the community, who 'with the meekness of the fear of God' (RB 66:4) welcomes the visitors and the poor (cf. RB 66:3). And with what charity guests are received, especially pilgrims and the poor to whom great courtesy is shown (cf. RB 53:9) and for whom one bears the very love due Christ himself (RB 53:7, 15)! The abbot admits them to his own table to the point that he seems to leave the monks to themselves in order truly to occupy himself with the guests (cf. RB 56). One might say that in a community where the retired nature of monastic life permits it and where relations with the brethren in the outside world require it, St Benedict wills that the abbot, the cellarer (cf. RB 31:9), the monks, and the community itself—excel in an exquisite charity, especially toward the weak and the poor, so that they, through contact with the monastery, may be able to find Christ and to be saved by means of the modest and humble charity of the monks, true disciples of Christ.

The Christian vocation, and even more the monastic vocation, therefore commits the disciple of St Benedict to practice the charity which goes so far as to give one's life for his brethren and for the salvation of the world for which the Son of God became a 'slave' (Ph 2:7). It should have nothing in common with a sacred selfishness working for its own salvation without caring about others, under the pretence of cultivating a pitiful interior life which wishes to ignore that of his brethren. The monk should be convinced that he cannot sanctify himself without others, that he cannot save himself without having prayed, worked, and suffered for the salvation of the world. The correlations and mysterious interdependences within the mystical body of Christ are the domain of the Spirit who is the Soul of that Body and who presides over the movements and functions of each member and orders them for the good of the whole Body. The nun, and why not the monk, have their place in the heart of this— little Therese perceived this clearly. In fact, the function of the contemplative in the Church is the nearest to the heart of God and at the same time the most detached from selfish complacency because he does not generally know the positive results obtained by his prayers and penances. Thus the monk understands that his place is there where his Master is, and his work passes necessarily through the cross of renunciation: 'If anyone wishes to come after me, let him deny himself, take up his cross daily, and follow me' (Lk 9:23). If the monk advances faithfully along the path marked out by the Gospel and the Rule, the Holy Spirit takes it upon himself, by secret arrangements and without the monk's realizing it, to control the ebb and flow in the veins of the mystical body, of the liberating blood flowing from the universal cross of Christ, to which are joined in due subordination, the modest crosses of his disciples.

The monk, therefore, has no need to mingle with the human throng in order to learn how to do good. If he were to go outside, unless, of course, he were to receive a special call from the Church, he would even be betraying his vocation since, spiritually speaking, his vocation has led him outside of the city of men.

Paul VI, following John XXIII, has vigorously insisted on the special vocation of the monk, which is not to be confused with other clerical vocations. The Rule of St Benedict gives a precise image of it, different from other kinds of religious life.

THE MONK,
PRISONER OF CHRIST

Here we should describe the other direction taken in the monastic itinerary: a direction in appearance opposed to the first which assigns him a place in the midst of humankind, his brothers. Yes, he ought to be very near them even while withdrawing from their society: an awkward requirement and in appearance contradictory. It will even expose him to the temptation, according to his personal temperament inclined to give in too easily to attractions in one direction or the other, of dispersing himself in exterior things, or of withdrawing into himself. The only way of avoiding these dangers is to keep one's eye fixed on the Lord so as to remain master of one's life and so as not to allow oneself to be deceived by illusions of imaginary duties, by the fantasies and the ill-defined inclinations of the flesh. Only recourse to the Spirit who leads him, in company with Jesus in the desert (cf. Mt. 4:1) will help him maintain his liberty of soul.

Yes, we are treating here of liberty. The monk makes himself a prisoner of Christ in order to assure that liberty. He is basically a man in love with freedom. The desert where he allows himself to be led by the Spirit, is for him a synonym for the fresh air of freedom. In the world he discovered around himself too many chains of gold and silver fettering his free flight toward the Lord and also too many shackles of baubles to doubt what he saw vaguely at the beginning: that is to say, the liberating power of the Spirit. He discovers with time, more and more clearly, that the Lord is Spirit, and where the Spirit is 'there is liberty' (2 Co 3:17). The young man searches in vain for freedom on the high sea, in love, in evasion, or even in drugs.

'That which is born of the flesh' (Jn 3:6) cannot free from the bonds of the flesh. The monk no longer allows himself to be duped by the illusions of freedom with their deceiving appearances; he even refuses to serve noble ideals of passing value. But if he renounces *that* liberty, it is in order to acquire *liberty*. He freely makes himself with St Paul, the 'prisoner of Jesus Christ' (Eph 3:1), much less in order to free himself from liberties which lead to slavery than to set free within himself forces for the service of Christ eternal.

For certain people, the monastery may be a shelter at first, but even they will with time experience that 'constraint brings forth a crown' (cf. RB 7:33), and that charity ends by chasing out fear (cf. 1 Jn 4:18, RB 7:67), depression, and all kinds of interior oppression. The walls of the monastery, they soon realize, were not set up to serve as an obstacle, but were built to protect their freedom. St Benedict, it is true, is concerned not only with keeping them away from worldly agitation, but exhorts them not to go out without permission (cf. RB 66:7), in other words, without legitimate reasons recognized as such by the abbot. Of course, St Benedict allows valid reasons and the goings out imposed by the necessity of providing for the needs of the monastery (cf. RB 67). It is to be noted here that the economic self-sufficiency foreseen by the Rule (cf. RB 66:6f) would cost too much today, given the modern economic system and the socialization of our society.

But to look at the matter closely, St Benedict, in showing himself severe in the matter of fraudulent departures, has as his only aim the erection of walls in order to preserve the monks from useless and harmful contacts. He was a student at Rome. He saw there the perversity of the world and was convinced of the need to withdraw from it rather than expose weak nature to the seductive influences of a way of life lacking vigor. Rome did not suit his soul. With the same determination with which he left Rome, he later left Subiaco so as not to put in danger the vocation of his young monks, tempted by an unscrupulous priest. No one has the right to think himself the strongest. He speaks, therefore, from experience. St Benedict, then, in order to avert his monks' contact with the outside world, decides that everything necessary for the proper functioning of the monastery should be found within its enclosure for, he says, it is not good for them to 'run outside' in every direction (cf. RB 66:7). His concern for souls causes him to write sentences capable today of displeasing certain readers imbued with the idea that the person of our day does not need such petty rules. However, St Benedict expresses without ambiguity his conviction of the existence of the taint left in us by Adam's sin. This matter, in any case, does not have an exclusive meaning for the use of monks alone. No one, except the Virgin Mary, can claim to be safe from the influences of perversity. The eyes of the monk are turned toward the God of purity. His protection against insidious influences ought, therefore, to be reinforced. The thorny bushes of Subiaco delivered St Benedict from the illusions of the imagination and of the memory. This discovery has no need of interpretation. It explains, however, why he insists on the necessity of asking the abbot and the brethren for prayer before leaving the monastery, and why the community prays for the absent brethren, and finally why the monk, once he has returned, commends himself again, in choir, to the common prayer of the brethren in order to expiate possible faults of curiosity and loquacity (cf. RB 67:1-4).

THE MONK:
GATE OF ENTRY FOR THE WORLD

For the same reasons, St Benedict forbids the monks returning to the monastery to tell others what they have seen or heard outside (cf. RB 67:5). As a matter of fact, although today it would not be realistic to want to impose this rule to the letter with the same strictness in all monasteries and on all their occupants without distinction, it nevertheless remains true that everything cannot be told to just anyone without causing havoc in souls. St Benedict, in formulating this restrictive phrase, indicates that all his monks may not have enough discernment to make the distinction between that which may be useful and that which is not. Moreover, a monastic community does not particularly do honor to itself by becoming the choice territory for story-tellers, idle speech, and vain curiosity.

Today the world scales the walls of the monastery by way of the mass media, particularly television. Surely, the Spirit of God does not often speak on airwaves where there more commonly reigns an attitude of indifference, of reducing everything to the lowest level, of reversing moral values, of secularism, and even a certain cynicism. The danger of slow intoxication for the habitual viewer lies less in manifest errors cleverly presented than in half-truths, the abuse of the sensational, the daily bludgeoning of slogans, and in a presentation where religion, the Gospel, God himself, are found on the same level as sporting events and movie stars. Little by little, error succeeds in perverting minds. It is the 'prince of this world' (Jn 12:31, etc.) who too often exercises 'dominion of the air' (Eph 2:2) and takes over this marvelous invention made by technology for the service of God and humankind.

A monastic community whose members frequently meet around the television set without making a strict selection of programs, will see its spirit change. In the long run, that little television screen will have more influence over the spirit of the community than does *lectio divina*. Interest in the passing events of this world will take precedence over the contemplation of the things of God. The monastic day, instead of ending with the prayer of Compline and the banishing of the evil spirits—'Visit, we beseech you, O Lord, this house and repel far from it all snares of the enemy' (collect at Compline)— will end with the latest news or even things useless for the soul, and gossip. St Benedict did not want to hear read at Compline the books of the Heptateuch or of Kings because these scriptural passages were not suitable at that hour for impressionable souls (cf. RB 42:4). Is the monk of today less impressionable? Or were his predecessors of the sixth century another race? Might he thank God that he is not like the rest of men (cf. Lk 18:11) for whom these shows provide a distraction at that hour? Television used without discernment in monasteries is out of place.

Those religious consecrated to the active life, organized according to their own proper needs, find themselves confronted every day with the real world. They are able to profit from the useful contributions of television. Experience united to prayer will furnish them with the principles of discipline which they need in order to restrict the use of television to what is useful to them and necessary to know. For the monk, in general, it makes little difference if he learns about the latest events with some delay. This wise deliberateness helps his interior calm, his wisdom, and allows him to maintain his distance concerning all that is passing without, however, cutting him off from the real world.

What was just said applies, in all due proportion, to certain other means of communication. There is no need to insist on it.

The monastery, therefore, ought to have, symbolically speaking, gates that are not wide open to all comers, but antennas controlled by the Holy Spirit to sort out the useful and the useless, or even the harmful, so that communications with the outside arrive wisely seasoned with the knowledge of the brethren in charge, who are capable of incorporating them into their general vision of the world and of life and then of making them bear fruit for the rest of the community without agitation or anxiety (cf. RB 64:16). The means of communication cause questionable, false, or subversive theories to penetrate into the monastery. The abbot and his associates should be watchful to identify and neutralize them; then they should provide the means for sound doctrine to sprout and mature in the climate of openness and healthy criticism. There is no uniform level of culture among the members of the same monastery. Thus it would be a mistake to allow diverse information transmitted by the air-waves to enter without distinction. They would cause confusion by their lack of formative value. As a matter of fact, at the time of St Benedict, the monks lived in a world which was not yet profoundly Christianized. Today we belong to a society which is largely de-christianized, and the monks, once they have withdrawn into the solitude of the cloister, have the right to expect to be spared the promiscuity of useless ideas which would take away from them that pure spiritual and intellectual atmosphere necessary for their sublime commitments. With St Paul they ought to be able to say: 'Let us, therefore, be children no longer, tossed to and fro, carried about by every wind of doctrine that has its origin in human trickery and skill in proposing error. Rather, let us profess the truth in love and let us grow to the full maturity of Christ, our Head' (Eph 4:14f).

It is said that the religious in the Church, because they have been more sensitized than others to the enthusiasm of renewal advocated by the Second Vatican Council, have been to a greater extent the victims of the confusion of ideas, of misunderstandings, and of a lack of discretion in the face of the new movements which arose as a consequence of that renewal. Their life-styles, well regulated and similar to each other up to the Council, were too brusquely shaken by an excessive and poorly controlled openness. As for the monks, they find themselves in a more secure position. The shock of rapid change comes to them with a diminished violence and causes less havoc.

CHRIST,
GATE OF THE MONASTERY

All this illustrates that the meaning of the monastic enclosure is more spiritual than material. Every person should take care to place a guard on his heart. He is the temple of the Holy Spirit, and he ought to guard it from baneful influences coming from outside. The monastery is the dwelling place of the Spirit. Its gates are open to all that comes from him and closed to all the rest. The enclosure retains all of its meaning as long as man bears within himself the wound of corruptibility. A false optimism has no place and would risk betraying the fortified city of the Spirit. The Lord calls to vigilance, and so that it might not be the carelessness of the shepherds which causes the flock to suffer the incursions of evil, he makes himself the 'gate for the sheep' (Jn 10:7)

In this conference, we have spoken first of openness, then, in the second part, of shutting. Is there not a contradiction here? No. Opening and closing serve the same end and complete each other. The gates of the monastery are made to leave outside the useless and the evil, and to open to the good. St Benedict appoints a 'wise old man' (RB 66:1) as gatekeeper. Indeed, for the discernment of spirits, there is needed a wise man 'who recognizes things as they truly are' (St Bernard, *On The Song of Songs, Sermon* 50), that is to say, who judges them according to their true nature.

The gates of the monastery ought to open and close for the Lord's sake. This is what is important. He should be the gate (cf. Jn 10:7). The gate of the monastery, therefore, does not close in order to isolate it; it does not open in order to be prey to every whim. Entrances and departures are made for the Lord and to serve his plans. The extent and the conditions of those departures are found in the Rule, and it is not orders from outside that have the force of law for the monk. The privilege of exemption is also a duty for monasteries: a privilege, because in that domain only the Sovereign Pontiff can impose from outside what he recognizes as just; a duty, because the abbot and the chapter are obliged before God to solve the problems that arise from it for his service and for the good of souls.

The monk, in choosing the monastic life, has found in it the most appropriate form for allowing him to follow and imitate Jesus. In placing his formula of profession on the altar, he has desired to lose his life for him, having been struck by the words: 'He who loses his life for my sake and the Gospel, will save it' (Mk 8:35).

The whole question of enclosure, and especially its intellectual dimension, is commanded by the love and service of Christ. As soon as one becomes lost in casuistry, one loses the meaning. The Lord has willed to enter into life through the narrow door of death, and he has shown us the path that we might follow him by renouncing our life, organized according to our personal views, and no longer living for ourselves, but for him who died and rose for us (cf. 2 Co 5:15).

Thus the monk loses his life for Christ, not in the somewhat selfish perspective of saving himself alone, but according to the word of the Lord: 'For my sake and for the Gospel' (Mk 8:35). The monastic life becomes, for him, a personal and fertile witness for the Kingdom of God.

THE MISSION
OF THE ABBOT

THE AUTHORITY OF THE ABBOT is situated in the same sort of mission as that of the apostles, emissaries of Christ—of Christ who is emissary of the Father—but especially as the mission of the Holy Spirit, sent by the Father and the Son. The apostles' mission was prior to Pentecost, but it received its confirmation, its power, its implementation, and its development from the Holy Spirit. Before the descent of the Spirit, the apostles were fearful, undecided, uncertain of the future. Dynamism, clarity of judgment, and courage were not their distinctive traits, yet they faithfully followed the counsel of their Lord and awaited 'that which the Father has promised...the Holy Spirit' (Ac 2:4f). Having returned to Jerusalem after the Ascension of their Master 'all with one accord gave themselves wholeheartedly to prayer...with Mary, the Mother of Jesus' (Ac 1:14). Then comes the memorable event. On the day of Pentecost 'all were filled with the Holy Spirit' (Ac 2:4), 'with grace and power' (cf. Ac 6:8), 'with wisdom' (cf. Ac 6:3) and received the *sacrum septenarium*, the seven gifts of the Spirit.

'The Spirit fills the universe' (Ws 1:7). He pours himself out over all the land. But God gives him to 'those who obey him' (Ac 5:32), so that they might be animated by the Spirit (cf. Rm 8:14), each according to the gift he has received and the ministry with which he has been invested. For in the Body of Christ 'the members do not all have the same function' (cf. Rm 12:4). It is the Spirit 'who gives to some to be apostles...or pastors and teachers....' (cf. Eph 4:11). Each one ought to make use of the gift he has received, 'if it is a ministry, then he should serve; if one is a teacher, he should teach; if one has the gift of exhortation, then he should exhort' (Rm 12:7f) 'in order to build up the Body of Christ' (Eph 4:12).

43

THE ABBOT,
CO-WORKER WITH THE SPIRIT

The authority of the abbot is situated in this context. Elected by his brethren, he will be invested by the Spirit with the mission of 'ruler of souls' (cf. RB 2:31, 34, 37). Now souls belong to the Holy Spirit; he lives in them and leads them to their eternal destiny. The abbot ought, therefore, to rule them in accordance with him and in total dependence on him. He has the obligation of listening continually to the Spirit, and he must learn to distinguish between his personal opinions and the voice of the Spirit who makes himself heard through spiritual illuminations, or through the voice of another, or through the signs of times and events: in short, in a thousand ways. It is in prayer, in the reading of Holy Scripture, but also in profiting by everything useful that experience and authorized advice may offer him that he will be capable, with divine grace, of developing in himself the incomparable gift of the discernment of spirits (cf. 1 Jn 4:1), to be able to judge if the spirits come from God (cf. RB 58:2) or from the flesh.

By accepting his election, the abbot allows the Spirit to invest him. We have only to page through Holy Scripture to see how he takes the entire person in hand, and in proportion to that grasp, the human person becomes a useful and powerful instrument in his hands.

The abbot, co-worker with the Holy Spirit, will try little by little, to make the manners and actions of the Spirit his own. One sees in the Rule how much St Benedict himself was an attentive disciple of the Spirit, and in following its texts, we can easily reap the fruits of the meditations and experiences of our legislator. He presents the abbot—or himself—as a 'loving father' (RB prol. 1, cf. ch. 2:24, 37:3), in imitation of the Holy Spirit, sent as Paraclete, as Consoler (cf. Jn 24:26). He presents him as a master and teacher, properties of the Holy Spirit, as good shepherd and physician in charge of healing the wounds of the soul.

THE ABBOT,
MASTER AND TEACHER

The abbot, co-worker with the Spirit, should strive not to rely on his own authority, nor on his own energy or know-how, but on the 'power of the Holy Spirit' (cf. Ac 1:8, Rm 15:13). The less he affirms himself personally in his way of asking and commanding, the more he will obtain the desired results. Let him think of St Paul writing to his Corinthians, his preoccupations. It is a fact, but also a pledge of great apostolic joys: 'I came among you weak, fearful, and with great trembling, and my word and my message had none of the persuasive force of wisdom. It was rather the convincing power of the Spirit, so that your faith might not be based on the wisdom of men, but on the power of God' (1 Co 2:3-5).

Thus the abbot is, for his brothers, the depository of the Word of God, their evangelist, the master and teacher in charge of 'teaching the precepts of the Lord' (cf. RB 2:4, prol. 1, ch. 3:6, 6:6), for the Gospel carries within itself the power of conversion. In weighing the words of the Rule, we note that this is teaching not only of an intellectual, but also of a moral type, and that the master ought to carry it out much more by his way of acting than by his words (cf. RB 2:1, 12f). He must show himself energetic when necessary, and make use of the whole range of exhortations, reproaches, and reprimands (cf. RB 2:23ff) of which the apostle speaks (cf. 2 Tm 4:2) when his example alone does not obtain the hoped-for result for the good of souls. An abbot who knows how to say the right word at the proper time, gently and firmly, will spare his community and himself many problems. He ought, for that reason, to understand the psychology of each (cf. RB 2:24f, 27:6), to be able to adapt himself to temperaments that are quite different (cf. RB 2:31f). He must have great patience, prudence, and discretion, so as to break nothing (cf. RB 64:12), while still seeing to it that abuses are not allowed to develop (cf. RB 64:14).

It is also his duty to help the brothers put off the old man. In this way, he will purify himself of his personal faults (cf. RB 2:40).

The abbot should take into account the immense responsibility with which he is entrusted, and his own weakness (cf. RB 64:13). He should therefore take the greatest pains to instruct himself in sacred knowledge (cf. RB 64:9), in the widest sense of that term, so as to place himself continually at the school of the Spirit of truth, sent to instruct him thoroughly (cf. Jn 16:13). Thus he, in his turn, will be a good teacher in the 'school of the Lord's service' (RB prol. 45). With St Bernard he will petition the Father to receive the Spirit as the sovereign unction (*magistrum habere Unctionem Spiritus*).

From his intimate relations with the Spirit of God, he will draw solidly-founded judgments concerning past and present currents of human thought (cf. RB 64:9) so as to be able to accompany his brothers, young or old, in their intellectual and spiritual problems. For the abbot is, whether he likes it or not, the educator of his monks insofar as that expression can be applied in his relations even with adult monks. His ordinary behavior, his judgments on values and non-values, his example, in the long run exert a profound influence in proportion to the authority emanating from his moral person. He is, according to the receptivity of each, the chief teacher of his community. By his prayer, the Holy Spirit will open up means of understanding and amendment in the souls of those whose mind's and heart's are still but little open to his action.

Among the ancients, the master was concerned not only with the knowledge of the disciples gathered around him—Jesus with the twelve and the other disciples is the best example—but still more with their moral and human formation. St Benedict uses the same procedure in the matter of the different personalities of disciples gathered around the abbot. It is not in every way an elite group. Here we are still far from the divorce between knowledge and life which rationalism set in motion. In fact, the dialogues of St Gregory teach us that St Benedict, in admitting his postulants, regarded not their natural dispositions, but their vocation received from God. The abbot should not reject them, but discern their will to respond to the call of the Lord. There are, therefore, among the disciples of this master, who is the abbot, types of people who are quite different, and even rude persons who lack intelligence, who have hard and difficult characters, in any case, are not very easy to manage (cf. RB 2:25-29). The prisons of the monasteries of the Middle Ages, used here and there up until the time of the French Revolution, are easily accounted for. Has the situation changed today? Under the influence of the more recent Orders and especially because of the profound changes in our present society, not only the prisons have disappeared from the monasteries, but candidates to the monastic life are not accepted unless they give solid guarantees of a sociable character and a lively intelligence. The screening is, therefore, more severe. Modern psychology, by penetrating into the depths of the soul, is able to distinguish between moral attitudes and psychological traits which formerly were often interpreted on the moral plane in the hope of therefore being able to cure them.

Besides these pathological cases, the abbot ought not, in the selection of candidates, to judge according to natural criteria, but pay attention to the ways of acting of the Spirit, according to the words of the prophet: 'What was fat and of fine appearance, you took to yourself, and what was weak you cast aside' (cf. Ezk 34:3f, RB 27:7). In doubtful cases, the abbot should not allow himself to be prevailed upon by reasons which come from a false charity, and admit a young man in cases where true charity would oblige him to send the candidate away as unfit for monastic life, because sooner or later, that vocation will become a burden to him.

THE ABBOT, GOOD SHEPHERD

Let us now examine one characteristic of the abbot which makes him particularly attractive because of the closer resemblance with Christ: that of a shepherd. As a matter of fact, by taking his place, he cannot but be a Good Shepherd. When the Lord invested Peter with the office of governing the Church, he did not say to him: Be a fisher of men (cf. Mt 4:19), or, Be a rock against which hell will not prevail (cf. Mt 16:18), and certainly not, Show yourself as first among your brethren. He said to him simply: Feed my sheep, thus specifying the character, the spirit, the method of his government.

St Benedict retains this image, and his recommendations to the abbot enter into this symbolism of the Good Shepherd. He should not govern like a mercenary (cf. Jn 10:12), seeking remuneration for himself, but he ought to put himself entirely at the service of his brothers. He no longer belongs to himself, but all his strength, his talents, his interests, his time, and even his health, belong to the brethren. For 'the Good Shepherd gives his life for his sheep' (Jn 10:11).

St Benedict brings out this image of the Good Shepherd in order to recommend to the abbot particularly, discretion and gentleness. It is necessary and useful for him to let himself become penetrated with these admirable parables (cf. Jn 10) in all the fullness of their meaning. By means of them, the Lord allows us to cast a wondering glance into his divine and human heart.

The abbot should long to penetrate ever deeper into the heart of Jesus in order to become, little by little, like him. If the Good

Shepherd is able to procure the good of the flock as such and the good of each sheep in particular, then the abbot himself also should apply himself to reconciling in the same way the common good and the particular aspirations of his community, and the good of the community in each individual, since these points of view are correlative and inseparable for one another.

People react more quickly taken individually than in a group, even on the spiritual plane. The abbot, if he is by nature ardent and dynamic should take into account the wisdom of Jacob cited by St Benedict: 'If I drive my flocks too hard, they will all die in a single day' (cf. RB 64:18). A Benedictine monastery is strongly attached to its traditions and its usages, even if they come from a later period, and every community knows about the eternal tensions between those who want a speedy march toward reforms and those who perseveringly hold them back. The abbot, therefore, should use all his prudence as Good Shepherd to respond to the needs of both sides and to maintain peace. It is also necessary for him to maintain a wise equilibrium between the 'strong' who are capable of more austerity, and the 'weaker' brethren (cf. RB 64:19). Let him be careful not to leave his monastery outside the great spiritual aspirations of the Church and of the world; this without rushing the process of a necessary evolution. In order to be equal to this task, let him keep himself informed, but most of all, let him have a great deal of tact, for by forcing the pace of his brethren too hard, he might offend and hurt them (cf. RB 64:18). If, on the other hand, he were to remain deaf to the signs of the times, to the rapid changes characteristic of our age, he would risk leading his community to slow asphyxiation. This healthy evolution depends, for a large part, on his own initiatives. He will not obtain results unless he takes the time to incite his brethren with firm gentleness. If the good shepherd goes forward with a sure, prudent, and patient step, his flock follows little by little without too much balking. In other words, the abbot should precede those entrusted to him and fix his ideal a little higher than that of the majority of his brothers.

Let us not pass over in silence the case of sheep who have gone astray. Not only should the abbot not allow them to get lost in their dangerous paths, but as a good shepherd, he should go to seek them and to lead them back to the fold (cf. Lk 15:4, RB 2:8f, ch. 27). The Lord, in abandoning the ninety-nine sheep to retrieve the lost lamb, teaches the abbot that he ought to use all his know-how not to lose any of the brothers confided to his care (cf. RB 2:32, 27:5). Let him keep in mind the accounts that he will render to Christ not only concerning the government of the community, but concerning each brother, since in accepting the position of abbot, he has accepted the duty of taking care of each one individually (cf. RB 2:37–39). Thus he should refuse no fatigue, no service which might be useful in facilitating the return of the erring brother. He should take all the more care inasmuch as he realizes that the social life of today, with the escapes available to those who wish to withdraw from the authority of the superior, does not offer itself to him as an ally for this delicate work. The good shepherd prays for them and never loses hope of leading them back to the fold.

In any case, this solicitude should not rest upon the abbot alone. If a brother begins to isolate himself, to separate himself inwardly from the others, to live on the fringe of the community by seeking the satisfactions of social life elsewhere, all the members should work to bring him back, because tearing off a member from the body is just as cruel when it take place imperceptibly. The Holy Spirit who animates the community and assures its unity is not only offended by desertions, but also by separations which take place even within the group.

ABBA — FATHER

The monastery is often compared to a family; the comparison with a natural family is far from perfect, however. It is proper to look to a more elevated plane to find there the One whom Jesus came to make known to us as the prototype of all paternity (cf. Eph 3:15). He is the true Father of the monastic family whose members have received 'the spirit of adopted children' (RB 2:3) of that Father. They have been invited by the voice of the Lord (cf. RB prol. 19), they aspire to spiritual gifts (cf. 1 Co 14:12), they are incorporated by the Spirit of God into the monastic family and recognize in the abbot their spiritual father, substitute for the true Father. The brethren who have entered the monastery, stimulated at first by motives of the natural order, are unable in the long run to be happy and in their true place except to the extent that their heart opens itself to the Spirit and they realize that in this area the best natural motives are of no avail (cf. Jn 6:63).

For his part, the abbot should be deeply convinced that in order to carry out his duty properly and to act as a real father, he needs the help of the Holy Spirit who already fills his brethren, granting that they are adoptive sons in Christ. Only in this way will they find in the abbot the reflection of him whose substitute he is.

The Church has known periods when faith in the mission of Christ's envoys created no problem; even when their life was not in accord with their words (cf. RB 4:61) people believed them and tolerated an abbot who was a good administrator and left the care of souls to others (cf. RB 2:33ff). Today, on the contrary, our secularized humanity is sensitive to the 'manifestations of the Spirit' (1 Co 12:7), and where he appears in his works, faith is kindled, and a spiritual relationship awakens in the hearts of those called and carries them along after him. The abbot is pardoned for being weak, for lacking a certain human formation, for not having detached himself from economic and political affairs, but he is not pardoned if he lacks the Spirit.

The true authority of the abbot comes to him from his spiritual paternity. He is *abbas* and ought to be conscious of it. This is considerably different from the authority of other ecclesiastical superiors—not in its theological basis, but in the manner of its exercise. The abbot should not allow himself to be absorbed by the demands of administration like a simple moderator. He should be a father, and even a mother. Of course, this does not mean that he should not treat his brothers as adults or manifest his authority. Toward the seniors he will show the respect of the father of a family toward those of his children who have arrived at the full possession of their personality. As a father loves in his son that which they have in common, in the same way, the abbot will love in his brothers the deep spiritual relationship built up by the Spirit. This assumes, transcends, and absorbs the natural differences of the flesh. Only in this way will the abbot succeed, little by little, in transforming his community, which is at first, perhaps, united more by common occupations or common interests than it is joined in Christ as a truly evangelical community, bearing witness before the world of the brotherhood which he has taught us and from which the world is so distant. The abbot ought to be convinced that this brotherhood is not built by initiative from below. The father ought to lay its foundation through the exercise of his own personal responsibility, which he cannot shift onto someone else. St Benedict places the chapter about the abbot at the beginning of the Rule and not at the end, as certain constitutions have believed it should be done, thus misunderstanding his true role, for the father precedes the sons, and without him, the family does not exist, or exists even less in the spirit than in the flesh.

Above all, the abbot is a father, and that quality gives him the right to resolve the problems raised by the often extremely individualistic nature of the person of today: the conflicts between conscience and obedience, personality and structures, finally, the desire for contacts and the limitations imposed out of respect for the community. A father occupies a privileged place so as never to sacrifice the worker to the work, the monk to the precepts or usages, and his son to an ideology. Because he is a father, he knows how to cause the person concerned to mature, and how to reconcile the irreconcilable. If one studies the problems of many religious who belong to more recent institutes, one gets the impression he is dealing with men and women who are truly brothers and sisters, but who, in fact, lack a father. The abbot, then, will endeavor to unite these two qualities: to be a brother among brothers, while still remaining the father of all. In the Most Blessed Trinity, the Father and the Son are absolutely equal, and only the relation of paternity and filiation distinguishes them. In the same way, the abbot recognizes himself to be a brother among brothers in a basic equality, and the relation of paternity is the only thing that distinguishes him.

The father of all without distinction: St Benedict insists greatly on this point. Since God does not respect the differences of race, social origin, or talents, in short, purely human qualities, neither should the abbot allow himself to be impressed by a person's superficial qualities (cf. RB 2:16–22). There is no question, of course, of behaving identically toward everyone, for love adapts itself spontaneously to the needs of the beloved and thus expresses itself differently according to each case. Some are more skilled than others at making requests, at imposing themselves, at flattering. The abbot will surround with solicitude the modest, the humble, those who are content with little, the 'poor in spirit' (Mt 5:3), and who do not put themselves forward in the community. He will take care not to prefer those of his sons who are inclined to love him (cf. Mt 5:46) to those who are quarrelsome. Love which lacks generosity toward one's neighbor runs the risk of being love of self. If the abbot loves sincerely and does not spare himself, he will win all his brethren to the right and will lead them to the Lord. Love is prudent. It knows how to wait for the right moment to plant a good word in another's heart. Thus the abbot will not rush those of good will who are slow at making up their minds, and will not force them to make spontaneous decisions except with affection—or humor. His choices will never be arbitrary. He will be neither impulsive nor turbulent (cf. RB 64:16), because in this way he would run the risk of disturbing the harmonious development of the personality of others and of changing his brothers into timid people. Far from creating an atmosphere of fear about himself—reverential fear has nothing in common with this—he will try to win the hearts of his brothers by his affection (cf. Rb 64:15, 72:10), for love causes one to accept the truth. He should know how to inspire confidence so as to encourage good initiatives in the community in an atmosphere of joy and sincerity. He should be entirely sober, just, and positive in his judgments of his brethren and should know how to love them without dissimulating their faults or their vices (cf. RB 64:11). Rashness of speech in this area can cause him to lose the confidence of the offended brethren completely.

THE ABBOT:
SERVANT OF ALL

Love descended from heaven to become the servant of our salvation. The mission of the abbot finds its place in the service of the love of the Lord 'who came to serve and not to be served' (Mt 20:28). Our age is greatly tempted to 'demythologize' the hierarchy and superiors. If such a process applies itself to the suppression of a cult of poor taste concerning the person, the distinctions of a worldly character, or the privileges that lack theological foundation, then it is necessary. But if it so attacks the sacred character of the abbatial function, its religious foundations, as to lower the abbot to the rank of a simple moderator of discipline or of an animator of a community and its works, then this would be a matter of a democratization of bad quality, because the abbot is not a simple administrator of goods nor simply 'the one responsible', and to see things in this way would be to miss the specific character of the Benedictine monastic life and to misunderstand its original inspiration, which is neither that of a spiritual enterprise nor that of a charismatic group.

The abbot is his brothers' servant exactly in the way that Christ became the servant of all. He is the vicar of the Lord and therefore at the service of his brothers' salvation. This function requires sometimes that he show himself as the master and lord—St Benedict calls him this—without usurpation or pretention, but 'for the honor and love of Christ' (cf. RB 63:13) and for the love of the brethren whom he should serve in proportion to the intelligence and to the temperament of each one (cf. RB 2:31). United to Jesus, he carries the cross of each of his monks, and the cross which he actually has on his breast reminds him at every moment of that service of Simon of Cyrene in regard to his brethren.

Little by little the abbot will discover his own style of government by carefully studying in the Rule all the nuances which St Benedict uses to paint a portrait of the abbot. The Lord will be his model—'learn of me', he has said (Mt 11:29). He will be solicitous of himself and of the flock over which the Holy Spirit has placed him as shepherd (cf. Ac 20:28). He will be humble in this service without losing his dignity, sincere without seeking popularity, and efficient without bothering with trifles. A poorly understood democratization would have him lose his authority and have him lose for his brethren the supernatural sense of filiation. In the measure that he belongs entirely to the Lord, he will be able to be all things to everyone through his deeply religious attitude. He is the servant, not of the brothers, but of their salvation. In this sense he serves the community even on the human plane. Is this not the indispensable foundation of the economy of salvation?

The abbot should leave to everyone, and especially to his closest co-workers, a true freedom of action by avoiding every kind of inopportune and disconcerting meddling; yet he must remain ready, in case of necessity, to fill in gaps so that the community will not suffer any detriment.

THE ABBOT AND HIS COADJUTORS

The distribution of responsibilities is of great psychological importance in the community. St Benedict envisages the reasons in favor of this distribution (cf. RB 65:14) although he is laconic enough concerning the matter itself (cf. RB 21; 65, etc.). The abbot holds, however, the advantage of being able in all security to confide a part of his responsibility (cf. RB 21:3) to others, his delegates, that they may exercise their office in dependence on him and may share with him the ministry of edification. Their authority, therefore, is situated at the level of the mission of the abbot and along the line of that of the Spirit. These delegates receive from the Spirit, along with the grace of state, the gift of obedience, so that not only peace and concord, fruits of being united around the abbot, might not be disturbed, but that they might truly be 'peacemakers' (Mt 5:9), bearers of happiness and serenity for their brothers. We have here an evangelical vision of this mission. This is why it is easy to understand the harshness which St Benedict shows toward rebellious deans or priors (cf. RB 21; 65). Established as ministers of charity and obedience in the Body of Christ, how is it that they sow trouble and discord there?

In order to avoid such abuses and to safeguard peace and charity, the Rule gives the abbot the power to organize the life of his monastery as he wishes (cf. RB 65:11). However, if he should notice a less faithful associate at his side, he should nevertheless not allow himself to be influenced by slander, by his own impatience, by any other not very religious motive (cf. RB 65:7, 8, 22), but to meditate on the attitude of the Lord in the face of the weaknesses of his apostles. If, on the other hand, the abbot has truly religious men as associates he will back them in every way possible in the exercise of their mandate. This kind of trusting identification will permit him more easily to correct their deficiencies or their errors than by an attitude of discontentment or disappointment. Above all, he will never forget his own limitations and will practice the words of the Lord: 'When you have done all that which was prescribed for you, say: "we are unprofitable servants"' (Lk 27:10). He will say it with much more conviction because he knows from experience 'how difficult and arduous it is to lead souls' (RB 2:31). The abbot recognizes his duties and his limitations and the boundaries of his field of action. On the one hand, there are the accounts to be rendered of his administration to Christ the Judge (cf. RB 2:39,

64:21). On the other hand, to constrain his action, there are the limitations of his personal resources, those coming from his brethren, the course of the present age, and a thousand limiting circumstances. He ought to show at the same time a deep humility and a great confidence in the Lord. His humility should never become a passivity born of a feeling of powerlessness, but should strengthen him in an ardent faith in the Lord, the Master of men and times who leads all things toward the good. The abbot should apply himself to put into practice that which his obedience to the Church inspires. He will live the Gospel, knowing well that, in giving the lie to our calculations, the Lord makes his own plans and grants the success. Thus the abbot will consider himself as the Lord's servant with the hope of one day hearing from the mouth of his Master the word of absolution: 'Well done, good and faithful servant, enter into the joy of your Lord' (Mt 25:21).

One impression stands out very quickly if we allow ourselves to become impregnated by the spirit of the Rule. St Benedict knew how to contemplate the Holy Spirit organizing and leading the Church, but also leading each soul in particular. He paints for us a portrait of the abbot in which he has clearly gathered all the practical wisdom which appears in the works of the Holy Spirit. It is, then, divine charity personified in the Spirit which is deployed in the prudence, justice, fortitude, and temperance, in the discretion and clairvoyance, in the humility and patience, in the goodness and tenderness, in the calm and in the energy which St Benedict would like to make take root, to implant in the soul of the abbot by placing him entirely under the guidance of the Spirit.

The monastic community is, in effect, a family of God's children, begotten by the Spirit (cf. Rm 8:14). He infuses into them the spirit of adopted children (cf. RB 2:3) and unites them into a family in which the abbot, his representative, holds his place as father. It is a unique and sublime responsibility, and the abbot should have a keen consciousness of it while placing himself without reserve under the guidance of the Spirit, true soul of this family which is totally his.

For their part, the children, lest they betray their sonship, should allow themselves to be impregnated with the spirit of filiaton which makes them consider their abbot as *Abba*, Father (cf. RB 2:3). To live the monastic life under the guidance of the abbot is to live the relationship of the child of God with the Father. What a lofty view of the monastic state according to the admirable and so true concept of its legislator! The line is right from the Father, through the Son, by the working of the Spirit, toward his children of adoption for whom the Spirit 'sanctifies' the abbot, the father, as vicar of Christ in his function of visible reflection of the universal Father.

THE GIFT OF
THE COUNSEL

MONKS, AND ESPECIALLY THEIR HEAD, the abbot, are privileged subjects for the gift of counsel given by the Holy Spirit. Children of the Father, of the family of God, they are gathered together for his glory with the specific intention of glorifying God in all things (cf. RB 57:9). They have entered the school of the service of God (cf. RB prol. 45) with the desire to learn to organize their life in such a way that God may truly be first served. Children of God, they want to be truly consecrated to Christ and to prefer nothing to his love (cf. RB 4:21). All their life belongs to the Lord. To him is entirely consecrated everything from their work, their prayer, their fatigue, and their rest, even to the smallest manifestations of their existence, even sleep. Is it not the Lord himself who, through his Church, accepts this consecration made by monastic profession, and who offers the monk the promises of his covenant?

IN THE LIFE OF THE INDIVIDUAL

How could monks remain faithful to their commitments if they did not enjoy the special guidance of the Spirit of God? How could they fail to fall back continually into seeking a simply human reason as the directing principle of their actions, thus organizing their life on rationalization according to the manner of the natural man? How could they bring to a good conclusion the work of the sanctification of their life without the all-powerful help of him who alone is holy, who alone is sanctifier? To arrive at union with Christ, through how many nights one must pass, how many humiliating failures one must undergo! The human spirit is radically incapable of finding the paths which, through the underbrush of its personal history, arrive at God, our goal. The spirit alone is the light on these paths and makes a secure march possible.

It is comforting to know that the greater the requirements and the more exalted the commitments undertaken for the Lord, the more intense is the assistance of the Spirit of God who inspires these actions and guides them to a good conclusion. He it is who creates all things and presides at the returning of all creation, especially of the rational creature, toward God. Only the Spirit, through his gifts, can make the whole life of the monk concur in the exclusive service of the Lord, and inflame him with an ever more faithful and generous love.

Through the gift of counsel, the Spirit guides his chosen ones in total security in the right paths toward the Father. Has not the son acquired, along with the gift of adoptive sonship, the right to be led personally and directly by the Spirit of the Father? Yes, the Father cares for his children. He looks on them from on high (cf. RB 4:49, 7:13) with kindness. Moreover, he follows them step by step and guides them along the paths that lead to him and, if it is necessary, sets them back on it continually. Can monks believe without presumption that they are able to count on his favors absolutely? If they desire to serve the Father without compromise, why should they not enjoy in return a constant, loving attention on his part? Yes, he will not be content to help them by his actual grace. Through his Spirit he will grant them the gift of counsel and a sort of divine instinct, a flexibility of soul receptive to the direct divine action. This intervention of the Spirit, far from cowing the liberty of the children of God, spurs them to action to channel their forces along the line of the suggestions of the Spirit and under his direct influence.

In the prologue (cf. RB prol. 9) St Benedict alludes to the 'deifying light'. Is he not also thinking of that light which, thanks to the gift of counsel, penetrates a person, transforms him, and causes him to judge and act under the immediate impulse of the Spirit, in a deiform manner, after the manner of God?

Are we conscious of this fact, this truth that is so simple and so astounding? Or are we ignorant about the powers which the goodness of the Father grants us to enable us to discern and to judge, to decide and to act, as children of God worthy of the name, in the thousands of contingencies of daily life?

IN THE LIFE
OF THE COMMUNITY

The abbot cares for each of his children individually, but also for the community of monks vowed to the Father's service. The community needs to be well orientated to be in all truth an instrument of salvation and a sign of God to each of its members. The person who has the duty of governing it was elected and established by the Spirit, under his inspiration. The gift of counsel, with its lights and its inspiration, makes him particularly close to the Holy Spirit. If he is open to his action, if he knows how to recognize and accept his movements with gratitude and humility, then he will become more and more aware both of the gratuity of his interventions and of their brightness, even in the darkness of faith. He is the substitute for Christ and directs his brethren toward the Father; therefore he can count with absolute confidence on the practical and concrete counsels of His Spirit.

Certainly, the inspirations of the Spirit are discreet and leave the abbot or the monk his full freedom of action; they are even scarcely perceptible, but nevertheless very real, however conditioned they may be in their efficacy by the greater or lesser degree of fervent receptiveness which is given them.

On the level of the activity of the gifts of the Holy Spirit, the gift of counsel corresponds to the cardinal virtue of prudence on the level of the moral virtues. Already Pope St Gregory the Great pointed out the remarkable prudence which St Benedict shows in his Rule 'which excels by its discretion'. Under the attractive symbol of the flock of sheep led by Jacob with obliging patience, St Benedict advises the abbot to use great discretion in governing his brethren (cf. RB 64:17-19) so as not to lose any of them (cf. RB 27:5). The virtue of prudence commands and balances all those things that it wishes to see in the abbot. He ought to find the right balance between gentleness and threats, sometimes to show himself the severe master, sometimes the indulgent father (cf. RB 2:24). He should know how to adapt himself to the different temperaments and to the degree of intelligence of each one (RB 2:31f), 'according to what he judges expedient in each case' (RB 64:14). Let him remain moderate in his reprimands 'lest by scraping away the rust he break the vessel' (RB 64:12). Let him not be quick-tempered or obstinate, but provident and circumspect in his judgments (cf. RB 64:16f). This is the spiritual profile of a leader who is capable in all things of observing the proper measure.

Let us not be surprised that we do not find in the Rule an explicit mention of what theology was only later able to elaborate concerning the 'gifts of the Holy Spirit'. It does not mean, for all of that, that St Benedict saw in discretion an exclusively moral virtue. Without any doubt, he knew through personal experience that when a monk enters further into union with God, he enters at the same time under a different type of divine guidance where the Holy Spirit becomes more directly the guide of his soul. St Benedict, we know, is extremely discreet concerning his own spiritual experiences. Therefore we must not expect from him distinctions in those matters where for him all is sacred and under the direction of the Spirit. We have been able to notice in the Rule the absence of well-defined limits between the natural and the supernatural, because the entire monastic life is oriented, even in its most ordinary manifestations, toward a goal which transcends the horizons of nature.

Yet allusions to the direct action of the Spirit are not lacking in the Rule. Lent is a particularly favorable time for his intervention, since the soul, purified of its vices (cf. RB 49:4) finds itself more at liberty regarding the desires of the body and, because of this, more accessible to the peace that surpasses all understanding (cf. Ph 4:7) and to joy, the gift of the Spirit (cf. Ga 5:22), so as to await, in this joy, the holy feast of Easter (cf. RB 49:7).

St Benedict seems to refer more explicitly to what theology calls the gift of counsel in the chapter which deals with the abbot's council, because he asks him to convoke all of the brethren, for he says, 'God often inspires the youngest with the best suggestions' (cf. RB 3:3). The gift of counsel is offered to every Christian, just as the Holy Spirit is entirely in the head of the Church, entirely in its body, and entirely in each of its members. The abbot is not the only one to receive the illuminations of the Spirit, who can speak more clearly through the humblest member of his community. The Spirit is free; he breathes where he wills. In the same way as in the Church, the great movements of renewal have not generally come from the hierarchy, but as they say, from below—St Benedict and his monastic order are a striking example of this—so inspirations may come from its midst.

What, then, is the role of the abbot? He also has his special task, exclusively his, a task imposed by the Spirit. St Benedict describes his role in these words: 'He should listen to the advice of his brothers, he should ponder it maturely in his own heart, and then he should do what he judges to be the most suitable' (RB 3:2, 5). After having listened attentively for the voice of the Spirit, if he reveals himself through the mouth of one of the brethren, it is for the abbot to discover, to discern, and to separate it from every other human word. That is the most delicate task of all. For the abbot does not enjoy the gift of revelations. But he more than the others, also has the gift of counsel in accomplishing his duty concerning the discernment of spirits. Sometimes the Holy Spirit will enlighten him suddenly in order to make him choose with a tranquil certainty; in other circumstances he will lead him step by step while helping him with his light. Above all, the abbot should never fail to invoke his aid. Moreover, he should not isolate himself in making a decision, and he should remain open to supplementary information and to asking other advice. He has his official councillors for ordinary matters (cf. RB 3:12). What is stopping him from asking them for useful advice which may put him on the right track? The process of investigation will not be ended until the moment he has made his decision. Without doubt, the Holy Spirit will have granted him his assistance which does not, however, render his decision infallible, just as it does not dispense anyone from the research which prudence may require.

Is the gift of counsel distinct from the virtue of prudence? The difference is fundamental, since the gift of counsel disposes a person to accept the action of the Spirit with alacrity, whereas prudence relies on natural reasoning enlightened by faith.

All those who have the responsibility of making important decisions—let us think of the abbot first of all, next the master of novices, whose duty consists in the discernment of spirits to know if they come from God—find themselves seriously obligated to give a generous reception to the gift of counsel, to the Holy Spirit himself, because they have great need of this great gift, first of all, so as not to allow themselves to be carried away by superficial judgments, conceived in agitation under the impulse of passing impressions or nourished by feelings of sympathy or antipathy, or even extorted under pressure from persons or events. The monastery is the house of God and belongs to him entirely, with all its persons, its institutions, its traditions, and its laws, even to its smallest objects. The abbot and his associates are only its administrators. How much the abbot needs the Spirit of Christ in order to escape the threat of judgment (cf. RB 2:37-39), and in order to merit the ultimate praise

addressed by the Lord to the conscientious servant who distributed
food at the proper time to his working companions (cf. RB 64:21f)!

THE GIFT OF COUNSEL:
BASIS OF THE GOVERNMENT
OF THE MONASTERY

As nothing in human works is absolute so there is no ideal form
of government either. If, in order to avoid the disadvantages
which a recent experience has brought into the spotlight, one thinks
it good to change the structures, he immediately falls into other
disadvantages which previous experience had avoided. The Benedictine formula is not paternalistic, nor monarchic, nor oligarchic,
nor democratic. According to the Rule, it ought to be theocratic. The
abbot is not the true master; he is 'lord' insofar as he is the Lord's
substitute. Also he ought to show in words and in deeds that Christ
governs the house through his Spirit, and that all the institutions and
decisions of the monastery are inspired and ratified through Him. In
the measure that the abbot, through a deep humility and a great
sincerity, is able to disappear behind him who appointed him to take
his place, he will be able to occupy that place in the name of Christ
with firmness and gentleness. Having received the mandate of governing his brothers, his equals in all things, he will neglect nothing so
as to recognize, thanks to them, the will of Christ, his Master, for
them and for the community. The monastery, then, will be living a
sort of theocratic democracy where, except for the purely material
questions, the law of the majority will not predominate, but where a
sincere seeking, which is everyone's job will flourish—a seeking for
the will of the Spirit working through his gift of counsel.

The monastery ought, therefore, in spite of its incorporation into
terrestrial reality, to be oriented and directed in view of attaining
that religious goal to which all the manifestations of its vitality
should remain subordinate. This state of things imposes on those
responsible for its government a very demanding and sincere discernment so as to tend continually toward it, to remove everything
that might pervert it, and to subordinate the secondary to the unique
choice. Since it concerns the things of God, his honor is at stake, and
where men sincerely seek his glory, he looks after things through his
Spirit. The abbot can count on the light of the Spirit in the measure

that he seeks only His glory. Certainly, the monastery is a social body governed by the abbot with his council, but for the believer, the Spirit really presides over its destiny and leads those responsible by his lights in order to make everything converge on the goal to which it is consecrated. In this sense and under these conditions, the monastery is a theocracy in which everything is directed by the Spirit to the praise of God's glory.

THE SOUL OF
THE MONASTIC
COMMUNITY

CAN A HUMAN GROUP
HAVE A SOUL?

INCORPORATION INTO A COMMUNITY is an incorporation into a human group. What psychology teaches us about groups must therefore be applied to the group which is the monastic community. The developments and consequences of this psychology find in the monastic setting an exceptional territory for verification. A monastic group is related in many ways to a family and its traditions, or to a regiment where *esprit de corps*, unwritten laws, and special ritual, unite the soldiers to one another not only on the occasion of their feasts and special days, but all through their daily life. A human group has its special goals, its methods for attaining them, its experiences, and its doctrines. It holds up certain virtues. We monks wear the same habit, an exterior sign of the unity of our groups, and it is one way among others of making us the same. Common ways of viewing things and of acting let the soul of the group, its spirituality, be born.

Now, in order to understand better the importance of the group and what distinguishes it and what ought to differentiate it from the masses, the crowd, we need to have clear ideas about the latter. A crowd, as distinguished from a group, is a multitude which is not constituted nor organized. It is united by chance. In a specific but limited sense, many men whose character is not well-tempered and whose formation is deficient, allow themselves to be influenced by forces which can manipulate them and induce them to act in ways that respond to secret impulses and hidden needs in themselves, to the point that they let these be manifest at the whim of circumstances; they react through uniform conduct, sometimes according to a scheme prepared in advance, but often in unexpected and irrational manifestations where uncontrollable and blind passions arise and violently sweep along whatever they find in their path.

The psychology of the crowd teaches us that it follows its own dynamics and that its laws are often far removed from those of the individuals who constitute it. In the midst of the crowd an escalade is produced; it is like the multiplier of each person's personal sentiments, and its behavior, therefore, is often more violent, more aggressive, and more tumultuous than that of the individuals who comprise it taken separately. In a crowd there is no longer the logic of reason, there is no longer intelligence or a spirit of responsibility which acts, but instinct and the deployment of animal forces, so that the individual for a moment loses his personality, finds himself, as it were, drugged, and follows blindly those who surround him. A new spirit leads the crowd: the spirit, the soul of the crowd. It is not a matter of a collective soul, but of the principle of collective behavior, of common opinions, of uncontrolled impulses going in one direction concerted by feelings and pushed by its own proper dynamics.

A typical example of the intoxication of a crowd is the trial of Jesus. The people — the very same who were present at his miracles, those people whose curiosity made them run all over where there was something to see — those who triumphantly welcomed the Lord a few days earlier, allow themselves to be turned against him when they see him bound and accused. A few leaders throw out the word of command: 'Crucify him'! and see these poor people — misdirected, excited, incapable of reasoning — allow themselves to be fanaticized and incited into the detestable condemnation of an innocent man, crying first of all with a certain reserve, and in the end with all their strength, 'Crucify him'!

Today, urbanization reduces distances, and modern man finds it more difficult to escape the influence of the crowd's collectivity. Television exercises its tyranny over millions of individuals and, unconsciously, they end up by submitting and adopting the opinions, the attitudes, the judgments heard and continually repeated. Style binds stringently. The press, the doctrine and discipline of the parties, exercise a dogmatism difficult to escape. Ever-present advertising and its thought, which follows the laws of psychology, stirs up the desire to acquire and develops the consumer society.

The study of the psychology of the crowd helps us understand better the importance, but also the ambivalence, of the group. The group is not a crowd; it is the opposite. It is a union, more or less close, of persons pursuing the same goal, having the same principles which they use as a means of stimulation and protection against the crowd and its inroads. In contrast to the individual, and even to the natural family, which is often defenseless today against the contamination of the spirit of the crowd, the monastic community which embraces all sectors of life, all the monk's interest, all his love, animates them, strengthens, multiplies by its cenobitic structure, is like a strong fortress able to defend itself against unhealthy influences coming from outside, but still more, for the mind and the heart, it is a holy city of culture of which Christ is the great light.

The group, then, exercises a function so vital that in founding the Church the Lord built it on a group, the twelve apostles, a number recognized even by modern science as ideal for its efficacy. Through this, we understand why, according to monastic tradition, new foundations of monasteries were made and should be made by a group of at least twelve monks, not counting the abbot. There is here more than a pious symbolism recalling the Lord's gesture.

Let us examine in a more detailed fashion the imminent dynamics of the group. It goes without saying that a group is not exempt from the dangers that threaten the crowd. It can allow itself to be carried away and even fanaticized and to transform its objectives into idols capable of making its members lose their real moral features, even to the point of perversion. But we are speaking here of monastic communities whose goal is to lead to the perfection of charity. This objective is, as it were, the catalyst of all physical and psychic efforts, the only enterprise which occupies the mind, the power of reasoning, the spirit of inventiveness and creativity of its members. In the heart of the monastic group there is created a concord, a harmony of intentions and actions. It becomes united, it becomes more and more welded together and becomes what the Acts of the Apostles has called 'one heart and one soul'.

Psychology shows that within a group, the social distance diminishes little by little to the benefit of social contact. Each member of the monastic community is a world, a unique personality. But by dint of the psychological mechanism, the distances among individuals lessen, contacts increase and become more and more intimate.

Then the flourishing contacts within the group leads each person to limit relations with and recourse to the outside. To the extent that the community becomes united, one same spirit becomes formed with its unwritten laws of behavior, of common understanding, and influences coming from outside and judged unsuitable for the group are rejected. At this stage of development, the auto-control of the community and a healthy critical attitude toward the positions or principles acquired is of primary importance. It is only by this condition that the inward union does not become a tyranny for the individual member and does not lead to effects similar to what we today call brain-washing.

Moreover, the ideal group has the effect of revealing, liberating, and developing the abilities of each member. Perhaps the subject himself had only a confused knowledge of this. Instinctively, in such a case, each person shows his good side, his qualities, and his talents — recall the chapter of the Rule on the artisans of the monastery — of which the community is able to make use.

These experiences lead to distinguishing the most capable to become leader of the group. The same thing applies to other responsibilities. Each one, then, occupies his proper place and his rank— humbly, while recognizing the qualities of the others.

If the leader is prudent and competent, solidarity will resist centrifugal forces which are never wanting. It will also resist corruptive forces which, in wanting to affirm or 'humanize' the relations, would run the risk of paralyzing them. Finally, solidarity in a monastic community goes far beyond productivity, whether of the intellectual type as in the common works of the apostolate, or of the economic type.

The objective of monastic common life occupies all the human forces; thus unanimity extends to all the manifestations of the life. Mutual help includes not only the needs of the body, but also those of the soul. Even the silence is an understanding. A gesture, a smile is enough to make oneself understood. In this sense, it is interesting to recall that the monks of the Middle Ages invented signs: a language of the hands, gestures, and eyes.

On the moral plane, the efficacy of the group penetrates right to the bottom of the soul. The fact of wanting to live truly together necessarily diminishes selfishness. This or that difficult character trait softens in contact with others. Knowing one another is a help to a better understanding of oneself as well as to a more vivid understanding of one's neighbor. A group forms character; isolation fashions eccentrics. The social sense becomes clairvoyant and makes one humble and modest in one's demands. Openness to others moderates the passions. The life of the group opens our eyes not only to the faults of others, but even more to the fullness of their personalities and makes us discover good qualities there, virtues well able to nourish a healthy emulation which is a frequent source of initiatives both small and great and of good example.

We therefore fulfill ourselves in community. The abbot, through his example and his teaching, exercises a decisive spiritual influence; but the formation of each monk takes place above all in the concrete living out of community life. For this life is the exercise of active charity, often deficient, it is true, but always generous to eyes disposed to observe it with benevolence. Every concrete act of genuine charity, like the sun on seeds and plants, exercises an effect of growth on all that is truly human, good, and beautiful. Not only does it preserve the character from deformation, from a lack of balance, from the loss of true interior liberty, but charity, being harmony and beauty, forms men in sociability, in respect, in magnanimity. It lifts up good qualities, ennobles abilities, encourages initiative, and awakens the spirit of inventiveness.

THE HOLY SPIRIT, SOUL OF THE MONASTIC COMMUNITY

The monastic community itself is, therefore, a spiritual force on an exceptional scale. The monks construct it themselves and bring to it their personal values. They are its riches, its vigor which in turn spreads its treasures over all its members and even, by extension, over all those who receive their light and stimulation.

It is altogether fitting to speak of the soul of the community. This metaphorical expression, borrowed from psychology, responds to a reality which is very true and extremely rich. To grasp the full measure of it, however, we should go yet another step forward. As a matter of fact, our investigation has rested up to now on a human, psychological plane. Now, if we were to limit the dynamics of a monastic assembly to that level alone, we would understand it incompletely. Above the natural laws of the group, but working within the laws of its psychology, there is in the monastic community another power which comes down from above (cf. Ac 1:8): the Holy Spirit. It is not flesh and blood, that is to say, natural powers, which form the group; but the Holy Spirit while making use of the natural dispositions of men and their laws, fashions the Christian community, the ecclesiastical community, the monastic community.

The group of the apostles is the typical example. Before Pentecost, they accompanied Our Lord. He lived with them and was the point of reference for each of them. The assembly of the apostles was not yet well welded together. And, in fact, as soon as the Shepherd was struck, the flock was scattered. But see how at Pentecost there occurs an altogether extraordinary event in their regard. Suddenly we see them appear together in front of the people. Group consciousness has been created: 'We', they say; we the group. They have a leader, in fact. They recognize him; he speaks in their name. Their collegial identity has been established. They are the Twelve, the twelve chosen by the Lord. In reflecting on the fact that they are no longer twelve, they search the Scriptures and find, in Psalm 108, the instruction they seek, giving them the right to replace Judas, fallen from his position of member of the group.

The objective becomes clear. They have a mission to fulfill, and they are conscious of that mission and of their responsibility to announce the Gospel not only around themselves but to the entire world—an immense task for a small community. But this community is moved by the power of the Spirit and realizes that it is united to the Spirit which Jesus had promised them. It is not flesh and blood which makes them decide to depart to the ends of the earth, but the Spirit who is the Spirit of the group.

We might complete and amplify this picture still more; however, this brief glance is enough for us to understand better the interior dynamics of the monastic community which is copied, according to tradition, from the life of the apostles. The Fathers of the monastic order, St Bernard among others, commonly attribute to the monastic life the character of 'apostolic life'—not in the sense that the expression is used today—for the ancient Fathers, the monastic life was an imitation of the life of the apostles following Christ and the life of the primitive Church.

As a matter of fact, the monastic community is formed around Christ. One enters there in order to seek God, the Christ. That desire does not come from flesh and blood; it comes from grace. The group, then, is formed through adoption, through incorporation. In order to fill the place left vacant by Judas, the apostles use a rite. In the same way, the monastic community receives its members according to an exterior rite (cf. RB 58:17, 28) which underlines the incorporation of a newcomer.

There are members, then. But someone who says 'members' also says 'body'. There is, then, the body, the spirit of the body, the spirit of union, the spirit of the group. It is not the spirit of the flesh which is at the base of the monastic community's formation. In fact, wherever the field of action left to the Spirit is too restrained, wherever the flesh has the tendency to unite the members, the cenobitic life according to the monastic style becomes unworkable and the group dissolves. What makes the common life possible is specifically the Holy Spirit. It is the consciousness of seeking and the will to seek Christ together, to have in common a point of reference, powerful but situated outside each person: the Christ. No one can say Jesus, if not through the Spirit (cf. 1 Co 12:3). It is in the Spirit that we recognize a leader: the Christ, and his representative, the abbot. And it is in the Spirit that we have one faith, one hope, one rule, and that we live 'in one charity and with the same customs' (*una caritate similibusque moribus — Charta Caritatis O. Cist.*). There is one and the same discipline for all (RB 2:22), one and the same love for all (RB 2:16), each has the same rights (cf. RB 3), each has the same chance to live, the same opportunities to develop himself according to the ideal of the Christian and monastic life in seeking the Lord. No one in that group attributes anything whatever as if it belonged to himself as his own, but recognizes even in the way he speaks that everything belongs to everyone (RB 33:6). That is not the work of the flesh, and everyone is conscious of working under the influence of the Spirit. Through him the group has the same goals and the same basic desires. Matters are dealt with together and always have as their ultimate reference the Kingdom of God. Charity is the convincing argument for coming to a decision. Just as the Spirit of God is the property of all, so everything is shared in the monastic community. For we cannot speak of only one heart and one soul where there are reservations and holding back. Sharing, if it is to be true and real, should not stop at material things. To be truly evangelical, our readiness to serve others (cf. RB 7:42) and our mutual obedience (cf. RB 72:6) should not stop with trifling matters. The Spirit is given without measure (Jn 3:34). The common life, lived with generosity, opens our eyes to the needs of others and encourages emulation in mutual service.

The person who is isolated by his own selfish desires and wishes withdraws into himself and is only at his own personal service. In his caprices he sees his rights; in his desires, so many demands on others. Attempts at life in common tried by certain people as a means of obtaining cheaply the services they desire are basically different from groups in religious life. These latter put their lives at the service of others; the former put others at their personal service. The monastic community, far from being a simple non-profit co-operative capable of assuring the life-style of male or female celibates, is essentially and radically oriented in the opposite direction. God is love. A life consecrated to his service is a life consecrated to the service of others.

The community whose soul is the Spirit of God is most naturally a community of common prayer and liturgy, for the Spirit leads those who live under his shadow to a continual meeting with the Father and with Christ. He places on their lips and in their hearts the eternal words which he has confided to his prophets. He renews the community unceasingly by uniting its members through the Body and Blood of Christ 'in one body and one spirit' (Canon of the Mass), by transmitting to it in the eucharistic union the impulses of the life of the Trinity. In this way, there is deepened what Urs von Balthasar has called *intercommunion*: the union of hearts among the members of the community according to the degree of participation of each in it. Let us add that, according to the same author, this *intercommunion* presupposes the *interconfession*: mutual openness in the humble avowal of one's own weaknesses, to which the chapter of faults gives an institutionalized expression. Sincerity without reserve is the condition for total sharing, in which the sharing of the eucharistic bread may acquire its full human dimension and its full social efficacy. The Spirit of God, *unus Spiritus*, is the artisan of this unity in charity and perfect humility.

And in this way is fulfilled the axiom: *All for one and one for all*. The service of all for each and all leads to the distribution of duties exercised in the name of the community. These duties differentiate and unite us. The monk cannot make his position his own property, a quasi-personal domain; rather, the more important the position is, the more he ought to feel united with and bound to the community. It is not in his own name that he exercises his responsibilities. No. Since the responsibility comes completely from the community, he should be all the more on guard for what can become its own end. In this sense, all those who have some responsibility, from the abbot down to the least monk, are mandataries of the community. That does not, however, make them depend in everything on a majority vote of the conventual chapter, but it gives them the obligation of acting for its true good. The final court of appeal for decisions belongs, not to the judgment of each person in charge or to the vote of the community, but to the Holy Spirit, its Soul.

We know that laws coming from groups tend to form a composite of goals, traditions, customs, behavior, and master ideas which one might rightly call the spirit or the soul of the group. The monastic community, a group of men or women united for a specific goal with means adapted to that goal, in no way escapes these laws. The soul of the group manifests its efficacy on the natural plane according to whether it is strong or less strong. But the reason for existence of the monastic community is found principally on a higher plane which transcends human goals and means. Would the group then have two souls? God forbid! That would bring in a disturbing parallelism, an unlivable dichotomy. In the same way as the group of apostles, through the outpouring of the Spirit, received a new and unifying orientation, so in the monastic community, tendencies, often divergent or poorly matched according to the natural laws of the human group, find themselves elevated to the essentially higher plane of a group united in the Holy Spirit — on the condition, however, that in the community, and in particular in the abbot who is chiefly responsible, faith, hope, and divine charity are the motives for all movements and orientations. Then, to that same extent, the Spirit takes direction of that community and becomes its soul. In this way it is no longer a group animated by laws of flesh and blood, but one heart and one soul in Christ Jesus.

IN THE LOCAL CHURCH

CONCERN WITH SITUATING the monastery and the life led there in the context of human society, whether civil or religious, appears rather insignificant at first to the reader of the Rule. There are no remarks on the state of society of the time. There are few considerations concerning contacts with it, except those indispensable for assuring the proper functioning of the monastery or for avoiding distressing situations for the monks. The sobriety of St Benedict's language and the purity of his intentions made him avoid observations which were not strictly necessary. His objective was to write a rule of life for cenobites (cf. RB 1:13) and nothing more.

This voluntary limitation explains, without any doubt, the reason for his silence concerning the place of the monastery in the local Church and its relations with it. Only once does he mention the Church of Rome, in regard to the order to be observed in the divine office (cf. RB 13:10). This reference, however accidental it may seem to be, has a specific and decisive meaning. The Roman Church possessed for St Benedict a normative authority, and we are in no danger of going beyond the facts if we conclude, on the basis of this, that for St Benedict, the authority of the Church of Rome extended well beyond liturgical questions. Apart from this little remark, the Rule does not directly mention either the local Church or the universal Church.

And nevertheless, the monastery is obviously an integral part of the Church. According to the Rule, the little circle of the monastic community appeals to the bishop in two specific cases where his direct intervention is desirable or necessary: the abbot has had a priest ordained (cf. RB 62:1); if he behaves badly, as a final recourse he should be denounced to the bishop (cf. RB 62:9). In other words, the bishop who ordained him retains some right of surveillance over him.

The second case treats of a badly conducted abbatial election. There too, the bishop retains a right of intervention. For 'if even a

75

whole community should conspire to choose a man who goes along with its evil ways, and if this should come to the knowledge of the bishop of the diocese to which the monastery belongs, then he himself or the abbots and Christians of the area ought to block the success of this wicked conspiracy and set a worthy administrator in charge of the house of God' (RB 64:3-4). If the bishop is not said to have the sole right of intervention, the reason implicit in the text has to do with the distances and the difficulties of communication which may prevent the bishop from being aware of the matter.

In these two cases, the Rule attributes to the bishop of the diocese the right and even the duty to intervene. He is, therefore, considered the final appeal. And as a matter of fact, the ancient discipline of the Church provided that the bishop had a right of oversight over the monasteries of his diocese. The difficulties and abuses which flowed from this during the course of the centuries caused the development of the right of exemption. As a matter of fact, the role of the bishop according to the Rule—the two cases prove it—was a right and a duty of *protection* to assure the good discipline of the house of God, but not a right of direction over the life of the community, a right which St Benedict attributed exclusively and formally to the abbot. If St Benedict in the sixty-fifth chapter does not speak explicitly of having the prior of the monastery established by the bishop, this case is nevertheless implicitly present in the text (cf. RB 65:3). It is remarkable to observe with what energy St Benedict rejects this possibility as absurd.

In the course of time, seeking to free themselves from sometimes inopportune or harmful interventions in maintaining monastic discipline, obedience, and peace, the abbots obtained from the Apostolic See disproportionate privileges which made their monasteries into quasi-dioceses and transformed the abbots into the bishops' rivals. St Bernard (*De officiis episcoporum*, 9.33) set himself against this excessive seeking of exemption as a lack of humility, while he allowed it where exemption from the bishop was a condition of the founders.

The purpose of this overview is not to paint an exhaustive picture of the problem. What interests us is reconciling the role of the bishop with the requirements of the Rule, which attribute exclusively to the abbot the responsibility and the organization of his monastery (cf. RB 65:11).

Today we have a more developed sense of integration into the Church, a requirement solidly based on the Gospels, the Acts of the Apostles, and the Epistles, particularly those of St Paul, where the bishop appears as shepherd of his flock. 'Keep watch over yourselves', says St Paul to the elders of the Church of Ephesus, 'and over the whole flock of which the Holy Spirit has established you as guardians to shepherd the Church of God' (Ac 20:28). St Paul does not set up any exception to this rule. There is no church within the Church; there are no sheep outside the flock. All the faithful of a local Church recognize the same bishop, appointed for this service in the power of the Holy Spirit.

Now, the bishop is the high priest of his diocese; he is the sanctifier of all his faithful without exception. He holds the ordinary *magisterium* in his Church in union with Peter and in dependence on him. He is the shepherd of the faithful. It would therefore be erroneous to attribute to the bishop only the job of co-ordinator of general pastoral work. All the sacramental life of his diocese takes place in dependence on him and in union with him. In this sense there is no exemption for anyone at all.

On the other hand, the abbot is the spiritual father of his monks. He admits postulants to the monastery, novices to the noviciate, monks to profession, and he presents to the bishop those who are to be ordained to the diaconate or the priesthood (cf. RB 62:1). He directs the spiritual life of his sons while being also responsible for monastic discipline.

Nevertheless, the bishop is the principal animator of the religious life in his diocese. He is responsible for the fruit of holiness produced by his Church under the breath of the Holy Spirit. He is the head of the body of his local Church within whose communion is produced the flow of the sacramental graces of the Spirit and outside of which there is no stable supernatural life.

Yet, while the bishop remains chief in charge of the religious life in his diocese, he respects the concrete forms of the religious life. Although the discernment of spirits is within his competency and although he may in a special case find himself obliged to correct errors, it is not his role to call into question or to correct the charisms which the authority of the universal Church has recognized as bearing the mark of the Spirit. The control which he exercises over the various forms of the life of his faithful will therefore be highly discreet and respectful regarding the manifestations of organized religious life. On the other hand, the realization of the particular vocation of the monastery requires a continual study of the actual state of human society, its expectations and needs, so the monastery may be a mecca for the work of salvation for people of today. Union with the bishop is necessary to constantly reinterpret this proper vocation in the light of the requirements of the world and of the Gospel.

The monks, conscious of the the bishop's sanctifying role, will therefore live in close union with him, knowing that the Holy Spirit has placed in him the power of distributing the Word of God and the consecrated Bread for their earthly pilgrimage. They will have for him the veneration due the representative of Christ established by the Holy Spirit. This faith will remove nothing from the veneration due their abbot, who is their spiritual father on the level of the monastic life which embraces life in its totality. The abbot also is their true shepherd (cf. RB 2:7, 8, 9, 39; 27:8) and their master and teacher (cf. RB prol. 1, ch. 2 *passim*; 5:6) in union with the bishop of the diocese, and in dependence on the supreme teacher and pastor, the sovereign Pontiff. The abbot ought also to teach the divine law (cf. RB 64:9) in its full extent. He should do this with everything he is, 'more by his actions than by his words' (RB 2:12), so that the nature of his teaching is more orthopraxis than orthodoxy. If St Benedict specifies that 'the abbot should not teach, establish, or command anything which would deviate from the Lord's doctrine', he means that his teaching should be in accordance with that of the Church and the teachers established by her.

The authority of the bishop, rightly understood, does not, therefore, take anything away from the abbot. On the contrary, the bishop is the link by which the abbot and his monks are integrated into the Church. *Extra episcopum non est ecclesia*—apart from the bishop there is no Church. Apart from the bishop there is no Eucharist, no total communion with Christ. Moreover, this union with the bishop should not in any way diminish the charism proper to the monastery, but should make it bear more mature fruits of salvation.

The monastery contains in itself certain notes which characterize the local Church: communion in charity rendered permanent by the vow of stability, the source of certain of the abbot's prerogatives and of his jurisdiction. Another note distinctive of the Church is verified in the monastery: the liturgy celebrated in a stable and solemn fashion as a service of adoration of the Lord in the name of the people of God. But, on the other hand, the essential mark of the local Church, that is to say, the apostolic succession which establishes divine right, is lacking in the monastery.

This exceptional position makes the monastery a pivot to the local Church. In it is realized intensely the *communio* gathered by the Holy Spirit to contemplate the mysteries of God, to live in the intimacy of the trinitarian life of the Son in the Holy Spirit, to tarry at the feet of Jesus to hear the Word of God. A monastic community that lives its life of communion near Jesus and in him is not only a privileged audience for the Holy Spirit for the whole diocese; it is, as it were, a concentration of religious forces of the Church in which is condensed the life of penance and purification, of seeking the Lord and faithful service to him, of adoration and contemplation of his goodness and his majesty. It is a privileged place for receiving the illuminating and inspiring action of the Holy Spirit, a place thus disposed for the prophetic task of discerning the signs of the times in the light of the Gospel within the local Church. Souls which are touched by grace feel themselves attracted to the monastery which lives its consecrated life with fervor. Burning with love for the Lord, they desire to be joined to the community where the gifts of the spirit are manifested, in a hidden way, of course, but where one learns to pray and to serve the Lord in the humiliations and the cares of daily life.

A monastery which takes its ecclesial vocation seriously is, therefore, surely a 'nursery of edification for the Christian people' (*Perfectae Caritatis*, 9) for the neighborhood and irradiates the spirit of the Beatitudes. Within the limitations which the common life imposes, bearing witness by this abandonment to the transitory nature of worldly values and at the same time to the absoluteness of God, the monks incarnate the life of the pilgrim Church travelling to its destination (cf. Encyclical *Evangelii nuntiandi*, 69). A monastery should be like the column of fire that led the people of Israel through the desert nights, a beacon for those searching in the night.

Let us not forget that the existence of a monastery poses almost insoluble questions to the minds of men who have lost, along with the faith of their forefathers, the sense of ecclesiastical institutions.

The size of certain monasteries, their majestic appearance, the impression of wealth they give, their apparent inaccessibility, prevents people who are led mainly by curiosity from finding a truly adequate answer to what seems to them to be a puzzle.

St Benedict did not have to deal with these false problems, which in fact boil down to the incorporation of a community into the social and ecclesial context of the world. What then was his formula? The monastery of that time, let us note first of all, could be of considerable size while having rather modest buildings. The description of the monastery at Subiaco given by St Gregory the Great in his *Dialogues* lets us realize this. But St Benedict, by the practice of very generous hospitality (cf. RB 53), was able to integrate it with simplicity and naturalness into the world which surrounded it. The poor were received there as special guests, and they did not call the monastic institution into question. St Benedict scarcely considered rich visitors. On the other hand, sharing with the poor and pilgrims he held close to his heart, because 'in them Christ is received' (cf. RB 53:15). He was not naive, however, and did not open the door easily to all comers, and the method for distinguishing real guests from undesirable passers-by was simple: those arriving were first of all taken to prayer (cf. RB 53:4). There their behavior revealed their state of mind. Moreover, St Benedict intended to preserve the solitude of his monks from the invasion of guests by prohibiting them from speaking together (cf. RB 53:23f). In observing these precautions well, it became possible to welcome people of every social class, to show them the monastery and the life within it, and thus to prevent any unpleasant talk concerning it. The guest house could not give the impression of wealthiness; care was taken that it be furnished with simplicity (cf. RB 53:22) and set apart for the abbot and guests. The food there (cf. RB 53:16; ch. 56) was without elegance but not subject to the rules of fasting (cf. RB 53:10). Thus the guest house reflected the simple, poor life of the monks.

The incorporation of the monastery into the daily life of the times did not occur, therefore, through the monks' going out — St Benedict shows himself little disposed to that (cf. RB 66:7; ch. 67)—but through the discreet openness of the monastery.

Would this not be a good formula for our times? The fervent life of the community, the manifestation of its internal unity lived out in charity and common work, the seriousness of the life of prayer, penance, and silence, and above all, the unfolding of its devout and well-prepared liturgy, are so many sermons which the Church and the world expect of a monastery today. Its openness to the truly poor would act as a very effective means of communication for neighboring people and for our world in distress. However, we are not concealing the fact that for an increasing number of our contemporaries, monasteries remain a question mark. Prejudices derived from accounts of a poorly informed or even hostile historiography do not help them to form correct ideas. On the other hand, it seems that among people of some culture, even unbelievers, we notice an increasing interest in monasteries. There they find in action values which they seek elsewhere in vain.

Basically, every community should discover how it can respond, in its own particular social context, to the expectations and to the quest of men of today who are led by a true religious sense, while still living to the core, an authentic monastic life, without compromising with naive condescension to ideas in vogue. It is enough for the community to agree, with ever renewed generosity to be a sign of salvation for the greater number of people.

As for the ecclesiology of St Benedict, one might find it at first glance but little developed. Looking at it more closely, one realizes that the Rule contains important, even basic, elements of it. Its principles are set out in a concrete way, which is all the more specific and striking. Following the teaching of St Benedict to its conclusion: seeing Christ in every person, and seeing therefore a brother, the Church becomes incarnate, and the monastery exercises its function as a rallying point where this body becomes a permanent reality. The community with the abbot at its head is its catalyst and represents Christ at work beyond the walls of the enclosure. The Eucharist is the central point of the Church, and the monastic community, through its solemn liturgy, is the assembly of the adorers of Christ; a monastery is by its very vocation a religious mecca, a true sanctuary of the local Church.

Let us not forget that the monastic life, contrary to what a superficial reading of the Rule might lead us to believe, is a charism given by God for the service of his Church. And this charism, proper to the monastic life, is to live the comtemplative dimension of the Christian life and to communicate it, that is to say, to cause the whole Church, especially the local Church, to share in it. Thus, as St Bernard expresses it, communicating this gift to the Church should not be done after the manner of channels, emptying their reserves too quickly, but after the manner of reservoirs which discharge their overflow. May monks and nuns realize that they are responsible for this gift which they owe to the Church whose debtors they are.

OBEDIENCE IN THE SPIRIT

THE PSYCHOLOGY OF OBEDIENCE

THE RULE PRESENTS OBEDIENCE to us essentially as a submission of our will to the will of another. The monk accepts the order received and exercises all his human faculties in carrying it out. Let us remind ourselves here that the psychology of obedience touches a man in the most sensitive part of his personality, his right to self-determination and his freedom of thought and action. The obedient man renounces following his own will in order to do the will of another. To obey—and this is essential to obedience—does not consist in being convinced of the merits of the order received and of carrying it out, although such a judgment may exist and is desirable. If our action is principally motivated by our personal judgment, we are only accomplishing our own will, while at the same time being commanded by another. In the same way, a purely external obedience carried out unwillingly (cf. RB 5:14, 17-19), is not true obedience, since it must be a real submission to the will of the one who is commanding.

Obedience is, therefore, precisely the submission of our will to another will. Now, is this not a mutilation of the personality, submitting oneself, on principle, to the will of another?

Before answering this question, let us pause at the concept of *self-will*. It goes without saying that we are not talking about the will as faculty of the soul and priceless endowment of human nature. *Self-will* is the too-natural tendency of a man to turn his will in opposition to that of another: the affirmation of self against orders from outside.

SELF-WILL

Let us leave the area of psychology and enter that of theology. Here we find ourselves before the opposition between the will of

God and that of sinful man. Self–will under that aspect is, therefore, simply the human will insofar as it is opposed to divine law. Against this self–will St Benedict demands that we go to war (cf. RB 7:21) as in the matter of the desires of the flesh (cf. RB 4:59, 7:12, 23).

Now a large share of daily decisions do not pertain to the category where evil opposes good but where choices which are in themselves morally indifferent meet face to face; that is to say, where a man could choose freely without clashing with the contrary will of God who in his eternal plans disposes all things while mysteriously respecting human freedom. There should not be any difficulties here for a man in choosing good and following right reason. Alas! Selfishness, calculating self–will creeps right into the choice of morally indifferent acts. And the desires of the flesh, deeply marked by original sin, too often cause the will to incline toward evil, so that our will, through this inclination to evil, can become 'self–will' in the sense intended by the Rule: that of a will stained with evil.

This state of affairs is so much more frightful, as all our acts, even our thoughts and our desires, our words and our most secret aspirations thus find themselves under the hammer of this encroaching tendency.

How to escape from the danger of this condition? How to flee from this *self–will* which is our misfortune, just as the gift of a free will is our good fortune? 'Turn away from your desires', advises St Benedict (RB 7:19) quoting Scripture. But how to do this?

To turn us away from evil, the Rule proposes that we take the 'narrow road' (RB 5:11), but the road which is sure and leads to life, thus avoiding the broad way that leads to perdition (cf. Mt 7:13F).

THE GOSPEL FOUNDATION FOR OBEDIENCE

In what does this narrow road consist? This will be the road of obedience where the room for freedom of action becomes more restricted, where man lives no longer according to his personal judgments, desires, and caprices, but at the good pleasure and according to the will of another: 'another will bind your belt and lead you where you would not' (Jn 21:18). We will practice this renunciation of ourselves and of our self–will (cf. Mt 16:24) under the direction of an abbot (cf. RB 5:12) and in the restricted area of a community.

What is, therefore, the Gospel foundation for such a counsel? Can I really confide the direction of my will to the judgment and the orders of another? Is it reasonable to renounce following the lights of my conscience and, in place of seeking in all sincerity day by day to discern the holy Will of God myself, to place my will in the hands of another who is fragile and limited like me and perhaps very far from holiness? Reason flinches at such a perspective, and yet St Benedict insists.

This attitude is evangelical, for the Lord has given us the example. He appeared among us precisely in order to make us see how we ought to submit our will to that of the Father: 'I have not come to do my own will, but the will of him who sent me' (RB 5:13 citing Jn 6:38). And, 'He became obedient even unto death' (RB 7:34 citing Ph 2:8).

Of course, the adversary answers within us: it would be easy for us to obey the Father if he would deign to make known his desires to us. In other words, the analogy between the obedience of Jesus to his Father and our obedience to a superior is far from being perfect. Moreover, Jesus does not seem to have given his apostles or anyone else the commission of imitating him in his obedience to the Father by submitting to this or that person, as if by that attitude, that fiction, we would be assured of obeying God himself.

How does St Benedict, and with him ancient monastic tradition, understand this obedience? Without any doubt, for them it was in all truth founded on the Word of God.

Christ's disciple should urgently and at all costs defend himself against tendencies to self-will. This is a necessity. We pause, there-fore, before the example of our Master, who insists on making us understand that he does not do his own will, but the will of him who sent him. The monk desires ardently to follow Jesus, chaste and poor. He desires, too, with all his strength to follow the obedient Jesus. St Benedict, therefore, comes to his aid to assure him that in submitting to the orders of a superior, he is obeying God, if the superior is commissioned by Christ. This is the indispensable condi-tion if the obedience is to end at God in person. Christ obeyed God. In the same way the monk wants to be absolutely sure that his obedience goes directly to God. This need is of prime importance, and we find ourselves here at the crucial point of monastic obe-dience. If the obedience of the monk were not directed to God it would be simply human—satisfying perhaps and comforting for feckless temperaments, but absolutely insufficient for monks seeking God. On the other hand, God does not speak to us heart to heart, but 'dwells in inaccessible light which no man has seen nor can see' (1 Tm 6:16). If he speaks to us without a veil, it is through his Son made man. Jesus himself left us, declaring, 'It is better for you that I leave, because if I do not leave, the Paraclete will not come to you' (Jn 16:7), and again, 'As the Father has sent me, so I send you' (Jn 20:21). Through this solemn parallelism, Jesus wishes to make us understand the incomparable authority with which he invests the men set up in his place, and it is on this foundation that St Benedict and his predecessors base the abbot's authority: 'He holds the place of Christ in the monastery' and bears the name attributed to Christ: 'Abba, Father' (cf. RB 2:2f). The Rule, then, rightly insists that obedience rendered to superiors is rendered to God according to His words (Lk 10:16): 'He who hears you, hears me' (cf. RB 5:15). This substitution of the abbot and the superiors for the Lord allows the monk to accept in faith what is commanded him: God himself has given the order (cf. RB 5:4).

'As if God himself had given the order'. Is this a pious fiction sustained by faith? The Church, holder of the power with which her Founder invested his apostles and their successors, can, without any doubt, commission religious superiors to hold the place of Christ in their communities. As she has been 'sent', she also can 'send'. For today's monk, the question of the authenticity of his superiors' power does not arise; thus he is secure to undertake his spiritual adventure without fear: to imitate the obedient Jesus. He will use the abbot and the community as an instrument for escaping from his own self-will and for clinging to the will of God.

OBEDIENCE AND REASON

Let us take up our question from the beginning again: how can we reconcile our need for and our right to freedom when the superior disposes of our talents according to his personal judgment and when that judgment may seem to us to be lacking in intelligence and in any case, contrary to what our competence in the matter sees as better. There is sometimes a question of making decisions which touch the most sensitive part of our personality. How is it possible, then, not to have a justifiable fear about the choices where passions, lack of know-how, and a thousand other factors risk inciting the abbot to command us to do something morally less than virtuous in our own eyes? Cases of this sort may present themselves endlessly.

In short, the question is a delicate one: granted that I submit myself to the superior's orders to avoid self-will, to sanctify myself, and even to do the will of God subjectively. But man is endowed with intelligence and freedom, and ought to act according to his conscience, that is to say, always able to judge whether the thing to be done is not morally wrong. This said, can he transfer the responsibility for his acts to another person who is, perhaps, poorly informed on the decisions to be made? Can he in conscience unburden himself to the superior if he sees him making a wrong decision?

St Benedict, in a certain way, foresees this realistic case of conscience in the sixty-eighth chapter. One may give a very broad, but at the same time, strictly faithful, interpretation of the meaning of this chapter and of the procedure he recommends to include all the conflicting situations between the demands of a situation and the discretionary power of the superior. In fact, the 'right' to obedience no more excuses the monk from pointing out questionable aspects of the order to the abbot than it excuses the abbot from seriously considering the objections modestly presented by the monk.

This remark retains all its weight in the case of 'functional' obedience which, while being essentially a submission to the will of the superior, is exercised in carrying out a task or a work. Monastic obedience, on the contrary, is less often involved in cases of this sort. The obedience of which the Rule speaks is chiefly obedience of an ascetic nature, which, for all of that, does not restrict it to a purely individualistic view. For this ascetic obedience less frequently results from an explicit order by the superiors than from the requirements of community life: presence at the Divine Office, the daily schedule, events that come up to change the ordinary program of our life where we, perhaps, would have wished something altogether different. This religious obedience imposed by the cenobitic life touches another which is required of us in the much larger frame of society, the Church and all of humanity, whose destinies foreseen by providence often affect our life in a decisive way. Faith in God and trust in his all-powerful love enable us to submit religiously to what happens beyond our power, knowing how to discern there the hand of Providence, which is able to draw good from evil for his chosen ones.

OBEDIENCE, FRUIT OF THE HOLY SPIRIT

Obedience—up to now we perhaps have given a more crucifying than beatifying impression—and yet it is absolutely at the center of our salvation, itself won through obedience (cf. Rm 5:19). Also, imitating the obedient Christ cannot allow the painful aspect to predominate for us. Certainly, it is not a matter of weakening obedience by presenting it in a false light, but the Lord who has once for all associated joy with the cross wants us to know how always to find life in mortification.

We must, therefore, dig deeper to find the true face of monastic obedience. The ascetic consideration of obedience underlines especially 'the labor of obedience' (RB prol. 2), thus the effort to be made. But it is necessary to do justice to the Holy Spirit, the Inspirer of every good work, who is at the center and the origin of a person's decision to set out 'on the road of obedience' (RB 71:2) in order to go to God, and also at the heart of his attitude of submission. Under the Spirit's touch, obedience becomes continually more perfect and more and more agreeable to God and pleasant to men' (RB 5:14). The reading of the fifth chapter makes us think of the Spirit, and the formulae which the Rule uses to describe this obedience are full of vigor and savor: signs of the passing of the Spirit. How, in fact, can the monk abandon immediately—without trouble, without delay, without half-heartedness, and without murmuring (RB 5:14)—his occupations of the moment and his own will in order to go promptly where he is commanded to go (cf. RB 5:8), leaving his work unfinished—if not under the influence of the Spirit who gently disposes the soul to free acts done willingly and joyously (cf. RB 5:16). Such ease and promptitude in running the way of the commandments (cf. RB prol. 49) cannot be explained otherwise than by the ardor of love poured into the monk's heart by the Holy Spirit (cf. Rm 5:5). Where nature alone labors and lags behind, the Spirit stimulates, invites, helps, and sustains the modest efforts of the one who has chosen to mount courageously the ladder of humility and obedience, but who, deprived of the Spirit's strength, would find himself out of breath, tired, discouraged, beaten by the inclinations of a nature quick to give in to the most varied influences.

Yes, the merciful and loving action of the Holy Spirit is indispensable here for gaining the victory, because nature presents a thousand excuses as a substitute for obedience and for the order legitimately given—an obedience to other imperatives which are perhaps more convincing, or indeed to philosophical, psychological, or sociological theories which take exception to monastic obedience as contrary to the dignity of the human person, to the structure of the intellect and to the pretended inalienable freedom of thought and action. The intervention of the Holy Spirit, which is never polemic, helps, then, to discern with clarity errors based on the illusion of human autonomy, and to overcome all the barriers opposed to an honest and joyful submission. His intervention helps to accomplish acts of great liberty, conceived in the most intimate part of our being. It teaches us to entrust the direction of our liberty to God so that he himself might so guide the intellect and the will of his representatives as to make all things work together for good for those who love him (cf. Rm 8:28). Those monks, far from doing themselves violence by obeying, or of giving the painful impression of living under constraint, are capable not only of obeying 'without delay' (RB 5:1) but show on their faces the reflection of their interior freedom.

It is not surprising, then, if the monk who has, under the influence of the Spirit, arrived at that liberty is capable of obeying even when obedience becomes crucifying or when the superior's injustice or conceit wounds his soul in the profoundest depths of his being. He remains unshaken in his love for God and submits himself, imitating Christ who became obedient to the Father even to the point of accepting death (cf. RB 7:34) imposed by unworthy men. Thus the monk remembers his vow of obedience and follows in the footsteps of his Master whose life was an uninterrupted series of submissions with death undergone through obedience for the salvation of men as its termination. He understands the soteriological sense of his own obedience which, through the mystical death of the effacement of self-will, unites him intimately with the redemptive work of his Lord, so he can share in the cosmic work of human liberation and of liberation of the world in the resurrection.

Have we all not been incorporated into the death of Christ through baptism in the Holy Spirit (cf. Mt 3:11, 28:19) so as to be raised from the dead with him (cf. Rm 6:3f)? Since baptism, there-fore, we bear within us the 'marks of Jesus' (Ga 6:17), 'the sufferings of the death of Jesus' (2 Co 4:10), participation in his obedience even unto death (cf. Ph. 2:8). Our modest individual obedience, however holy it may be, would not be anything if it were not included in that of Christ. See where the paths of obedience end? It joins the saving efficacy of Jesus' obedience to the Father.

It has yet another deep dimension for ourselves. Neither monastic obedience, nor even functional obedience, is an end in itself or in the mission to be accomplished; it goes further and prepares the ear of the monk to be more capable of discerning the gentle voice of the Holy Spirit who speaks mysteriously to the humble and receptive heart or inclines it to good in an ineffable manner. The monk who is capable of hearing the one who commands him liberates his heart from obstacles and nothing prevents him from being attentive to the Spirit anymore. This is the theme and the goal of the Rule: 'Listen, O my son'.

To carry out this program, he is not alone. Already at baptism he received the Holy Spirit with all his gifts, and he does not obey only with his own powers. To obey in listening to the Holy Spirit is not only a natural virtue, and the monk who is ready to incline the ear of his heart (cf. RB prol. 1) to the ineffable voice of him who dwells in it since the day of his baptism, obeys 'through the power of the Holy Spirit' (Rm 15:13). 'When, therefore, our nature finds something beyond our strength, let us pray to the Lord that he may deign to grant us the help of his grace' (RB prol. 41); the power of the Spirit sustains him, in other words. He makes us share in the redemptive obedience of Christ in whom we can do all things (cf. Ph 4:13). Thus obedience, far from browbeating our will, will strengthen our per-sonality in Christ and will be recognized as a liberator, obtaining for our heart the satisfaction of true joy.

OBEDIENCE AND LOVE

Obedience is an answer of love. One who loves, obeys. If we do not obey through love, we do not really obey, or rather, the love, the charity, the kindness in our hearts—fruits of the indwelling of the Holy Spirit—ought to reign over our whole life.

Today it is common to hear people speak of the alienation of liberty through obedience. They see obedience as a sort of outside interference with the will which, if not truly accepted, is viewed as hostile to our freedom and our personal development.

Now, we are in need of unity within ourselves. The phenomenon of rejection, so common in medicine in cases of grafting from one body to another, is an illustration of this. Everything brought into our personality from outside, if it is not assimilated, attacks the unity of our Ego. We may force ourselves to impose it on ourselves; if it is against our nature, that effort will be doomed to failure. How, then, can one accept an obedience, a command, which, in the final analysis, may appear to us impossible to assimilate, and against which our will, our feelings, and our judgment revolt? The monk who has solemnly promised to obey could find himself in this situation.

Now the process of assimilation in a human being takes place in accordance with its nature. The intellect and the will play a decisive role in this. In the concrete, no true assimilation takes place in man without love. Love alone has the capacity for receptivity.

From this it must be concluded that every obedience without an attitude of receptive love remains like an alien body, provoking a sort of moral indigestion. Perhaps the will bends itself beneath the yoke, but it remains intimately alien from what it is doing and carries it out in spite of itself. Let us note in passing that for the one who obeys, it is sufficient to accept the command and to carry it out willingly; the adherence of the mind to what is commanded is not necessary.

To examine these truths deeply, let us first of all look at Jesus. When he speaks of his Father's will—and he does it often—we are struck by one thing: there is such an accent of tenderness in his words, especially in his way of speaking to his Father, that we are deeply moved. This attitude certainly explains one of the reasons why 'many believed in him' (Jn 8:30) when he spoke to them of the Father: 'He who has sent me is with me; he has not left me alone, because I do always what pleases him' (Jn 8:29). 'Father, the hour has come. Glorify your Son so that your Son may glorify you' (Jn 17:1). 'All that is mine is yours, and what is yours is mine' (Jn 17:10). Jesus gives us the secret of his touching intimacy with his Father. It is explained by the complete and limitless union of the two wills. It is the love of the Son for the Father and the love of the Father putting all of his complaisance in his Son which explains everything. If we weigh that word 'Father' every time we hear it from the Son's lips, we will perceive there an infinite, immeasurable tenderness. Jesus is the loving Son of his Father; how then would he not do the will of the heavenly Father with an unspeakable joy?

Look at a little child who deeply loves his parents. He runs at their command, and it is a joy for him to respond to their desires. Now this is a very imperfect human analogy, we know. Look at Our Lord, child of his Father, an infinitely loving child. He need ask no question to know what will please him most. Love prevents any kind of withdrawal into self and transcends every kind of consideration. In this mirror we understand better how St Benedict can demand an 'obedience without delay' (RB 5:1) quoting the Psalm (Ps 17:45): 'As soon as the ear heard, he obeyed me' (RB 5:5). Let us not say flippantly: 'It was easy for Jesus to obey since the heavenly Father could not ask him unreasonable or impossible things'. Was there ever in the history of the world a thing less comprehensible for the human intellect or more difficult than that demand of the Father on his own Son, who was most innocent of all, to die 'for the wicked' (Rm 5:6)? The obedience of Christ was not only immediate, generous, and heroic, but eager, carried on the wings of love.

Obedience poses serious problems for us; Holy Scripture teaches us this from the first pages. Our inclinations, left to themselves, follow the tendency of Adam. 'For the flesh lusts against the spirit' (Gal 5:17), and this even under the New Covenant of the Holy Spirit. But since grace superabounds (cf. Rm 5:20) in those who have been reconciled and are animated by the Spirit of God, obedience, although it remains a 'labor' (RB prol. 2), an effort to be made, is no longer the insupportable yoke of our fathers (cf. Ac 15:10), for it is dictated by love and not by fear.

Yes, by love. We know it: the characteristic of the Son is to obey the Father, because he is the Son begotten by the Father in an act of infinite love and who returns love for love through the Holy Spirit. In the same way, we have been 'led to the obedience of faith' (Rm 16:26), chosen as adopted children of the Father through Jesus Christ (cf. Ehp 1:5). This is for us the great mystery of our religion: to have been 'set apart' (cf. Eph 1:11) so that the Father might discover the admirable countenance of his Son in the features of countless chosen ones who have become well-beloved sons.

This reality is truly the most beautiful of the contrivances of the Father's love for humankind. From his creation, this mystery can be perceived. The human person, created in the image of God, carries already within himself the seed of a child of God. But to make of us sons in his image was the work reserved for the Son.

And thus the Son incites us to his love for the Father and to his obedience through love—to what we call, rightly, 'filial' obedience.

For the monk who proposes to obey in order to return through the labor of obedience to him from whom he was estranged through the laxity of disobedience (cf. RB prol. 2), the only formula worthy of an adopted son of the heavenly Father is filial obedience, that is to say, dictated by filial love.

St Benedict, with piercing vision, penetrates to the very depths of the mystery and expresses the motive of the monk's obedience in a masterly fashion: the abbot is considered 'as holding the place of Christ in the monastery': that is why he bears the very name given to the Lord, according to these words of the apostle (Rm 8:15): 'You have received the spirit of children of adoption which cries out in us: *Abba*, that is, Father' (RB 2:2f). This says it all. To see in the abbot the one who takes the place of Christ, as Christ is the one who takes the place of the Father, incites us to an obedience of a true son, and therefore, of a loving son. This whole problem finds its solution in filial love, outside of which there is no solution which is theologically and psychologically satisfying.

Let us leave aside here the question of how and in what sense the abbot holds the place of Christ. To obey him as a representative of Christ in faith elevates our obedience to a higher plane and at the same time eliminates all false problems. For the minute the monk begins to complicate the act of obedience with 'buts' that come from psychology, he is changing his ground and is leaving that of the theology of divine paternity and filiation to enter into the philosophical realm with all its usual opinions and counter-opinions.

We are speaking here of monastic obedience as the Rule presents it. St Benedict keeps no more than two motives capable of leading his sons on the path of salvation: either the fear that the Father 'after having deigned to count us among the number of his sons might be saddened by our evil actions and come, like an angry father, to disinherit his children' (RB prol. 5f) or, indeed, the love of Christ, as the reflection of the Father manifesting itself in his service (cf. RB 5:2f). Only that reference to the Father makes it possible to receive an obedience 'as if God himself had given the order' (RB 5:4), and only in this way can the monk carry out the order received with the eagerness of love, 'without trouble, without delay, without half-heartedness, without murmuring, without a word of resistance' (RB 5:14). Filial love causes one to run in the paths of the Lord's commandments (cf. RB prol. 49).

Let us leave aside for the moment the right, and even the duty, which the monk has, as a son, to make his father abbot aware of this or that error of judgment which he may have committed in giving an order all of the consequences of which he had not grasped. The sixty-eighth chapter of the Rule is based on this consideration. Obedience is by no means blind. But just as filial love will not allow the monk to let his abbot fall into manifest error, so also it will not permit him the audacity of arguing with the abbot (cf. RB 3:9) by attempting to maintain his opinion insolently (cf. RB 3:4).

Nor will we speak here of the duty of the abbot to act always as a loving father. The love of the father logically precedes the love of the son. And as the love of the son incites the reciprocal love of the father, so the filial obedience of the monk incites his abbot to be attentive, devoted, and prudent in the orders he gives.

All these considerations do not hide from us the trials inherent in obedience; yet the problem it poses has the advantage of being simple, and the monk has only two possible alternatives: either to turn his back and refuse to comply, or, in fact, to obey. In this second alternative, the only one worthy of him, he will have Christ as a model and will imitate him in his frank, free, and noble obedience. With his grace, the monk will be with him, and his portion will be the joy of knowing that he is deeply united as a faithful son to the Father who is as lovable as he is great.

Obedience carried out with filial love is the keystone of the monastic life. This life, therefore, is loved under the rule of the Spirit and of his gifts. It would be difficult to imagine how it could be a happy life without this great peace, the fruit of obedience, which has become a basic attitude of the soul.

OBEDIENCE AND SPONTANEITY

During the season of Lent, St Benedict recommends that the monk spontaneously offer the Lord something extra: *propria voluntate* (cf. RB 49:6). On the other hand, he condemns, nearly ten times in the Rule, 'self-will'. It risks leading a person to the path to hell (cf. RB 7:21). Obedience is the way that leads to God (cf. RB 71:2). This *propria voluntas* then, should make us present a free and spontaneous offering to the Lord, and at the same time be pursued as the principal enemy of our salvation.

A real problem is hidden under this literary inconsistency. It is necessary, on the one hand, 'to hate one's own will' (RB 4:60) by submitting it in obedience to that of the Lord and his representative; and, on the other hand, to cultivate in ourselves the will—the supreme gift of the Creator to human nature, counterpart to the intellect. Is it, therefore, reasonable to renounce this self-will and, consequently one's freedom of action? Do we not in this way run the risk of shirking the necessary duty of being responsible for our actions? And then, obedience is a heavy responsibility. Why should we suppress our spontaneity? It makes a person so attractive and so youthful. Why choke the spontaneous burst of initiative? Does the vow of obedience not run the risk of deforming a person, of mutilating his nature, of taking away from him the freshness of his first reactions? In submitting to the will of another, does a person not put himself in danger of sinking into a thousand complexes, of distorting himself, and of living in the almost institutionalized fear of going beyond the narrow limits of obedience?

Before answering, it would be useful to note that outside the world of religious obedience, the conditioning of modern man is manifold. The 'society of the masses' exercises such an impact on the individual who lacks the firm foundations of a well-assimilated religious conviction that his freedom is seriously endangered or reduced to nothing. Let us consider the masters of thought in our society: the television, the radio, the newspapers, and their influence; then the tyranny of fashion, of public opinion, of advertising, and of social constraints! If one were to add yet the propaganda of political parties and the demagogy of their methods, it would be necessary to recognize that the obedience of modern man is deprived of all sacred character and goes much further in its constraints than that of the monk whose obedience is freely accepted and founded on a solid theology. The modern situation urges humankind more than at any other moment in its history to dream and speak of liberation. Distorted, contracted, complex, seeking an easing of tension at all costs, we flee large agglomerations as much as we can, so as at last to find and to be ourself.

This realistic vision of the conditions of modern human life allows us more easily to approach the problem mentioned above, which may be reduced to the following question: Is there opposition between spontaneity and obedience?

Let us begin with certain specifics; they already contribute the beginning of a response. Spontaneity is not necessarily a virtue. It can degenerate, whether in words, gestures, or actions, into an attitude of slovenliness, vulgarity or violence. It is necessary, therefore, to educate it, to free and purify it from many wild deformations to allow it to become the likable and attractive quality we designate by that name. Now, education is, in a large degree, the combined effort of authority and obedience. If, under the pretext of not hindering the development of spontaneity, some parents undertook to bring up their children with 'anti-authoritarian' methods, the bitter fruits of that education were not long in coming. Certain modern experiments exist to dissuade us from dreaming according to the manner of Jean-Jacques Rousseau.

Spontaneity, in the fully human sense of the word, is therefore the work of education and obedience.

This realization allows us to examine more closely our question: how to combine spontaneity and obedience? It is necessary therefore to find the reconciliation of opposites, the *compositio oppositorum*, since it may happen that what comes to our mind and passes spontaneously into our words or actions, is not in conformity with the demands of law and obedience. How therefore, can the monk be preserved from more or less frequent conflicts arising between what spontaneously inspires his mind or his will — good or indifferent in itself — and what obedience due to the Rule of the superior dictates to him?

THE EXAMPLE OF JESUS

Let us look at Jesus, our great Model. Was there a dilemma in him between the two contrasting possibilities of his own will—his spontaneous freedom of action on the one hand, and the will of the Father on the other hand? Certain theologians attempted to eliminate this problem by attributing to Christ, in spite of his two natures, only one will (monothelitism), that of God. The very words of Jesus pronounced on the Mount of Olives: 'Father, not my will but thine be done' (Lk 22:42) ought to have inspired them better, because it distinguishes clearly his own (human) will from that of the Father. As for our present problem, the words of Christ give us the solution, and what at first seems opposed is in agreement. Jesus submits his (human) will to that of his Father, as always, since he came down from heaven not to do his own will, but the will of Him who sent him (cf. Jn 6:38). We have only to page through the Gospels to find, to a surprising degree, Christ's affirmations, unceasingly repeated, of continually conforming his will to that of the Father.

We have always known this great example and our desire is to follow it. Yet we need not only this simple and clear doctrine, but we have to know how, in the psychology of Jesus, this process of subordination or co-ordination of the two wills is explained. It goes without saying that we also want to obey the heavenly Father, but our problem is to learn how to harmonize our will with that of the Father, or more generally, with the will of those who have the right and duty to command us in the name of the Father.

Our problem is not of the moral or theological order, but of the psychological. We desire not only to obey in such a way that it will not create in us dissociations, complexes, and unresolved conflicts, but we want the values of the human person to remain intact, and still more, that obedience may forge our personality and educate our spontaneity to that freedom and greatness of soul which we admire in Our Lord and, with all due proportion, in the saints.

Has this problem of the two wills, then, been resolved in Jesus' soul? The answer is very simple. In the final analysis there is no opposition or subordination or co-ordination. There is a transcending of the apparent opposition, and that transcendence is the love for the almighty Father in the soul of Jesus. There is no problem, or rather, the problem resolves itself. No manner of difficulty, no manner of opposition, of contestation, of hesitation, presents itself to Jesus, who loves his Father with that unspeakable love which is nevertheless so very human. Jesus loves his Father, and it is therefore his great desire, his very food, to do the will of that Father (Jn 4:34). This love of the Father, far from mutilating or stemming his spontaneity, makes it lucid, strong, and admirable in its human manifestation.

TRANSCENDENCE IN LOVE

After having contemplated that mirror of perfection which is Jesus, let us return to ourselves. The problem posed is of an extreme importance for us. If in accepting obedience, we have not known how to incorporate it into our ego, there arises the question of a mental health problem; or if we evade the obedience in order, as we imagine, to safeguard our personality, there arises then the question of a moral rectitude problem. If a monk, confronted with the demands of obedience, tries only to fulfil the precept, saying to himself that it is necessary to submit, to bend, to fall in line with what obedience requires, that monk remains on the surface of the virtue. He runs the risk of feeling himself passed over, exploited, constrained, and ultimately frustrated in his attempt. He is in danger of rejecting obedience at some point and moreover, perhaps more interiorly than exteriorly, trying to avoid what is displeasing to nature. If it comes to this, his spontaneity will suffer seriously, and he will be in danger not only of drawing no profit from obedience, but even of deforming himself through a wrongly understood or wrongly accepted obedience.

The only true integration of obedience takes place through love. St Benedict says this: 'The third degree of humility requires submission to the superior in all obedience for the love of God' (RB 7:34). And St Benedict quotes: 'He became obedient even unto death' (Ph 2:8). To give one's life freely and through obedience comes from the greatest love (cf. Jn 15:13). Jesus loved his Father. There was no problem there. For the disciple of Jesus, obedience causes no problem if his love for God has arrived at maturity. The Lord has said: 'If anyone loves me, he will keep my word' (Jn 14:23). Love does not tolerate or accept the least dissonance with the will of the beloved, and the monk could not run the path of God's commandments except with a heart enlarged by the sweetness of love (cf. RB prol. 49). With a lukewarm love, or without love, he would not run, but he would loiter on the way and would seek detours and evasions. Obedience would always remain a painful yoke for him with all the moral and psychological consequences which follow from this.

And spontaneity? How difficult it is to be sincerely spontaneous toward those whom we do not love or those who are ill-disposed toward us! On the contrary, mutual sympathy generates spontaneity. Where disobedience extends like ice over the relations between the monk and the abbot, spontaneity dies or becomes a deceptive facade; on the contrary, it increases where obedience is cordial and docile. As the spirit of insubmission brings either impudence or inhibitions, so the person who is open to the desires and the orders of those over him retains his natural and sincere spontaneity, the fruit, not of levity or calculation, but of a heart which is loving and receptive out of virtue.

There arises here an important point in monastic pedagogy and of human education in general. The novice who hears of obedience, of the Rule and of the usages, the prescriptions large and small which regulate the common life, can find himself intimidated and crushed, especially if he has the impression that the eye of the master is watching him. But when he feels himself loved, and when he is offered, along with the pill of obedience which is a bit bitter for nature, the motivation of the love of the Lord, he will be capable of swallowing the austere asceticism of the struggle against self-will and of incorporating it into the joy of the sincerely-loved service of the Lord. That novice not only will not lose any of his trustful spontaneity, but will become capable of ennobling his first reaction with the considerateness of charity, the gift of the Holy Spirit, by manifesting a docile, joyous, and free obedience. He will be a true son, spontaneous toward his father and his brethren because he loves them.

Love is the true and only master of cordial and sincere obedience. 'Walk in love' (Eph 5:2). That was the secret of Jesus' astounding obedience toward his Father. For Jesus to be doing the will of the Father was a vital need because for him loving his Father was a vital need. His life was bathed in the Father's love. To advance in love, to follow the path of love, *ambulare in dilectione*: this was the whole life of Jesus, even to the supreme sacrifice, a life given for humankind, his brethren, through love for his Father.

In the light of these truths, it is important to notice how mistaken are the attempts to mutilate obedience in order to protect freedom and spontaneity. Obedience does not destroy the spirit of responsibility and does not cause problems. In fact, to wish to submit love or obedience, the expression of the love of God, to self-seeking calculations, is to make of the monk a mediocre man with wings broken by false problems.

St Benedict, following in the path of Jesus' message, is of another opinion. For him, obedience is *sine mora* (RB 5:1), that is to say, spontaneous, without delay. Whence comes this obedience without self-interest? It comes from love. It is the way of someone who loves, and the characteristic of 'those who hold nothing dearer than Christ' (RB 5:2).

Obedience, then, emerges into love. One who loves does not have a 'problem with obedience'. Love frees it from the chains which someone who loves only imperfectly might feel. 'Obedience is proper to those who hold nothing dearer than Christ' (RB 5:2). To love Christ is to be animated by the Spirit (cf. Rm 8:14). Obedience practised as St Benedict describes it (RB 5) is an authentic manifestation of the Holy Spirit. For the monk, 'to run' in the name of obedience is to be all love, all spontaneity. He thus arrives at the full 'liberty of the glory of the children of God' (Rm 8:21).

St Benedict, when he treats explicitly of the obedience due the abbot, the brethren, the Rule, goes far beyond that framework, we have no doubt, and he shows us that in this way the monk is obeying God. Is that all? Let us leave aside other obediences, for the monk belongs to the Church and to civil society, and let us see how God is able to rule us without passing through men and institutions.

God speaks to us through his Word. It demands all our attention and our obedience. 'Is there, in fact, a word of divine authority in the Old and New Testament which is not a very exact norm for the conduct of human life?' (RB 73:3). Through *lectio divina* we sit at the feet of our Master, and he teaches us himself. Did St John not write to his Christians: 'You have received the unction coming from the Holy One, and you all possess knowledge' (1 Jn 2:20)? Has Jesus not told us: 'You have only one Master, and you are all brothers' (Mt 23:8)?

God has given us his Spirit (1 Jn 4:13), making us his adopted sons. Through his Spirit, the Father speaks to his children, enlightens their mind, and inspires their will.

Now what is more normal for the sons of God than to let themselves be guided by the Spirit of their Father and to obey him? St Benedict teaches us this. The whole Rule is arranged to teach the monk to recognize and follow the voice of the Spirit. The asceticism of monastic obedience is so contrived to exercise the monk and to make him obedient to the Spirit as a son. Monastic silence liberates him from the noise of 'idle words' (RB 6:8), enclosure and solitude help him 'break with the ways of the world' (RB 4:20), the prayerful atmosphere of the monastery sustains him in his efforts to be recollected, and finally, the teaching of the abbot and the example of the community encourage him to open himself to the Spirit.

The Holy Spirit, in fact, visits the monk; the Rule presupposes this. Has the Spirit not called him to the monastery? Without the mysterious fruitfulness of the Spirit, no human word would penetrate to the depths of the heart to bear fruit there. Certainly, the prologue of the Rule is an eloquent sermon, but the Holy Spirit should 'open the ear of his heart' (RB prol. 1) to persuade a man to set out and embrace the monastic life so as to make him 'listen to what the Spirit says to the Churches' (RB prol. 22 quoting Rv 2:7). The Lord himself 'seeks his laborer in the multitude of the people' (RB prol. 14).

Once enrolled, the monk, with the help of the abbot and his brethren 'with the Gospel as a guide' (RB prol. 21), with the Rule as master (RB 3:7), 'runs' and 'ascends' the paths and ladders of the Lord, and advances under the influence of the Holy Spirit who alone has the power to touch the soul from inside. From rising in the morning (cf RB 22:6) until the great silence of the evening, at the moment when the monastic day ends with the prayer of Compline (cf. RB 42), it is the Spirit who incites him to fervor and prevents him from falling into mediocrity or negligence, which St Benedict flogs in various passages of the Rule. If the monk is well-disposed, the Spirit will inspire him to a prayer that is longer and more intense (cf. RB 20:4). During Lent, it is the Spirit who fills his heart and makes him offer God supererogatory acts born of the joy resulting from spiritual desire (cf. RB 49:6). It is the Holy Spirit who excites the hope of success in his heart, wholly occupied with ascending the rungs of the ladder of humility, and makes him arrive 'at the love of God which, if it is perfect, casts out fear', faintheartedness, and mediocrity; thus he arrives at a great liberty of soul, a soul purified of its faults and its sins by the Spirit's work (cf. RB 7:67-70, prol. 49).

At the beginning of his monastic life, the Holy Spirit's touches and invitations are barely perceptible to the monk, but to the extent that he obeys them, they become clearer and stronger to the docile soul. It is especially the conscious faithfulness to the call of monastic obedience soliciting the monk outwardly that causes the Spirit to become more insistent.

It is only after having received proof of little Samuel's obedience to the call he thought came from the High Priest that God led him to obey the mysterious voice of his Spirit. The faithful and steadfast obedience of the monk to the representatives delegated by God invites the Spirit to speak directly to his soul.

Let us mention again the special case of the abbot. He finds himself at the head of a community gathered in Christ's name. How could he govern it according to his own personal ideas, plans, emotions, or imagination? He would not be able to take the place of Christ unless the Spirit of Christ dwelt in him. Thus flesh and blood could not make him say before his monks: 'You are the adopted sons of the Most High'. Only in the Spirit of the Father will he be capable of being for them the foster father for the Eternal Father. We need only recall here one particular case where St Benedict expressly invites the abbot to be attentive to the voice of the Spirit manifesting himself through the advice of one of his disciples: 'The reason why we say that all should be called to counsel is that God often reveals what is better to someone younger' (RB 3:3).

Here then are a number of indications which allow us to discover the lavish board offered by the Rule. The monastery is the kingdom of the spirit. To see in the monastic community nothing but a congregation of men or women capable of loving each other, without grasping the intimate principle of their union, that is to say, the love of the Spirit, would be to understand nothing. Someone who does not grasp that the Spirit directs and unites them, even if among them some seem little concerned, has not penetrated the sacramental reality of community, united in the name of Christ who wills that they be one as he and the Father are one (cf. Jn 17:11-21).

Here the grandiose vision of the fourth Evangelist presents itself to our mind: the contrast between the world and the children of God, that world which, with its prince, always wants to gain territory in the Kingdom of God. A monastery is in no way sheltered from this contrast. The mutual assistance of all its members is needed so that the Holy Spirit may freely exercise his beneficial power. The docility of all toward his invitations is needed. To begin with, the simple and prompt obedience described by the rule is needed to cause all of the attempts of the Evil One to fail and to open the doors of our heart to the Spirit.

TRUTHFULNESS

AMONG THE DEGREES OF HUMILITY, the seventh might be considered the highest in a certain sense, because it demands of us an extreme abasement. For, according to the law of our daily growth, of our drawing closer to the Lord, it is necessary to descend in order to ascend (cf. RB 7:7). That is a fundamental law, and St Benedict explains it to us in the beginning of the chapter by emphasizing that in order to practise this seventh degree, it is not enough to call oneself the vilest of all, but to believe it *intimo cordis affectu*, with an intimate conviction of heart (RB 7:51).

St Benedict here puts his finger on a fundamental attitude of our behavior—the inward and the outward ought to be consistent with one another. It is in the *intimo cordis affectu*, according to the first sentence of the Rule's prologue, that we became disobedient. We must, therefore, become obedient again, and that to the very depths of the heart. The seventh degree shows us this. We are tempted not only to believe ourselves more obedient, just, and perfect than we are in reality, but also, after having understood the necessity of humility, to call everyone's attention to ourselves by words, actions, or display, to the low opinion we have of ourselves, without having our deep conviction anywhere near our external attitude. There is a discrepancy between our effort to be truthful and the depths of our heart. It is not an intentional difference. At least not usually. But the discrepancy between that toward which we are tending more or less efficaciously and the depths of our thought is a basic conflict in us since the lie of paradise: the prolongation of that lie is our existence. We experience in our being the backlash of the lie of which Adam was the victim, and often we have the tendency to put on a behavior, a facade, which does not wholly correspond to our inward reality. This ambiguity at the root of our being, this split between the truth of what we are and the appearance of what we want to be, this basic discord is, as it were, rooted in us. Sin causes us to experience another discord: the lack of harmony between what we are called to be and our refusal to follow that call. Moreover, the tendency to want to appear better than we are still weighs on us. Is it necessary to see in this the desire to anticipate our real situation by

103

presenting ourselves to others and to our own eyes as we would wish to be, or does the need to hide our unpleasant traits simply end up in convincing ourselves that we are different than what others seem to think about us? This tendency to deny our true inward characteristics leads us to create an imaginary portrait of ourselves. This is another illusion.

The seventh degree of humility tends to restore in us perfect harmony, conformity between the exterior and the interior, between the illusion and the truth. Modern man, in the midst of the great social disillusionments of our time, feels an imperative need for truthfulness, often going as far as a lack of respect, impoliteness, and rudeness. Clearly these excesses have nothing to do with truthfulness and are inexcusable in human relations. Being honest with ourselves puts us in relationship with the absolute before divine truth; for all that is true participates in truth. God is truth, and falsehood is opposed to God.

This truthfulness—how is it possible not to see it?—makes our whole being draw nearer original innocence, the ultimate purity where there is no fraud or falsehood or duplicity. The seventh degree of humility urges us, therefore, toward this simplicity—not to be confounded with ingenuousness or naiveté ('be prudent as serpents and simple as doves')—which is the veritable hallmark of the children of God united in the Holy Spirit (Mt 10:16). This truthfulness is indispensable to the monk who strives for the unification of his being. Is the *monachus* not the person who seeks to establish peace in his soul, domination of divine charity in man with the unifying grace of the Spirit, the Principle of unity, by detaching himself from everything that weighs down, encumbers, and falsifies his heart, from everything that attaches itself to him and hides him from his own eyes, that dissipates him, divides him, or turns him away from what is essential? To establish harmony between what we say and our inward convictions, *intimo cordis affectu*, is a process of unification for our heart.

Then how can we work at the unification of our being, at establishing a perfect truthfulness of life? How can we overcome our basic tendency to wear a mask, to disguise what we really are? How can we restore unity in ourselves? Only Christ, by the light of grace, can allow us to attain this goal. A purely human effort would not be enough. We can only restore the truthfulness of our being in Christ.

First of all, a continual gaze at him will cause us to discover and perceive the transparence of his personality, that of the day of the Transfiguration when he appeared whiter than snow in the splendor of total transparence. It is necessary for us also to arrive one day at that candor of being since no shadow may penetrate the kingdom of light, for it brooks no shadow, and the shadow is the deformity in us. The full light ought to produce complete transparence in us. Our whole life, according to the Gospel of St John, is a struggle between darkness and light. The progressive coming of the light should drive the darkness from the remotest regions of our heart that we may be light in the Lord and children of light (cf. Eph 5:8), and thus a lampstand for the world (cf. Mt 5:14f). To be witnesses of the light, is this not a duty for the disciples who are called to follow Christ more nearly by sharing his life?

This work of the harmonization of our being, this asceticism of truthfulness should occupy our entire life. The soul cannot arrive at ultimate transparency except at the price of a constant effort at purification. Have we not had the impression of resplendent serenity on the face of certain people who have died? The ineffable peace spread over their faces teaches us that already during their lifetime they had arrived at a very great unity between body and soul which banished from their countenance the distortion of the effort needed to appear to be what one is not. Between the soul and the body no deformity, no friction, and is the light on their face, fixed by death, not a final reflection of a struggle carried to a successful finish and of peacefulness, the fruit of the victory?

St Benedict uses the word *sincera* only once in the Rule, in the seventy-second chapter, the tenth verse, to encourage his monks to have for their abbot a humble and unfeigned love. This love, it is easily understood, could unconsciously be influenced by self seeking, or the pursuit of certain advantages. It could be vitiated by flattery, adulation, and illusion. The effort for sincerity ought not, however, to express itself by a reserve dictated by fear or by exaggerated manifestations of respect or humble love toward the abbot, or, on the contrary, by a distant attitude to avoid being considered a flatterer. The simplicity of a sincere veneration for the representative of Christ, whose place he really holds, will set the just measure for relations with the abbot.

The Rule insists a great deal on the sincerity of the relationships among the brethren. Not only should the monk not nourish insincerity in his heart (cf. RB 4:24), and speak the truth from the heart as from the mouth (cf. RB 4:28), but he should also be very careful even in his gestures not to be open to equivocation. Thus he should not give a hollow greeting of peace (cf. RB 4:25), that is to say, in manifesting it, his will should correspond entirely and loyally to the outward act. He should not accept any half-measures in the matter of truthfulness, but should explain himself clearly regarding the meaning of his actions. In certain cases, personal dignity requires the avoidance of any kind of gesture that might be open to ambiguous interpretation. There may be false brethren in the monastery, and St Benedict is careful to point this out. It is necessary, therefore, to know how to endure, in a Christian way, unjust and sometimes revolting procedures (cf. RB 7:43).

Obedience also can be stained by insincere ways of acting. We obey materially with the heart of a murmurer (cf. RB 5:17f), or we deviate from an order so as to do things our own way, under the pretext of doing it better. Those who are fanatical for sincerity would prefer, in a case of this nature, a refusal of obedience (cf. RB 5:14) to an act which they believe they cannot carry out sincerely.

In order to develop truthfulness in us, St Benedict recommends openness of soul (cf. RB 7:44) in the fifth degree of humility. Undoubtedly, the frequent admission of our faults encourages the examination of conscience and the healthy surveillance of our actions (cf. RB 7:12f), and consequently, truthfulness with ourselves. For no one deceives us so much as we do ourselves, and the tortuous meanderings of our excusing rationalizations equal the pleas of the best lawyers in the world. Only an energetic and determined sincerity will succeed in dismantling the cavils of our self-love.

Jesus, resplendent on the Mount of Transfiguration, struck the three apostles dumb. Let us realize well that we will never approach that limpidity by our own means. It is the Holy Spirit who transfigures us by making his dwelling in us. 'In him there is no darkness' (1 Jn 1:5). If every man since Adam is a liar, our being will only be purifed to the depths by the fire which is the Spirit. It is he who, on the day of Pentecost, made the apostles limpid, transparent men. Innocence is not within the grasp of our nature except through the grace of the Spirit with whom duplicity cannot co-exist, since he is 'the spirit of truth' (Jn 26:13). There are spots and shadows in the sun; in him all is brightness and light. May the Holy Spirit deign to enlighten our hearts and may everything in us become light, so as to make of us the 'light of the world' (Mt 5:14). Only the effacement of humility will allow him to work in us and deliver us from the pride which is essentially falsehood, so as to make us attain sincerity, that radiant honesty of our being.

OPUS DEI :
THE DIVINE OFFICE

DOES THE HOLY SPIRIT not cause us to sing: 'Let everything that breathes praise the Lord' (Ps 150:6)? From him we have the breath, the respiration to sing, at its rhythm, the glory, the power, the goodness, and the mercy of the Lord. The Holy Spirit is the Inspirer of the most beautiful words and melodies of our Divine Office, and he does not cease to inspire our expressions of adoration and homage, our requests (cf. Rm 8:26f) before the Lord. Who is able to praise the Lord worthily if not he who knows the very depths of God (cf. 1 Cor 2:10)? Let us listen, and we shall hear the whole of creation sing the Lord's praises, each creature after its own manner. Are they not, by their essence and existence, the voice of the Holy Spirit to the Lord's glory? The praise of the Church is like the rational creature's echo of the innumerable sounds of nature and the harmonization of the cosmic chant and its varied voices. The Divine Office of the monks is the solemn actualization of the voice of the Bride of the Holy Spirit, the Church.

Our faith, and indeed our reason, tell us that we are little nothings brought into existence by the Creator's love and by the art of the Spirit who wanted to make humanity the masterpiece of terrestrial creation. His powerful goodness gives us existence, and if God chose not to hold us in being, we would fall at that very moment into non-existence. We are in his hands, even to the least of our fibers.

It is in God, as a matter of fact, that 'we have life, movement, and being' (Ac 17:28). It is elementary logic that since we are beings endowed with intellect and will, entirely in the hands of God, that we should adore him and prostrate ourselves before him in continual praise. It is at Vigils, toward the end of the night, that we begin our day with an attitude that expresses—alas, very feebly!—our gratitude, our homage, our faith, and which continues until evening in the rhythmic praise of the Hours, only to begin again the next day.

THE DIVINE OFFICE,
WORK OF FAITH

God is always present to us. Is it possible for us to be absent from him, to forget his presence? Alas! Our nature is inclined to forgetfulness and distraction. The monk, seeker of God that he is, tries humbly to be present to him. That is why our ancestors instituted what the Rule calls the *Opus Dei* (*passim*), *Divina Opera* (RB 16), *Opus Divinum* (RB 19:2). Their living faith led them to recollect themselves not only by continual interior prayer, but by community praise from morning until evening, in this way mutually encouraging one another (cf. RB 22:8) to accomplish what their faith had inspired them to undertake. Conscious of the loving presence of the divine Majesty, they chose to assemble at the most important times of the day to renew their faith and to express again their love and homage to the Lord.

St Benedict was heir to these sentiments. He therefore organized for his monks, and—without clearly foreseeing it—for the monks of the West, what he calls in his Rule the *Opus Dei*, an expression which corresponds substantially to *Laus Divina*—'praise of the Creator' (RB 16:5), *Officium Divinum*—'Divine Office' (RB 8; 43:1).

THE STRUCTURE OF THE DIVINE OFFICE
(RB 8–18)

The Rule provides a longer Office toward the end of the night: Vigils. At sunrise, with Lauds, begins the day through which seven Offices are distributed (cf. RB 16:1–3): Prime, Tierce, Sext, None, Vespers, and Compline, the last two before nightfall (cf. RB 41:8f). This alternation of common prayer with other occupations clearly supposes the intention of returning ceaselessly to the Lord's praise and presence so that the monk may refresh himself continually in his faith and avoid forgetfulness of God (cf. RB 7:10). The rhythm of the *Laus Divina* distributed throughout the whole day ought to create, as the legislator intended, a sort of *Laus Perennis*—an easier returning to the attitude of prayer.

THE FORM OF THE DIVINE OFFICE

St Benedict is very sober about the external forms which accompany or sustain common prayer. That it should be sung, insofar as is possible, responds to the content of the sacred texts which sing the mercy, the power, and the glory of God and rise even to jubilation. How could we keep from singing of the joy of being in the service of the 'Lord God of the universe' (RB 20:2), the God of all goodness!

St Benedict barely mentions the different physical postures during the Office. The brethren are seated for the readings (cf. RB 9:5; 11:2), they rise from their seats 'out of honor and reverence for the Blessed Trinity' (RB 9:7, cf. 11:3), they stand to listen to the reading of the Gospel 'with respect and fear' (RB 11:9) and, it would seem, for the psalmody. Or should we suppose that the *Opus Dei* was recited or sung kneeling, if we refer to the ordinances laid down by St Benedict concerning the brethren who are working far from the oratory: 'The brethren...are to perform the Work of God where they are, on their knees out of reverence for God' (RB 50:3)?

However it may be, what interests us is the spirit of deep faith, reverence, and joy which is expressed through these few ordinances. The body is the countenance of the soul, and cannot remain insensible and unmoved when the heart enters into harmony with the Word of God. Liturgical gestures are meant to be expressions of the mind and the heart, of faith and of love. The undisciplined imagination provokes discord between the gesture and its intention, between the voice and the mind. It is an effort to be renewed each day so that 'our mind may be in harmony with our voice' (RB 19:7). In this sense, the *Opus Dei* wages a never-ending struggle of purification and unification between the outer man and his soul.

THE IMPORTANCE OF THE DIVINE OFFICE

The place the Divine Office holds in the monk's life is determined by his vocation. He is, by definition, the person who seeks God, who listens to his Word, who is turned toward him as to the magnetic pole of his being. He is, then, a contemplative person (which in no way excludes action). St Benedict's disciples have always faithfully observed his prescription with respect: *Nihil operi Dei praeponatur*—'Let nothing be preferred to the Work of God' (RB 43:3). Among all the occupations of the monk, among all of the obligations of the community, the Divine Office holds first place. The whole tenor of the Rule underlines the duty of organizing the monk's life, as far as it is possible, and especially the community's life in such a way as to give privileged place to the Work of God. The forceful phrase about letting nothing take preference over the Work of God is very close to another expression of the same construction: 'Let nothing be preferred to the love of Christ' (RB 4:21). The Divine Office, which is an especially strong manifestation of love for the Lord, shares, therefore, his privileged place.

This intransigent fidelity to the Divine Office conceived by the Rule is difficult to explain to someone in an age whose faith is vague and scanty. For him this insistence is exaggerated and contrary to the needs of the world. He pretends that through *labora* (work) the duty of *ora* (prayer) is amply compensated—that the service of the brethren is the most authentic expression of God's service and that the Lord has no need of our praise. There is no need to enter into apologetics. This is a matter of faith, and it alone can make us grasp the absoluteness of God and the relativeness of all the rest, with the true hierarchy of values. Only faith can understand why, for someone who performs the Divine Office, desiring in this way to seek the Kingdom of God and his justice before anything else, everything else will be added unto him (cf. Mt 6:33).

St Benedict is a witness to God because he is a man of absolute faith. We are therefore not surprised at the prescriptions with which he surrounds the primacy of the Divine Office. From the hour of rising, the monks should think of the Divine Office and should 'vie with one another to arrive at the Work of God' (RB 22:6, so much so that they will 'gently encourage one another, that those who are sleepy may have no excuse' (RB 22:8). How could the monk make the Lord wait, when he has given him the privilege of being called to his service! The importance of the Divine Office requires, therefore, first of all, punctuality to assure regularity in the observance of the canonical hours. St Benedict therefore obliges the abbot to see personally to the duty of announcing the Hours of the Office or to delegate it to a very conscientious brother on whom he can confidently rely (cf. RB 47:1). To this faithfulness corresponds the punctuality of the monks, who 'should always be ready. When the signal is given, they are to rise at once' (RB 22:6) to anticipate the hour of the *Opus Dei*. During the day 'at the hour of the Divine Office, as soon as the signal is heard, the monk will leave whatever he has in hand and hurry to it' (RB 43:1). The severity with which St Benedict punishes those who arrive late for the *Opus Dei* (cf. RB 43:4–12) also shows the importance he attached to it. In his words we can feel vibrations of 'zeal for the house of God' (Jn 2:17), zeal for the honor of God.

For St Benedict, the Divine Office is above all a duty for the community. This does not mean to say that this duty is not at the same time a personal duty for each monk. The brethren who are working far from the chapel, therefore, 'will perform the Work of God where they are and kneel out of respect for God' (RB 50:3), whereas the brethren who have been sent on a journey 'will not allow the prescribed Hours to pass; they will recite them as they are able, in private, and will not neglect to fulfil this duty of their service' (RB 50:4). Whereas in other areas St Benedict is less prolix in details, he thinks of all eventualities when it comes to the *Opus Dei*.

In the life of the monk, the *Opus Dei*, the service of God, therefore takes precedence over every other occupation. That is why if a novice lacks zeal for the *Opus Dei*—let us note that St Benedict requires a real zeal—this attitude would be a counter-indication of a vocation (cf. RB 58:7).

In setting out to establish a school for the service of the Lord (RB prol. 45), St Benedict embraced the entire range of the monastic life. But there is no doubt that the *Opus Dei* and the ritual and especially the spiritual apprenticeship for its performance, took the dominant place in his thought in this service—which place, in fact, he does attribute to it in the Rule.

THE DIVINE OFFICE, A SERVICE

Although the Rule of St Benedict presents God to us as a father (cf. RB 2:3, prol. 5f) whose children we are, the word 'Lord' is to be found there much more often. The fear of God, although it is filial fear, seems to correspond more to the mentality of the Rule than the love of Christ of which, however, it speaks admirably, or in any case, true love of God does not exist without fear (cf. RB 72:9). The Divine Office is a service due divine Majesty (cf. RB 16:2), and it is for us an inestimable honor to be always the servants of such a Lord now that Christ has made us his children and his friends. The Divine Office is a duty which we owe to the Lord and which we must render 'in the fear of God' (RB 50:3), and 'prescribed Hours' are an obligation of service before the throne of the Most High and must be observed as well as possible (cf. RB 50:4). It is, therefore, truly a service accepted freely by the promise of *conversio morum*, that is to say, living faithfully the monastic life described in the Rule.

THE DIVINE OFFICE PRODUCES THE UNITY OF THE MONASTIC LIFE

The Divine Office is called *Opus* (work): that is also a way of emphasizing a sense of duty, of service, which entails fatigue. This expression is related to the Greek word '*Litourgia*' which contains the word '*ergou*' = '*opus*'. The *Opus Dei* is an occupation, a labor alongside other labors, although it is the most noble and most important. It is the occupation first in dignity, but not the only one. It is not a substitute for other duties, nor does it supplant them, and it cannot become an excuse for avoiding works which may be more painful. As a matter of fact, it balances the other occupations of the day so that no other may absorb the monk too much or monopolize him.

On the other hand, the Divine Office being a work, albeit a holy work, reminds the monk that all his daily tasks should also be a holy work, an *Opus Dei* of which the Divine Office is only the first, that which begins and ends the day and presides over all the monk's activities. These are not governed by the rhythm of a profane work, but by the Work of God which gives them their meaning, their mood, their atmosphere. Every sort of labor is transformed, so to speak, into a prayer. Manual labor thus becomes a prolongation of the *Opus Dei*. Thus in the unity of the Holy Spirit is produced the unity of the monastic life; it is a 'labor' (RB prol. 2). The Lord searches for 'his laborer' (RB prol. 14) in the multitude of people that he may lead him into the workshop, that is to say, the cloister of the monastery and there make him 'work diligently with all the instruments' (RB 4:78) of good works until 'by the Holy Spirit he deigns to manifest in his laborer' (RB 7:70) the grace of purification. The monk is the workman of the Lord, the workman of his own salvation, and the *Opus Dei* is his principal work.

The Divine Office will produce the unity of our whole monastic life. Its purpose is that 'God may be glorified in all things' (RB 57:9). The monk wishes to place all his love in the fact that everything created is essentially for the glory of God. It is through the texts of the Divine Office that we will express our joys and our sorrows, our successes and our failures, our anxieties and our misplaced confidence, and it is from them that we will receive, as it were, the answers from the Spirit capable of putting everything back into place and giving us back peace and unity. We may arrive at the Office agitated; we will leave calm and comforted. We may be smarting under the weight of cares, and in prayer we will meet Christ carrying his cross just ahead of us. The Divine Office makes of the monk a person with one sole purpose, one sole aim which allows no other goals. He is the person who is seeking God; everything he meets along the way serves as a means to his one aim in life.

The Divine Office unites us to the prayer of the whole Church whose intentions we continually espouse: those of the Spirit of Christ. He unites us to his *opus redemptionis*, to the work of salvation in which we more and more become co-workers through the Divine Office and our whole monastic life. We are in solidarity with Christ and his work.

It is above all in the Divine Office that union in the spirit takes place with our brethren who glorify God with us 'with one heart and one voice' (Rm 15:6). In the Divine Office is produced and renewed the union of charity, the effect and sign of the operative presence of the Spirit. In spite of all the divergences of opinion and of activity which may separate the brethren, charity, the gift of the spirit, unites the monks gathered for the Divine Office in a common effort of praise of the Lord at a level of charity which goes beyond all the secondary differences, since their common good is faith, the love of the Lord Jesus, and divine praise. The Divine Office makes us meet again continually, in the unity of the Holy Spirit, those who are our travelling companions on our way to the Lord.

THE DIVINE OFFICE
PRODUCES COMMUNION

The Divine Office creates in each monk, and by way of consequence, in the House of God, a spiritual atmosphere where the presence of the Lord is strongly felt. The union with God present, with Christ, the Friend of each moment, becomes, even though subconsciously, more habitual. As the 'Jesus Prayer' leads little by little to a state of prayer, so, too, faithfulness to the Divine Office tends to produce in the monk's soul a habit of constantly returning to God, a continual attention to the Lord. The Holy Spirit takes hold of this total good will, of this desire for God. Even if we are distracted, he comes to the aid of our weakness, since we do not know how to pray as we should (cf. Rm 8:26). He makes, as it were, a sheaf out of the few wisps of our poor praise, of our sincere desires to pray, and offers them to the Father with 'ineffable groanings' (Rm 8:26). The Holy Spirit produces the communion of the monk with the Father and the Son, as well as the communion with the brethren, so that all might be one in him.

The communion prepared by the Divine Office faithfully performed and produced by the Holy Spirit finds its consummation in the eucharistic communion of the conventual Mass, the center and summit of the *Opus Dei*, in communion with Christ who is the unique good of the monk's undivided love.

LECTIO
MEDITATIO
ORATIO

BENEDICTINE SPIRITUALITY is distinguished by the trilogy: listen—meditate—pray. These activities follow one another naturally, blend themselves together, and prepare a person for intimate conversation with God.

To know, first of all, how to listen is, without doubt, the beginning of wisdom. Then—open the mind and the heart and become available and receptive like a child. How could one be otherwise? The Father speaks to us and sends us his Word but, alas, listening is not an easy thing. St Benedict tells us that the body and the soul are the two uprights upon which the rungs of the ladder of humility rest (cf. RB 7:9). We cannot undertake any spiritual activity without making our body participate in it as well. If it is not calm and relaxed, if it is not recollected, it will not leave the soul in peace. But if, without constraint, it assumes an attitude of respect and deference, it will help the soul keep itself humbly before the divine Majesty (cf. RB 20:1f) since he condescends to speak to us. To the extent that a person becomes rooted in the fear of God, a gift of the Holy Spirit, he becomes conscious of his unworthiness, of his fundamental impurity, but also of God's immense condescension.

God manifests himself. He speaks to us. No human person can attain to the Infinite by his natural powers, and he needs a special faculty to go beyond himself and grasp the mysteries of God. The gift of faith opens to him this divine world, hermetically sealed to the unbeliever who is deprived of the Spirit's unction.

The believer, purified by contrition and seeking to understand with uprightness, ought to listen. Listen to himself? No, but that admonition is not useless, for a person should make an effort to go out of himself. Withdrawn into himself, he easily falls into the error of letting himself be enlightened by human lights, or he imprisons

117

himself and contorts himself in a labyrinth of ideas his own size, haunted by the fear of losing his freedom if he should receive orders for living from a God distinct from himself. So he turns around in a circle, taken up with his own ridiculous little world.

To listen to God is to be able to have recourse to him who does not mislead, does not lie—to the just Judge, to Love itself. To listen to God is not to be alienated but to free oneself from a vicious circle.

LECTIO DIVINA

To listen to God in the reading of Holy Scriptures is first of all to be taught by the Spirit who speaks of the Son and the Father (cf. Jn 16:15). His mission is to lead us to all truth (cf. Jn 16:13). Can we understand how wonderful it is to be instructed by the Spirit, taught by him 'the mystery hidden from ages past...and now manifested to his saints' (Col 1:26) of which we are the beneficiaries 'chosen before the creation of the world' (Ep 1:4)? Let us not be surprised to see St Benedict reserve several hours of the day, especially in winter, to *lectio* (cf. RB 48). Today in our monasteries, we fall far below that provision! There would be so many things to say if we were to speak of its fruits in detail. Let us just recall that to the extent we set ourselves to be taught by the Spirit, unity is produced in our life— unity between doctrine and practice, unity between the desires of the Spirit and the desires of our heart, unity between the thoughts of God and the thoughts of man. For assiduous *lectio divina* gives the faithful soul a culture which has nothing of the superficial but is complete, perfect, profound, and has no other limits than the infinite knowledge and wisdom of God.

MEDITATIO

The passage from *lectio* to *meditatio* is almost imperceptible and overtakes a person. One feels the need to weigh the words, to penetrate their meaning and implications, and to draw practical lessons from them. The various methods correspond to the development of human thought. The more uncalculated they are, the more natural they remain, so much better is their chance of not weighing down the development of thought. Meditation should be made under the light of the Spirit without turning back too much on oneself. Far from leading to an egotistical concentration, it attempts to fix a simple and limpid gaze on Christ and on the work of the Father, and thus a person finds rest and fullness, answers to his questions, and solutions to his problems.

Let us not allow ourselves to be discouraged by an inability to meditate or by apparent failure, because such handicaps are not rare, and some people experience them to the end of their days. A fruitful meditation is not measured by the stop-watch. The very human admonition of St Benedict that 'prayer be short and pure' (RB 20:4) concerns meditation as well. Returning to *lectio* always remains the simplest remedy for escaping dryness or apathy.

ORATIO

It goes without saying that we should leave the problem of determining where the meditation ends and where the prayer begins to the psychologists. A true meditation is the surest way to prayer and, if it please God, to an experience of contemplation.

From meditation may spring up, as a natural conclusion, one of the prayers offered by the liturgy or the *Opus Dei*. The Spirit himself has formulated them, and he is the author of the soul's most beautiful invocations to God. No one, in fact, can say '*Abba*, Father' except in the Spirit (cf. Rm 8:15f). 'No one can say: "Jesus is Lord", except under the influence of the Holy Spirit' (1 Co 12:3).

The Old Testament gives us wonderful expressions of prayer. We take them and make them our own. The Psalms, for example, allow us to pour out into God's heart the most intimate feelings of our own: joy, thankfulness, supplication, distress, suffering, propitiation, and the seeking of the divine presence. The Church from the very beginning put into the mouths of Christians these same words of Scripture. The same Spirit inspired the just of the Old Testament as to how they should pray. Today he teaches us how to adore 'the Father in spirit and in truth' (Jn 4:23). The Spirit alone can give us the knowledge of prayer and make us fully penetrate its meaning. He alone can awaken in our soul the taste for it and joy in it. No one can speak to the Father without having received his Spirit. The Father is clothed in a light which dazzles us. He is the wholly *Other*. How could we speak to him without having been introduced by his Spirit into the mystery of the language with which his own Son speaks to his Father? Anyone who does not know how to gather from the lips of the Son the way to pray with him and in his name, or at least is not introduced by the Spirit to the sentiments of true prayer, will never know how to pray.

St Benedict gives us basic counsels to make our prayer genuine and 'pure' (RB 20:4). Pride is the basic impurity, and it brooks no domination. Now just as the kings and powerful of this earth do not hear favorably a request made with arrogance, in the same way God resists the proud (cf. 2 P 5:5). By what aberration can a man who is dust presume to be heard by the God of the universe if he does not pray with a humble consciousness of his nothingness, in all the purity of devotion of his heart, and with tears of compunction (cf. RB 20:1–3)? The publican deserves to be heard, whereas any kind of self-complacence is an obstacle to the Spirit and transforms the most sacred phrases into words devoid of meaning in the mouth of the proud.

'Sing praise wisely' (RB 19:4), St Benedict exhorts in the words of the psalmist (Ps 46:8). See to it that the mind follows intellectually what the mouth pronounces, that is to say, that the entire person is in harmony with the sentiments which the Holy Spirit puts into his heart and upon his lips. Now this identification with the wishes of the Spirit takes place at least in the will of a man, an identification which is required in order to present oneself with assurance 'before God and his angels' (RB 19:6) where alone truth is able to subsist in its pure state.

This requirement is even more necessary when the monk desires to pray privately and on his own initiative. During our participation in the common prayer of the Divine Office, we act through obedience. In private prayer, self-will, vanity, or other impure motives can more easily slip in.

St Benedict, to assure the purity of this prayer, *oratio*, wants it to be short 'unless it be prolonged under the impulse of the grace of the Spirit of God' (RB 20:4). When the heart is the prisoner of various attachments, its prayer of petition is restless and multiplies words (cf. RB 20:3). God wills our good with an infinite clairvoyance and favorably hears those who abandon themselves to his will. Tears and fervor of heart (RB 52:4) can be a sign of the genuineness of this prayer, this *oratio*. To remain in the oratory demands, therefore, an attitude of exterior silence, and the Rule does not allow noisy people to remain there lest they disturb those who desire to pray more intimately (cf. RB 52:5). Even their more or less idle presence disturbs the others. For the person who finds, in prayer, by the grace of the Spirit, a deep, even mystical, contact with his God, a certain material solitude, a calm, a silence, are desirable conditions. Did the Lord himself not demand them by requiring someone who wants to pray to retire into his chamber and close the door (cf. Mt 6:6) in order to be entirely alone with him? Certainly in this matter, the most important thing is solitude, liberty of the soul, knowing how to close the door of the heart to the hubbub of desires, inclinations, and imaginations, but without doubt, exterior tranquility helps chase out of ourself everything that can distract us from the encounter with the only true Love. So then, the Spirit of love manifests himself and makes the soul enter ever deeper into the life of the Trinity in making it be attentive to and share in the mysterious springing forth of the Word from the bosom of the Father, the Word who takes root deeply in the loving human heart and bears fruit there for eternal life.

The Spirit thus makes us fully conscious that we are adopted sons of God, an incomparable dignity before which we cry out in wonder: '*Abba*, Father' (cf. Rm 8:15f), and he introduces us into the spontaneity of divine intimacy. But although the Son has given us the power of considering ourselves no longer servants but friends (cf. Jn 15:15), at the same time the Spirit deepens in us the consciousness of being children by pure grace, without any natural merit. To the extent that we take our weakness into account and our inability to ask the Lord for what is suitable for us, it is the Spirit intimately united to our spirit who takes this in hand and prays in us 'with ineffable groanings' (Rm 8:26f). The more the Holy Spirit takes over the faculties of the soul to free it from its often sterile efforts and prays in it, the more that prayer becomes deeply linked to the divine will which is wholly love.

'No one can say 'Jesus is Lord', except under the influence of the Holy Spirit (1 Co 12:3). True prayer, that lifting of the soul to God, always takes place under the Spirit's influence. The Father sent him to us to teach us how to converse with him: *Abba*, that is to say, Father. Only the Holy Spirit can give us such authenticity to our conversation with him.

By ourselves we are not able to converse with the Father, because a good relationship with another implies having been able to find a person to person plain of correspondence with him. Moreover, an experimental knowledge of the other is necessary. It is necessary to be able to measure the distance and the nearness between him and ourselves and, by trial and error, to find an access to his mind and especially to his heart. This knowledge gained by experience controls the sentiments which our words and gestures express or imply—sentiments of fear, filial respect, friendship, confidence, or energetic insistence, according to the case.

Now when it comes to God, 'no one knows the Father except the Son and he to whom the Son has willed to reveal him' (Mt 11:27) through the Holy Spirit whom he has sent us in order to let us know the entire truth (cf. Jn 16:13). This truth is necessary for us. It is essential for adopted children to know how to talk to their Father. And Paul assures us that we have received that Spirit (cf. Rm 8:15).

It would be useless to seek the power to pray within ourselves. How can someone be led to talk to God if he does not have a glimmer of faith in a supreme being of total power and goodness? This beginning of faith does not come from himself but from the Spirit who inspires him to be attentive, insofar as he is able, to accept this grace. In any case, this first prayer might be very imperfect, centered more on man than on God 'for we do not know what to ask so as to pray as we ought' (Rm 8:26). On the other hand, prayer alone is able to produce in our hearts a true, beatifying conversion. This prayer, aided by grace, is able to obtain this renewal.

When St Benedict speaks of *pura oratio* (RB 20:4), he is thinking, surely, of that prayer where no petition is expressed, of that state of simple adoration before the Lord, of loving admiration, of thanksgiving, and of contemplation which, because of its gratuitousness and its abandonment to the Lord's sovereign will, its generous availability, is closely related to the high-priestly prayer of Jesus. This attitude of soul, inspired by the Holy Spirit, permits the Lord to operate there in total freedom. Basically, this prayer is the one that best suits the monk who stands before God like a lamp in the sanctuary. It approaches the deepest tonality of the texts offered by the Church at the Divine Office.

The entire Rule is orchestrated to allow the Holy Spirit to lead a person to this progression of the loving intimacy of a child toward its Father. The works of liberation, such as asceticism and humility, prepare the heart for the Spirit's action; fraternal charity stimulates the soul to generosity; *lectio divina* opens vast horizons to the works of divine love and gives birth to meditation and a prayer of admiration which introduces the soul to contemplation. The Holy Spirit, Love of the Father for us, who lives in us, who is nearer to us than we are to ourselves, stirs up, accompanies, supports, and brings about this transformation. The atmosphere of the monastery created by the rule, the conditions of the material and spiritual life in the monastic routine, all concur to make his influence more active, his voice more persuasive, and to create a climate of uninterrupted prayer in the monastery, well symbolized formerly by the *laus perennis* of some large communities.

Nowadays spontaneous prayer groups or charismatic assemblies are cropping up here and there. The *Book of the Acts of the Apostles* already mentions them (cf. Ac 2:42, 46; 4:24; 12:5). We find the same sentiments among monks gathered together for prayer and the common life, and joy makes them vie with each other to hurry to morning prayer (cf. RB 22:6) to meet the Lord. In fact, our happiness overflows at the thought that the Lord eagerly awaits us infinitely more than we him (cf. RB prol. 18 citing Is 58:9). Are we not the children of that loving Father who is always on the lookout and who is watching from afar to see if we will finally return home (cf. Lk 15:20)?

Let us also add in conclusion that we will rise from such prayer radiant and filled with tenderness and understanding for our brothers, the children of the same Father.

MONASTIC ASCETICISM

'ALLOW YOURSELVES to be led by the Spirit and you will not run the risk of satisfying carnal desires. For the flesh lusts against the spirit and the spirit against the flesh' (Gal 5:16f).

The flesh, in the biblical sense, is human weakness. The flesh is nature corrupted by sin, the heir of death. The spirit, creature of the Holy Spirit, made in his image and sustained by his good will, tends toward life. The struggle of the spirit against the flesh of sin, carried on under the guidance of the Holy Spirit, is necessary for anyone who 'wants to enjoy true and eternal life' (RB prol. 17), so that the darkness of death may not seize him (cf. RB prol. 13 quoting Jn 12:35). This primeval struggle, therefore, is essential for the monk who, by definition, is a seeker of God (cf. RB 58:7)—and therefore a seeker of life.

This struggle is waged on two fields of battle: that of the soul and that of the body. St Benedict presents these two fields of action to us as two steps on the ladder of humility. As a matter of fact, it is beneath the banner of humility that he concentrates this whole struggle—this entire asceticism—that of the will, which is the principal field of battle. This asceticism for the monk, therefore, is summed up practically in the submission of the will under the yoke of obedience, that is to say, in 'not loving one's own will and in not taking pleasure in fulfilling one's own desires' (RB 7:31).

Whereas elsewhere we have devoted our attention to the 'powerful and noble arms of obedience' (RB prol. 3), here we are going to study the thought of St Benedict on the asceticism of the body.

CORPORAL ASCETICISM

The body, like the spirit whose companion it is, is, of course, God's creature. We must treat it with respect. 'No one has ever hated his own flesh' (Eph 5:29), but ever since the sin of Adam, death is its heritage. Doubtless it will rise again on the Last Day; however, in

125

order to rise it should, servant of the spirit that it is, die like a seed to bear the fruit of eternal life.

The body is the seat of the flesh and bears its burden. Now the flesh rebels and flees death even though everything in it becomes extinguished, loses its strength, and becomes corrupt. The spirit by nature tends toward grandeur, liberty, the purity of the heights. As for the flesh, it is attracted toward base things, to what is easy and to the deceptive freedom of the senses and the passions. Yet certain people claim that this division between flesh and spirit is artificial and that one must follow a basically good nature. That is to let a blind person guide someone who should be able to see.

St Benedict, whose fatherly and moderate conduct in this matter is reassuring, is far from wanting to mistreat the body because of the proclivities of the flesh. He is equally distant from a false optimism as he is from a discouraging pessimism concerning the body. For him, the task of asceticism consists not in checkmating the powers of nature imprudently or in repressing them, but in disciplining them. Mistreating the body can lead to neurosis or to the danger of violent, intemperate outbursts. True asceticism cannot exist without prudence. St Benedict is clearly opposed to asceticism as an end in itself or to exercises which lack a *raison d'etre*, such as we read about in the narratives about certain desert fathers. Every false appearance of mortification—that word is not to be found in the Rule—ought to be avoided. 'When you fast, do not take on a gloomy look' (Mt 6:16). The opposition between the spirit and the flesh, far from producing negative effects, is a cause of progress and salvation. It awakens the best forces in a person by ennobling him and leading him to purity, which is the goal of all Christian and monastic asceticism.

Now, we have a duty to preserve our life. It is proper, therefore, to yield to certain desires of the flesh: for example, to nourish our body to keep it in good health. Suicide is forbidden by the fifth commandment. Humankind has the instinct for preservation of the species. The monk proposes to respond to it by sublimating it in a life of chastity.

Man is also preoccupied in assuring the security of his personal existence. How can one observe a wise policy in this area? Pious exhortations are not enough. It is necessary to offer specific and effective help to those of good will who examine themselves to discover superfluous demands, often hidden under the excuse of health or of maintaining one's physical strength when there is no real necessity. On the other hand, one sometimes meets monks who, through an exaggerated fear of sin or incited by a demon of misguided spirituality, destroy prematurely and without discretion the strength of their body through an imprudent asceticism.

PRACTICAL RULES

The Rule ought to give some norms and practical advice so that the struggle of the spirit, in union with its companion, the body, might be waged according to the rules of prudence and might produce results which would draw the approval and help of the Spirit.

One preliminary condition for the struggle is watchfulness over the movements of the flesh (cf. RB 7:23–25). The Office of Vigils is for the monk a continual warning to remain present before the Lord and to 'guard himself at all times...from the desires of the flesh' (RB 7:12), because 'God sees him at every moment' (RB 7:13). It is necessary, therefore, 'to watch at all times over the actions of one's life' (RB 4:48). This vigilance will lead him 'not to fulfil the desires of the flesh' (RB 4:59 quoting Gal 5:16).

In the fourth chapter, St Benedict offers some instruments of good works. These are rules, rather succinct, but they nevertheless give an orientation: 'To chastise the body, not to pamper oneself' (RB 4:11f). The counsel 'to love fasting' (RB 4:13) causes us to form a good attitude toward it. Borne as a burden, it weighs the soul down; accepted willingly, it becomes a means of regeneration for the spirit. We will see shortly how these counsels and others of the same type (RB 4:35–38) find their realization in daily life.

Fasting, for St Benedict, does not consist in restrictions or in the coarser quality of food so much as in the relatively late hours of the meals, on which he seems to have been rather conservative regarding customs introduced into the society of the time. This was a way of making the whole community fast together (cf. RB 41). We realize that this was the intention behind this ordinance, because at times when it is very hot or during heavier work, the time of the meal is advanced (cf. RB 41:4), and also the guests (cf. RB 53:10f, 16), the elderly and the children (cf. RB 37:3) did not have the same rigors imposed upon them. Let us note that the law of abstinence (cf. RB

39:11, 36:9) is added to the restrictions required by the late hours of the meals. This manner of fasting was intentional, as is confirmed by the fact that St Benedict used it also in punishing rebellious monks (cf. RB 24:5f, 25:5).

THE HAPPY MEDIUM

So that this general arrangement might not produce effects contrary to its aim, differences of temperaments must be taken into account: 'Everyone has received from God his special gift: one this and another that' (RB 40:1 quoting 1 Co 7:7). St Benedict knew that stomachs do not adapt themselves to every diet; so he gives a rule able to satisfy 'the needs of different temperaments' (RB 39:1–4) as regards the quantity and quality of food without giving in to personal tastes. He does not forbid wine and allows it to be used, although with reluctance (cf. RB 40:6f). A certain uneasiness is noticeable throughout the text of the Rule which establishes norms for food and drink: on one hand, the concern to do right (cf. RB 40:2), on the other, the fear of possible abuses (cf. RB 39:7–9). As a matter of fact, monastic life requires abnegation, and history teaches us that temptation has sometimes caused monks to seek compensation in good eating. St Benedict also recognized the danger of drinking more than was reasonable (cf. RB 40:1, 3) and puts his monks on their guard (cf. RB 40:6f). St Paul knew what he was talking about when he admonished the Ephesians: 'Do not become drunk with wine...but seek your fullness in the Spirit' (Eph 5:18).

It is therefore a matter of finding a happy medium. St Benedict has marked it out: not to indulge oneself to satiety, but to remain sober. *Non usque ad satietatem, sed parcius* (RB 40:6). The ancients had a rule of rising from the table with the feeling of not being totally satisfied. In the same spirit, St Benedict indicates a maximum measure: a generous pound of bread (cf. RB 39:4) and an hemina of wine (cf. RB 40:3). Let us not waste time seeking the exact measure of that hemina. Each one of us knows his limits. They differ from those of his neighbor. The deep sense of discretion (cf. RB 64:19) which characterized St Benedict suggested to him the happy medium for the strong as well as for the weak, for he was convinced that the Spirit is freedom from all servitude prompted by the body or by a misguided spirit.

THE BODY AT THE SERVICE
OF THE SPIRIT

The body needs sufficient food so that the spirit may remain efficient and agile. Nature itself has established these rules, but Christian asceticism has seized upon them to give them a religious meaning and to transform them into a sacrifice of praise for the Creator. It helps the human person, image of God that he is, to make that image grow in him more and more. Christian asceticism is also a means of penance, for fault-laden humanity. It helps him re-establish order within himself so as to be able to appear before the offended Lord.

Fasting and abstaining help a person—a monk—to free himself from the weight of the flesh. These practices, wisely understood, give him agility and resistance, make him fitter for the activities of body and spirit, more energetic and more courageous. Timidity, certain psychoses and neuroses sometimes arise from the dullness of a soul weighed down by a body which is too pampered. Since grace presupposes nature, the body as well as the soul should keep ready to receive the gift of God. A certain asceticism accepted by the body fosters agility of soul in regard to movements of the Spirit. Along the same line, the daily routine of the monastic life should offer a healthy alternation of prayer, reading, and manual labor, where each occupation has its place harmoniously assigned. Everything else is useful to the extent that it harmonizes with this basic plan and does not arrogate to itself an importance which does not by rights belong to it.

The monk often realizes too late that he has imprudently mis-treated his body, whether by unhealthy nourishment or by a lack of balance in his manner of living or working. He then finds himself obliged to re-establish a fragile balance with great trouble by artificial and often costly means. He is, indeed, in danger of settling himself into a sort of inescapable state where the service of God and of his brethren is subordinated to the needs of his own self. This remark, of course, does not concern the truly sick. They are in need of their brothers' aid.

This is why the monk should carefully observe St Benedict's wise prescription: not to undertake anything in the line of works of supererogatory mortification without the blessing and permission of the abbot (cf. RB 49:8–10). Some people bear the weight of their body painfully and, with St Paul, desire to be liberated from it (cf. Rm 7:24). They are tempted to want to rush ahead and to forget that it is necessary to leave the care of transforming our humble body up to the Lord at the time of his choosing, by configuring it to his glorious body (cf. Ph 3:21).

CHASTITY

Nevertheless, the monk can anticipate that hour because perfect chastity makes him in some way like the angels. The virginal love of his soul transfigures even his body. Does innocence of soul and of body not engender joy and generosity? When a person is not divided (cf. 1 Co 7:35) between God and his spouse (cf. 1 Co 7:32–34), or in other words, when God is also the Spouse, there is no bifurcation.

But ever since original sin, what is subject to sin deserves death. Like Christ in his body, nailed sin to the cross, our body should die little by little like the seed in the ground by means of 'extenuating the flesh so that the spirit might be saved in the day of the Lord' (1 Co 5:5, cf. RB 25:4). The putting off, the burying, of sin, takes place with the grace of the Spirit by the putting off, the mortification, that is to say, the putting to death, of the flesh by means of asceticism. Chastity draws the monk away from the demands of the impulses implanted in our nature by the Creator to assure the preservation of the species, so that he can convert them and sublimate them into impulses of charity, ruled by the Holy Spirit. Therefore physical asceticism helps the monk not to see chastity as a constraint. He loves it (cf. RB 4:64) because he discovers the wonderful liberty with which the Spirit favors him, girding him with strength (cf. Ps 17:33, 40).

CLOTHING AT THE SERVICE
OF THE SPIRIT

The food restrictions imposed by the Rule (RB 37:2) are therefore situated in the area of education offered to the monk by the Spirit to lead him to 'hasten toward perfection' (RB 73:2). The guidelines concerning clothing surely enter into the same perspective. There is for St Benedict not a matter of a purely material detail to be dealt with, but of a problem closely related to the monastic vocation.

During the Transfiguration, the Lord's garments, having become white as snow (cf. Mt 17:2) reflected the profound change that had taken place in him. Not just any clothing is suitable for the monk or nun. It ought to express effacement, modesty, poverty, the state of conversion, and ought to exclude every kind of elegance, vanity, luxury, and affirmation of personality. The fifty-fifth chapter of the Rule sets the tone for us with no uncertainty. The clothing is for covering the body and not for embellishing it. That is why, if certain adaptations of clothing become necessary, it is very important to follow these criteria and to have a sincere desire of giving the habit its religious meaning: poor and modest.

Should we abandon the religious habit to dress as lay people? That would be to fall into the other extreme by depriving clothing of its expressive force. If it contributes to a kind of transfiguration, then would secularizing it not mean that little by little certain personal attitudes of the monk that should remain his heritage would become dimmer? In the same way, the behavior concerning which the Rule instructs us in the seventh chapter from the ninth to the twelfth degrees of humility, becomes, when it is well assimilated, second nature for the monk, the man of God, the spiritual person. In this context, reassuming the clothes left on entering the monastery would be a wrong step. Have they not been abandoned on entering the monastery to be left in the wardrobe and kept there in case 'at the instigation of the devil, he should allow himself to be led to leave the monastery' (RB 58:27f)? By means of all the stipulations he made for monks concerning the body, St Benedict wanted to show us the action and the teaching of the Spirit who gives the proper measure to these actions imposed by our human nature by causing what pertains to the prudence of the flesh to die in them (cf. Rm 8:6). Thus the body, in its own way, contributes to the spiritual transformation from which, little by little, is born the new person (cf. Eph 4:23f) made in the image of Christ.

FOLLOWING THE POOR CHRIST

1. THE TEACHING OF THE RULE CONCERNING POVERTY

THE MODEL OF POVERTY FOR THE CENOBITE

ST BENEDICT WANTED TO BASE his teaching on poverty on the testimony of Scripture; he therefore cited the example of the community at Jerusalem and its way of practising poverty: 'distribution was made to each according to his needs' (RB 34:1 quoting Ac 4:35). But in referring to this community, he was well aware that it had been trying to imitate the life of the disciples with Jesus. Now Jesus lived in complete poverty and had nowhere to lay his head (cf. Mt 8:20). The apostles likewise had left everything to follow him. Peter was able to say: 'We have left everything and have followed you' (Mt 19:27).

They therefore possessed nothing personally; yet it is necessary to live. Luke tells us how Jesus and the Twelve were followed by several women 'who were keeping them out of their means' (Lk 8:3). Judas was the administrator of the common cash box (cf. Jn 12:6, 13:29) and provided, after the manner of a cellarer, for the necessities of all and sundry according to their needs.

Cenobitic monks, following the young Church of Jerusalem (cf. Ac 4:32, 34) wanted to copy in their own life the model which has since been called the 'apostolic life', that is to say, the community life of the apostles with Jesus. The monk, in fact, proposes, like the apostles, to follow Jesus: chaste, poor, and obedient to the Father.

The ideal of poverty has known diverse interpretations in the course of religious history. How does St Benedict understand it? Poverty for him, we may believe, consists in imitating that of Jesus and the apostles. It is important, therefore, to listen to Jesus in order to know his thought. If he declares the poor in spirit blessed (cf. Mt 5:3), he is aiming not only at a spiritual, platonic poverty compatible with the possession of great riches, but he means to speak of the truly poor, the little ones, the humble as opposed to the rich, as Luke (cf. Lk 6:20, 24) makes clear—on condition, of course, that this material poverty opens one's heart to spiritual riches and to the kingdom of heaven.

THE POVERTY OF THE MONK

Let us note, first of all, that St Benedict does not use the word 'poverty' when he expounds his thought. He simply prescribes that the monks 'not give or receive anything without the authorization of the abbot nor possess anything as their own, whatever it may be: not books, nor writing tablets, nor stylus for writing, in a word, absolutely nothing' (RB 33:2f, cf. 55:16–19). On the other hand, 'they ought to expect from the father of the monastery all that is necessary for themselves' (RB 33:5), and he recommends 'that all things be had in common for all' (RB 33:6 quoting Ac 4:32). The model of this monastic poverty is clear: Jesus with his apostles, as the primitive Church of Jerusalem had no individual possessions but received what was needed from what was common to all, even so the monk was to have no private possessions but would receive what was needed from the father of the monastery. We will speak later of the means of sustaining the community.

What does it mean, 'to have nothing as one's own'? The monk has things for his use, but whatever they may be, he does not become their 'owner'. The rule in two different places even draws up for us a short list of things needed for daily use (cf. RB 33.3; 55:15, 19). Today it might be lengthened with good reason. In order to be perfectly clear, St Benedict adds that the monk cannot even dispose freely of his own body and his own will (cf. RB 33:4). To have nothing as one's own is therefore evidently not to have the right of freely disposing of an object for personal use by reserving an exclusive right to it.

All these stipulations show a certain intentional austerity; and the 'poverty of the monk' is vindicated in a certain sense. Austerity is practised by him as a personal virtue with an authentic spirit of humble dependence on the 'father of the monastery' (RB 33:5) and his officers (cf. RB all of ch. 31), including careful attention to the objects received (cf. RB 32; 46:2), sobriety in food (cf. RB 39 and 40), and poverty concerning clothing (cf. RB 55:7, 10).

The Gospel does not speak explicitly of all these details; it is, however, permissible to believe that Jesus practised the renunciation of material poverty in a similiar way. The monk wishes to follow Jesus because he loves him and therefore desires to find in him the model of that poverty he undertakes to live.

THE GENUINENESS OF POVERTY

It is not easy to harmonize the notion of monastic poverty with the sociological notion of poverty. Basically, in speaking of what we call, for want of a more exact expression, 'poverty', we should follow the example of St Benedict. He does not use this term in the Rule, nor does he demand that the monk take a vow of poverty.

As a matter of fact, if we speak of poverty, we think of the lack of the means of biological sustenance: for example, to be without remunerative work, thus without a salary, not to enjoy a private income, to lack food or clothing, to be unable to attain a better professional formation. The cenobite monk is generally protected from this sociological poverty; it is not part of his vocation. To use more exact terms, it would be more proper to speak instead of 'renunciation of property', of 'community of goods', of 'thrift in the use of things', of 'dependence on the superior in the use of things'. All of these expressions being incomplete when taken separately, there is no other solution but to use the ordinary term 'poverty' while specifying its meaning.

In following Christ, therefore, the monk chooses for himself real material poverty and not only a spiritual poverty compatible with the possession of personal goods, licit for Christians living in the world. Is the poverty of the monk not an illusion, since in renouncing personal belongings, his living is nevertheless assured? Will he be truly in solidarity with the poor? Now, the poverty practised by Jesus and the apostles was not misery, because this cannot be presented as an ideal. The Creator, in giving humankind the world with its riches, willed that we make use of them in our life (cf. Gn 1:28f). On the other hand, the poverty of the monk should be real and not based on a juridical fiction or on casuistic *epikeia*.

To pretend that in order to be poor we need only depend on a superior and his at least tacit permission in using things, would be an error. Moreover, this pretence could be hypocrisy if the monk got to the point of considering the use of superfluous things licit for himself. From the phrase 'no one is allowed to have something that the abbot has not given or permitted' (RB 33:5, cf. 33:2), one cannot conclude that one may keep forever what the superior had given at a certain time. As a good jurist, the author of the Rule has expressed his idea well in an affirmative way: 'let no one have the audacity...to possess anything whatsoever as his own' (RB 33:2f).

During normal times, the livelihood of the monk is assured. His responsibility for practising a real material poverty in the sense that the Rule intends is that much greater. Casuistic kinds of excuses, pushing responsibility off on the abbot, cannot quiet his conscience. If it is not a matter of adopting literally the list of objects enumerated by the Rule, it is nevertheless not to be doubted that St Benedict required a thoroughgoing material poverty. It is for each person to ask himself what, according to the sound interpretations of his own community, corresponds to his desire to follow the poor Jesus.

In order to impress evangelical poverty on us, the Rule also specifies that the monk should have nothing superfluous. He might prevail upon the permission of the abbot to keep this and that thing for his personal use. This permission, which is juridically sufficient, is morally insufficient if the object in question, far from being necessary, is in the area of the superfluous, 'Anything more which one might have, is superfluous and should be taken away' (RB 55:11). In the same spirit, if a visiting monk requests hospitality in the monastery, he should be well received there as long as he does not trouble the community by idle demands by asking for things considered superfluous by the others (cf. RB 61:1–3). Evidently, St Benedict puts exaggerated concern with the color or the texture of clothing and shoes into the same category. One should be content with what is to be found in the area and what can be bought at a better price (cf. RB 55:7).

THAT EVERYTHING SHOULD BE IN COMMON

The evangelical poverty practised by Jesus and, following him, by apostles of the Church of Jerusalem, requires 'that everything be common to all' and 'that no one speak of anything as belonging to himself' (RB 33:6 quoting Ac 4:32). No object ought to be considered or kept as one's personal property (cf. RB 55:16–18). Receiving gifts from relatives or friends as personal belongings, or even simply 'letters, blessed objects, or small presents' (RB 54:1) particularly exposes the monk to this fault. Therefore let there be no exception! Let everything be truly in common! And let the monk, who has promised to follow the poor Jesus, not allow himself to be overcome by sadness in seeing the abbot dispose of the things he has received in favor of other brethren (cf. RB 54:4).

On the other hand, the monks have the right, or more exactly, the joy 'of expecting from the father of the monastery everything that they need' (RB 33:5). The fact of possessing makes a person independent; poverty makes a person depend on the good will of others. Christ submitted himself to a thousand dependences out of love of us. We renounce material dependence by embracing poverty for the love of Christ and of all our poor brothers whose poverty he shared in order to let them share his riches. The words of the Scripture: 'Distribution was made to each according to his needs' cited twice by St Benedict (RB 34:1, 55:20) implies not only the promise of receiving what is necessary 'for the present' (Mk 10:30) but also the Kingdom of Heaven itself.

To 'him who renounces the little bit that is his everything' in order to follow Christ, Christ will give his 'everything' which is God himself. He will give himself as a possession common to all his chosen. He will be for each and all the fullness of beatitude, their portion.

Having everything in common creates a spirit of sharing, first of all in material good within the community, but then it forms hearts in that fraternal spirit where hands are reaching out to us. Sharing, for monks, ought to express itself especially through 'sharing the Gospel', and their life should be a concrete putting into practice of the Word of God.

2. THE PRACTICE OF POVERTY

How could I pretend to love Christ, to follow him, without wishing to be poor like him? Love urges us to follow the beloved. And since Jesus has come among us to share the life of the poor, how could I follow him without trying to live as a poor person among the poor? Do most people not experience poverty under one form or another?

Jesus entered this world as a poor person. He lived thirty years with the small and the humble, those of whom history preserves no trace. His life was modest, and the Holy Scriptures themselves with few exceptions leave us hungry to know almost anything about his life on earth.

When he emerged from the obscurity of history, it was into a life as fertile in humiliation, in tribulation, and in apparent failure as it was rich in works of holiness and in magnificence. The Gospels describe that life for us as full of love in an ever increasing detachment and renunciation. The more he advanced in his public life, the more he saw the circle of his disciples diminish. Outside his immediate group, he was less and less understood. The hostilities of his enemies became stronger. The prospect of a painful end loomed. Then Jesus began his passion and saw the bands of his most faithful disciples disperse. The High Priests staged everything to destroy him. Even the people betrayed him. Dishonored, despised, he mounted the cross, stripped of his garments. The very earth no longer gave him support. He renounced his mother, giving her to St John. Finally, in an ultimate abandonment, he saw himself forsaken by his Father, and he gave up to him his life, all that was left to him.

In all this, even Jesus' final sigh, we see the ever greater embrace of poverty. He wanted to experience it with the most disinherited of this world: with the hungry and the thirsty, the strangers, the naked, the sick, and the prisoners (cf. Mt 25:35f). He wanted to experience poverty with the persecuted, the exiled, and the homeless, with the dishonored and the calumniated, with the exploited, the tortured, and those condemned to death. He even chose to be placed in the ranks of criminals (cf. Lk 22:37) and let himself be stripped right down to the ultimate degree of poverty.

Ought we follow Jesus that far? We never know what human malice or the turn of unfortunate circumstances has in store for us. Let us only remember that in all our suffering, if we are willing to remember it, we meet Christ on his Way of the Cross, and that by bearing the shame of following him, 'we participate in the sufferings of Christ and merit to have a place in his Kingdom' (RB prol. 50).

OUR LITTLE POVERTY

But this patience in destitution is learned by little acts of poverty and renunciation. The Rule offers us a thousand occasions for this. Let us examine often whether, among the objects set aside for our use, there are not some that are superfluous (cf. RB 55:11). Are we honestly content with what we are given, with our position, with our employment (cf. RB 7:49f)? Do we accept in good spirit, as a consequence of our vow of poverty, a certain insecurity—the heritage of the man of today—which might one day, God forbid, lead us into more or less unfavorable circumstances? Let us recognize, however, that our situation, in spite of the radical poverty which keeps us following Christ, is less uncertain than that of most lay people. With the exception of those in charge, we do not have to be concerned about tomorrow, about what we shall eat or what we shall wear. Moreover, poverty obliges us not to be concerned about little things, about our old age, or about the possibility of sickness. It also obliges us to make our frugal way of life, our thriftiness, our concern to take good care of the goods of the monastery, (cf. RB 32) profit the community and each of our brothers. Who does not know how costly negligence with tools, machines, clothing, and utensils is! Our age of consumerism encourages wastefulness, but the sense of thrift is a civic virtue, a matter of culture, and a manifestation of solidarity. The monk should exercise this virtue for the love of Christ and of his disinherited brothers.

The spirit of poverty teaches us to share. What belongs to me, belongs to my brothers since 'everything is common to everyone' (RB 33:6). Things that are for my use cannot be of my exclusive domain, and the brother who really has need of them has the right to use them. My responsibility in the community follows the same norms. My time should be at the service of others. I cannot shut myself up in an ivory tower in order to preserve my tranquillity. 'The boon of obedience is not to be rendered only to the abbot; it is also necessary for all the brethren to obey one another' (RB 71:1). 'Let no one seek what he considers useful for himself, but rather what is useful to others' (RB 72:7). 'The brethren should serve one another' (RB 35:1). Those who are not at the moment occupied with the demands of their duties should put themselves at the service of others (cf. RB 53:18–20). This spirit is, of course, very contrary to the selfish tendency to spare one's own efforts, to let someone else work while remaining on the sidelines, to care for one's own health to the detriment of a brother. The spirit of poverty thus joins with the virtue of charity and dedication to one's brothers. There is no charity without the gift of self. Now to give is, in a certain sense, to separate oneself, to detach oneself from something, to deprive oneself and thus to enrich someone else. Christ 'being rich, made himself poor for us so as to enrich us through his poverty' (2 Co 8:9).

This desire to use material goods in common opens the heart to sharing spiritual goods, first of all within the community, but also with all those who come to the monastery and especially with guests and friends. A monastic community is, per se, the depository of the goods of the Spirit. In all modesty, it should bear witness to this. One should not set the lamp under a bushel (cf. Mk 4:21). At the gatehouse it shares its bread with the poor; it should share the word of the Spirit with the hungry of this world.

Having everything in common also disposes the heart to be concerned for the poor and the pilgrims and to provide for their material needs (cf. RB 53:15, 55:9). The monastery accepts a real responsibility for them.

3. THE AIM OF MONASTIC POVERTY

Wealth makes one important; exercising poverty puts us in our place. We come into the world entirely naked; we will leave it entirely poor. Our life hangs between two dates. What does it represent in the ocean of human history? 'One age goes, another comes, and the earth endures continually' (Qo 1:4). We ought to accept these modest dimensions in advance. By imposing restrictions upon us, poverty helps us become conscious of our limitations. We experience our dependence, we become aware of the poverty of our being, our mediocrity, and we learn to accept ourselves as we are, with our nature, our temperament, our little defects and good qualities. We learn to renounce stupid ambitions, pride, exaggerated hopes. Poverty rightly practised leads to humility, that is to say, to an accurate appreciation of ourselves without overestimating nor underestimating what we are through the grace and will of the Creator and by the strengths and weaknesses received from our ancestors whose good and bad points we bear.

Accepting ourselves helps us accept our neighbor and allows us to appreciate him without envy or jealousy, to love him and help him. Discovering our poverty makes us humble, gentle and patient, understanding, flexible and prudent, sincere and honest. But knowing ourselves is also estimating our talents and good qualities, and undertaking with courage the tasks which fall to us. And this accurate knowledge of ourselves inclines us to thank the Lord for his innumerable gifts to us.

The practice of poverty leads a person to interior freedom. Little by little he becomes aware of the shackles and habits by which he is unconsciously bound, whereas poverty practised courageously makes him see that he can free himself from them without harm. Advancing on the way of liberation, he meets Jesus, the entirely free, because totally poor, Man according to the word of the One who was able to promise us: 'If the Son makes you free, you will be truly free' (Jn 8:36).

The monk desires to practise the 'theology of the liberation of man' by detaching himself from everything that could shackle his own freedom and, together with the poor, by practising poverty as liberation. If he feels himself in solidarity with the poor, his aim is not to console those who live in misery, nor to help them to become rich, for this would be contrary to his purpose. His intention is to follow Jesus by practising poverty as a road to the riches of the kingdom and by his life to preach the blessedness of poverty. Some people practise it with a certain ostentation in order to challenge the 'affluent society'. That is not enough. Christ has given it a sacred meaning, has made it a pathway and even a condition for true happiness.

An accurate understanding of poverty opens our eyes to the fact that we are sinners. St Benedict in the twelfth degree of humility teaches the monk to declare himself one by the modesty of his bearing, 'feeling himself at all times loaded down with his sins' (RB 7:64). Yet, having arrived at the summit of the ladder of humility, that is to say, of interior poverty, he is finally liberated from his sins and his vices (cf. RB 7:70). Poverty purifies the soul by the grace of the Lord. The great Poor Man on the cross detaches us utterly from clinging to sin to the extent that we are united to his total poverty, dead to sin: a liberated death, the source of salvation.

The monk, having arrived at this point in the spiritual journey, understands that this emptiness of detachment is not an end in itself, but the means used by the Holy Spirit in order to fill with the fullness of Christ the total emptiness left by total poverty. What shines forth in the monk who has become truly poor does not shine with a human perfection, but with the image of Christ in whom he is transformed by the action of the Spirit.

It is only after having profoundly realized the 'nothing' which we are of ourselves, after having become aware of that constitutive poverty become mortal through sin, that we have access to the vivifying Spirit of Christ. All the teaching of the Rule, of the ladder of humility, aims at the recognition of that poverty to allow the Holy Spirit freedom of action in the soul of the purified monk (cf. RB 7:70) and thus to make of him a *homo spiritualis, a 'person of God'*.

4. THE SUSTENANCE OF THE COMMUNITY

The Lord teaches us that the rich, that is to say, all those whose spirit is inclined to seek riches, will enter with difficulty into the kingdom of heaven, because opulence smothers the action of the Spirit, whereas the kingdom is promised to the poor. Material poverty, lived in the spirit of the Gospel, goes together with spiritual riches. Those who are satisfied do not await the Holy Spirit.

The danger which threatens even the monk today is to allow oneself to be influenced by the ways of our consumer society. We can settle into a spirit of self-sufficiency opposed to the visits and the gifts of the Spirit in a too comfortable community. Jesus, threatening the rich with excommunication from the kingdom, condemns this spirit of seeking wealth in the present life which causes one to seek money, not only to satisfy real needs, but in order to enjoy luxury, a thousand conveniences, or simply consumerism for its own sake, the increase of business figures, the accumulation of wealth, accompanied by the exercise of power.

The life of the monk ought to be the convincing antithesis of this comfortable society: a life of sobriety and reasonable restriction, freed from material cares, in which the spirit overshadows the body and its excessive demands. Therefore it should be neither a life of material production and gain for its own sake, nor a life of careless-ness and parasitism. Through his work he should acquire the right so to live as to blossom forth into a life in the Holy Spirit.

The monastic state, therefore, should be organized in such a way that 'the brethren might consecrate certain hours to manual labor and others to *Lectio Divina*' (cf. RB 48:1).

St Benedict, let us note in passing, doubtless did not have the intention of excluding intellectual work. His desire to adapt himself to each one according to his capacities and abilities—*multorum servire moribus*' (RB 2:31)—would not have let him force a monk who was poorly suited to manual labor but gifted for intellectual work, into an activity in which he would not be able to develop properly. The hours consecrated to reading incite, as it were necessarily, the monks who are capable of that effort, to work of the mind and the intellect.

The social aspect is also not lacking in this concept. After having completed a certain number of hours of work, a brother will not be tempted to say that he has done enough to earn his food. He is in solidarity with his brothers. Among them are the aged, the sick, the brothers in studies who live on the work of the community. Let us add to that the general expenses required by the service of God. The poor and the guests have always had a right to be welcomed at the monastery.

How does St Benedict envisage this problem of the material sustenance of the community without falling into a system of a money-making enterprise? Evidently, he admits the necessity of making a living, but wishes to keep the community removed from an abusive seeking for comfort and material security so as to assure its spiritual character.

St Benedict never wrote a treatise on the economic problem. The necessity of earning one's daily bread he simply presupposed. It is therefore necessary to work. It is with this that his reflection begins. He intends to organize the work under the heading of a spiritual aim of the monastery.

The monks, therefore, should work with their hands (cf. RB 48:1) and make their living, but not at the expense of their religious life. At the time of St Benedict, it seems that the monastery owned land (cf. RB 41:2, 4) since he speaks of harvests (cf. RB 48:7). He seems, though, to have wanted the administration to be arranged so as to permit the hiring of day laborers (cf. RB 48:7) since some monks were probably not used to heavy work. For this reason, St Benedict recommends that the abbot take care that the work be done with discretion (cf. RB 48:9, 64:17f). This text should not, however, be interpreted as an anticipation of the practice of the feudal system of the Middle Ages, which transformed the monks into actors in an almost uninterrupted and solemn liturgy and left the work to serfs; otherwise, St Benedict would not have written the chapter on manual labor with the instruction: 'the brethren ought to consecrate certain hours to to manual labor' (RB 48:1), nor would he have had to write the little chapter concerning the monks who are working at a distance (RB 50). The aim of the work is not necessarily to make money—the Rule gives that impression—yet in the chapter about craftsmen, St Benedict makes it understood that the products turned out by the monks can be sold and that such a craft might even support the community (cf. RB 57:4, 2).

Concerning the motivation for work, he seems to have wanted to avoid that of the material sustenance of the community, so the monastery might not be considered a kind of business. This does not, however, prevent him from wishing that 'the house of God be wisely administered by wise people' (RB 53:22). Thus he attributes to the work reasons of a disciplinary and spiritual character. First of all, it is a matter of avoiding idleness, which is an enemy of the soul (cf. RB 48:1). Next he adds another motive which gives us a glimpse of the mentality of monasticism at the time: 'If the brethren find themselves obliged to work at the harvest, let them not be distressed, for then they will be truly monks when they live from the work of their hands after the manner of our fathers and the apostles' (RB 48:7f). Through these lines we feel the vibration of a certain nostalgia for by-gone days, with the realization that ordinarily one could no longer ask monks to do the harvesting themselves. Why? One might suppose that this demanding work required a concentrated effort over a limited time and did not leave the brethren enough time to satisfy their liturgical and spiritual duties. The first Cistercians, who desired to deserve the praise of the Rule by being true monks living by the work of their hands, preferred in summertime to suppress the daily conventual Mass for two weeks in order to do the harvesting themselves. They aspired to total poverty by living by the work of their hands.

The aim of the monastic life is entirely spiritual. This clearly comes from the arrangements provided by St Benedict and from the organization of the material life. God, therefore, will provide for the needs of his own. St Benedict quotes the thirty-third Psalm: 'Nothing is wanting to those who fear God' (RB 2:36).

He exhorts the abbot not to be excessively preoccupied about the scantiness of his means. Let him rather remember what is written (Mt 6:33): 'Seek first the Kingdom of God and his justice; the rest will be given to you in addition' (cf. RB 2:35).

What are these means of sustenance for the community, according to the Rule? It does not seem possible to give a single answer to this question. St Benedict speaks of the 'substance' of the monastery (cf. RB 2:35) obviously in the sense of material resources for living, without, however, specifying its character. One cannot imagine stocks or investments. The reference to harvests leads us to think of the ownership of land which belonged to the community (cf. RB 48:7; 41:2, 4). The fifty-seventh chapter suggests handicraft as a means of support. Pastoral ministry might also be a means of support according to the words: 'The laborer is worthy of his hire' (cf. 1 Tm 5:18).

It is fitting to note here that it would be normal to see society fulfil a duty of financial support for the monastery since it undertakes man's obligation to adore the Lord and to present the requests of God's people to him.

In our day, many men and women want to regain their equilibrium of soul and spirit and to refresh themselves spiritually away from the unhealthy agitation of modern life and the tide of diverse influences which it carries along with it. The monastery guest house can offer them this beneficial contact where they can regain their balance and, at the same time, this hospitality can earn the monastery a small income.

It is not easy to draw the line between good administration and an excessive preoccupation for tomorrow, and the counsel of St Benedict to administer the monastery wisely (cf. RB 53:22) corresponds to the verse from the Book of Proverbs: 'Give me neither poverty nor riches; provide me only with food to eat' (Pr 30:8). The accumulation of material goods beyond what is necessary has never, in the last analysis, produced desirable results. As soon as a monastery acquires a reputation for being a profitable organization in the eyes of the people of the area, it loses its force as a witness against running after money and riches and is categorized as a business. Once its goal is secularized, then secularization, that is to say, turning the monastery's destination to civil ends, as history teaches us, is but a logical consequence.

The abbot who accepts responsibility as 'father of the monastery' (cf. RB 33:5) should busy himself with the distribution of the daily bread among his children. He should pay attention to the ancient proverb which, perhaps with too much of a culinary slant, says wisely and realistically: *bona coquina, bona disciplina* (good kitchen, good discipline). One cannot demand continual fasting without interrupting it for feasts, from a community of people who pray and work. Everyone is not capable of marching without respite on the heights of asceticism. St Benedict takes this into account when he lays down the measure of food (RB 39) and drink (RB 40)—dispositions dictated by 'reason of equity' (RB prol. 47).

Here again we grasp the specific character of what one might call poverty according to the concept of the Benedictine Rule. The promise of *conversio morum*, or monastic life, does not include the observance of a poverty comparable to that of a missionary who is careful to adapt himself to the way of life of the people he wishes to evangelize. The poverty of the monk does not demand the non-use of things owned by the community, but a sober use in the manner of a simple life. St Benedict places his monastery in an agricultural environment. The farmer lives on what nature gives him. He is not usually rich, but he is not in misery either. The Benedictine monastery as such, without being rich, escapes poverty, which does not prevent the monks in the community from living there in poverty, not in the destitution of those who live in shanty-town, but in accord with the simplicity of the way of life which every page of the Rule implies.

Here there arises a question which is often discussed: how can a monastic community appear poor if it lives in a great majestic edifice, often classified as an historical monument, a national or regional treasure? Is its sacred character sufficiently clear to the people of the world who are curious to see relics of the days of their ancestors? For St Benedict, the monastery is the 'House of God' (RB 31:19, 53:22, 64:5). It is, therefore, the city of God situated on the mountaintop, visible to all (cf. Mt 5:14). It is the temple of the Holy Spirit where the spirit takes precedence over the body. Its appearance may witness against its reality to people who have little or no idea of what a monastery is. But they can discover that reality in the very character of the liturgy as the service of Divine Majesty seeking to express itself by gestures marked with dignity (cf. RB 9:7, 7:60–63; 20; 22:6 etc.), and in a monastic life tending to beauty and beautiful balance. Is art not the child of liturgy? And it is surely because monastic art is usually bare and simple that its churches have a rare nobility and its monasteries impress us. Someone who has eyes to see easily perceives there the sacred, which has fashioned their style. It is true that many monasteries owe their grandeur to a period of economic ease. But at the same time, they witness to the strength of faith and to the religious energy which caused them to rise.

These, often grandiose-appearing, buildings can therefore give an impression of wealth. But anyone who has a practical understanding of life knows that their preservation usually means a heavy, even a crushing, burden on communities today. The contrast between the beauty of the buildings and the financial difficulties against which a number of communities are struggling excuses in some way the impressive spendid size of the monasteries, more so as the simple and laborious life of the monks and nuns quickens them with a spirit of real austerity.

But it cannot be denied that for many people in the world the still greater impression they receive of power, more than wealth, creates a real problem of ineffectual witness. This impression is nourished by prejudices, supplemented by narratives which present monks in an unfavorable light. Monastic communities, to appear as they should, as witnesses of the Spirit, ought therefore to exert every effort that a genuine religious vitality may animate their buildings, so as to be indisputably sources of life. It is not enough to be good traditionalists about the values of the Middle Ages. If the community faithfully lives its life of prayer and as a community celebrates a liturgy which is as dignified and as solemn as possible, it will be a witness to the faith and a sign of the worshipful presence of God's majesty. This beautiful liturgy will cause the beauty of the buildings to be understood and accepted as a connatural expression. On the other hand, a monastery whose community shirks its duties by reducing the liturgy to a minimum and by neglecting monastic work as a means of sustenance will draw upon itself the reproach of 'mortmain' and will be considered an alien body by its neighbors and hardly suitable for the community living in it. The number of monks or nuns is not, however, the determining factor; it is the sustaining force of their witness of faith and charity emphasized by the sobriety of their life. Let us leave aside those who judge the value of an institution only by its profitable material production, and also those who make the *raison d'etre* of a monastery depend on its pastoral effectiveness or its intellectual output. Yet even such people, if they were to approach a fervent community, would perceive the values of a simple and silent monastic life. These values, indeed, go beyond their expectations, but they themselves secretly feel an urgent need of them.

Manifestations of Christian charity on the part of the community and the superiors will be of great practical importance for families living in the vicinity of the monastery. It is they who will determine the way the community will be judged. If the community isolates itself by a reserve which people consider haughty, then it will be wanting at the same time in charity and in prudence. Simple gestures of delicate attention and sharing joys and sorrows under the form of help and advice, without useless departures from the monastery, lessen or do away with the sort of fear or even antipathy to which the impression of grandeur caused by the monastery buildings can give rise. By taking these imponderables into account, monastic communities will not be troubled by situations tangential to their life, and they may be nurseries for edifying Christian people (cf. Decr. *Perfectae Caritatis* 9).

TO THE GLORY OF GOD

THE HOLY SPIRIT, ARTISAN OF THE GLORIFICATION OF GOD

THE GLORIFICATION OF GOD is the work of the Holy Spirit. He scrutinizes the divine depths and knows its secrets (cf. 1 Co 2:10). To Him belongs the work of revealing the greatness of God's love. And everything the Spirit reveals to us of Him turns to the praise of his glory (cf. Eph 1:14). The work glorifies the master.

Creation is the language of the Spirit to show us the divine beauty of greatness. 'The heavens proclaim the glory of God' (Ps 18:1). Because He is love, the Spirit Creator expresses himself through beauty. Love is the discloser of beauty. Through it, love sings its joy, the ardor of its desire, its fullness. The Spirit is beauty and harmony by essence and cannot express Himself otherwise.

It is why He hovered over the waters (cf. Gn 1:2) and gave the earth the form that elicits human admiration, so that by seeing what is visible, we might be drawn to the love of the invisible. From unformed matter, the divine Artist drew the most beautiful work that exists—the universe, the earth and everything it contains. Should this work not be beautiful, when by it the Spirit gave at least a remote idea of the infinite perfection of God, of that transcendent God for whom creation is the many-colored vestment which reveals Him to us and at the same time hides Him from us?

The Spirit is the glorifier of divinity. Jesus, God become man, needed this work of the Spirit. 'He will glorify me' (Jn 16:14) He said, by revealing to the faithful the inner meaning that they might understand the divine mysteries entrusted to our ignorance.

The Holy Spirit glorifies God and His Son, Jesus Christ, not only by revealing the grandeur and the beauty of divine majesty, but by making us love them. The intellect alone can only guess at the immensity of God's fullness; it is love that grasps, esteems, and tastes

149

the lovingness—*benignitas et humanitas*,'the goodness of God our Saviour and his love for men' (Tt 3:4)—of God who is all love for us (cf. 1 Jn 4:8). It is the work of the God of love to reveal the love of God.

Now the Spirit Creator has chosen to communicate to human beings his ability to glorify God through works. He has breathed into man the magnanimous soul which desires magnificent works and is capable of producing and reproducing by using matter and the forces it contains—that matter which awaits from his hand the completion of its potentiality, its fulfillment, and its genius. The Spirit Creator has given life to *homo faber* while inspiring him to defend it, to develop it by using the nature which surrounds him to draw from his close union with it everything necessary and useful to his life.

Human action receives the seal of this beauty of nature where it develops. Thus every human task, from the smallest technical act to the greatest works of art, has its source of inspiration in the Spirit Creator who imparts to it a reflection of divine beauty. In constructive emulation, then, men admire the accomplishments of their brethren and glorify their Father who is in heaven (cf. Mt 5:16). All human creativity and the ability to produce have their origin in the Spirit, and it is the Spirit who refers them to God *ut in omnibus glorificetur Deus*—that in all things God might be glorified (RB 57:9 quoting 1 P 4:11). This motto, quoted by St Benedict in the chapter dealing with the monastery craftsmen, is given by St Peter as a program for all of the faithful. As a matter of fact, it is a program of life for every person, a reality for all of creation, and does not concern only the monk. And God is not only the beginning and the end of everything that exists; He is its reason for being. Since absolutely everything comes from Him, everything is ontologically ordained to His glory, and nothing can escape this law.

Now the human person, conscious and free, is the master of his actions, which he can perform for the glory or the dishonor of God. It is a liberty at once awesome and adorable. To all a person's thoughts, desires, acts, to his whole existence, it can give an upright and simple orientation which, while unifying him, makes him a person of only one fundamental idea, an upright and strong person whose flawless character preserves him from compromises and degrading cowardice. If, on the other hand, he allows the perversity of selfishness into his actions, he perverts them from their final goal and, at the same time, he loses the link which unites them in harmony and which unites him within himself.

THE CRAFTSMEN OF THE MONASTERY

That in all things God may be glorified. St Benedict gives this principle as an epilogue and ultimate reason in a chapter which seems to treat a relatively banal subject. It deals with the craftsmen of the monastery who, while serving the cause of the community by their talents and abilities, may fall into the fault of working more for themselves and their personal satisfaction than for the glory of God.

There is a second pitfall to avoid: that is to sell the products of the monastery while allowing oneself to be tempted by seeking economic profit and thus to lay oneself open to the temptation of dishonesty or avarice.

St Benedict's basic attitude in these two cases is to set the thought of God against these deviations: everything should be done for his honor. This is a general principle which rules not only the particular cases examined in this chapter, but the whole of life.

Let us pause at the practical applications and examine first of all the case of the craftsmen. At the time of St Benedict, these people were exposed to two very human snares: vanity, and the idea that they were indispensable to the life of the monastery. St Benedict sets humility against vanity and obedience against the pretension of assuring the community's material support. He does not deny that the labor and the works of art deserve praise. Likewise he recognizes that certain aptitudes and abilities benefit the community economically. These facts are obvious and deserve, sometimes, public recognition by the superiors and the community. But to do one's work in a spirit of self-sufficiency is contrary to the reality of a creature who receives his gifts and talents from the Spirit Creator and who ought to exercise them with a deep consciousness of being a secondary cause which could never create anything without the assistance of the supreme Artisan. Humility is nothing but the recognition of our real condition and it allows us, in thought and in action, to place ourselves in perfect conformity with existential reality.

It is entirely natural to draw satisfaction from one's know-how and to take pleasure in success. This helps us conquer timidity, inferiority complexes, lack of courage, and an unjustified mistrust of ourselves. This attitude, far from being harmful, stimulates a person to work, drives him to the spirit of conquest and to magnanimity. The Cistercians would never have been monastic builders without the enterprising spirit which animated them and which created in honor of God and the Blessed Virgin Mary monuments of such purity and so original and exceptional a style that its causes admiration in people today. 'Glory be to the Father and to the Son and to the Holy Spirit' passed from their mouth to their hands to become materialized in columns, arches, and trusses. Has the Holy Spirit not collaborated in these works? The Maurist Benedictines would never have become the prototypes of the learned and patient monk had they not edited hundreds of volumes of inestimable value and this, by and large, in the humility of anonymity. St Benedict does not condemn this spirit of dedication and enterprise, but he wants to preserve its purity so that in all things the Lord might truly be glorified—He and none other—and that there will be no form of idolatry diverting the honor due the Lord to a creature.

What means does he use to assure the right hierarchy of intentions? He has recourse, as usual, to obedience. As a matter of fact, this is the surest means of directing every action to the Lord, because it is to the Lord that true obedience is paid. Although other natural intentions, as we have seen, could creep into our work, what is done in sincere obedience receives the form of that virtue. To obtain this very necessary obedience, St Benedict has no intention of compromising. He would rather disappoint the proud monk and wound his honor as a man and an artisan than see him infringe on the honor due the Lord. Better to humble the pretentious monk and do without his work than to accept it, conceived and produced in a disposition of soul which removes its highest meaning, that of being accomplished in the Lord's honor. St Benedict prefers to give up material advantage where the spiritual advantage is in danger. Thus the Spirit of God cannot be pleased with a work produced by abilities that come from Him but are perverted, at least partially, from their original aim. Humble obedience ought to rectify the work of the artisan and only then could he be authorized to take up his work again.

Do the works of art accomplished by the builder-monks not attract our admiration by their simplicity and their purity—very near, if one may dare say so, to the simplicity of the Spirit of God?

Through these works of art God seems to reveal himself in his silent humble grandeur. Man disappears in the anonymity of history; thus the great Artist, who is the Spirit, manifests himself much more clearly. And the glory of God is assured by the humility of man. For where man puts himself forward, he affronts the glory of God, which is still the first cause and *raison d'etre* of the work.

THE GLORY OF GOD
AND THE GLORY OF MAN

Even if a man does his work with the intention of rendering homage to God, a more or less conscious intention of seeking his own glory gets mixed with it, according to his inclination to falsehood. And there we are, in danger of seeking our own, while pretending or naively believing that we are working for the glory of God whose honor thus becomes a pretext for seeking ourselves and an occasion of satisfying our own impulses, our inspirations, our personal desires, our satisfactions, and the wish to assert ourselves and make people talk about us.

It is a fact; we find ourselves with a delicate problem. On the one hand, a person should have a certain sense of his own value and his successes. His nature, inclined to underestimate the talents which the Spirit himself has placed in him — perhaps also inclined to passivity — requires this. The Spirit of God is not jealous to the point of not permitting an artisan, who somehow participates in His creative power, to have a part in the honor which results from the work created. For St Benedict, the solution of the problem is found in obedience. Once the person's intention applies itself to some work, but remains sincerely subordinated to obedience, then there is the matter of a secondary intention, or of the consequence of what we are doing in obedience. It is therefore ordered to the glory of God. In this sense, we can rejoice in success, in good results. We can find a just satisfaction there. St Francis de Sales in his picturesque language speaks of the smoke which is necessarily released where there is a fire. It is the smoke of contentment, the innocent vanity of having succeeded in doing some good work truly accomplished for the Lord in simplicity of heart. We can even attribute the paternity of our work to ourselves if we succeed in carrying it out with that

intention of heart—of doing honor to God 'from whom all paternity, in heaven and on earth, takes its name' (Eph 3:15), so that God
in all things may be glorified.

THE GLORY OF GOD
AND THE PROFIT-MOTIVE

To all this is added the problem of the sale of products.
St Benedict probably had concrete reasons for putting his monks on
guard against temptations to defraud in the process of selling. He
reminds those who would dare to commit fraud or deceit in selling
that they would fall under the scourge of the punishment of that
death in their soul which Ananias and Sapphira underwent in their
body. As they would be lying to the Holy Spirit by holding back a
part of the price of the sale of their goods, the monks would be
committing not only an injustice against the buyers, but an injury
against the Holy Spirit who presides at the destinies of the monastic
community gathered together in the name of Christ whose soul He
is. Never should there enter the monastery the idea or the practice
that business and politics have nothing to do with morals, or that an
administrator should not be bothered with scruples, and anyway,
'business is business'. It is well understood that in certain cases when
the monk is dealing with the children of this world, he ought, while
remaining a child of light, to realize that they are very astute with
their equals (cf. Lk 16:8), so as not to be duped by them. But he
should not be dishonest with the dishonest. It is necessary to have
the prudence of the serpent; he should not have its duplicity. The
simplicity of the dove, symbol of the Spirit, befits the spiritual man
and, according to the counsels of the fourth degree of humility, it is
better to let oneself be cheated than to seek one's own advantage (cf.
RB 7:42f) and better to suffer injustice and to allow oneself to be
despoiled than to risk doing injustice to another (cf. 2 Co 6:7f).

St Benedict also mentions another kind of sin which can be
committed on the occasion of a sale: avarice. There are reasons to
justify a high price for the monastery's products. Behind the wording of the Rule, there also seems to be a reminder of the possibility of
a time of want, of economic difficulty responsible for raising prices.
St Benedict not only puts his monks on guard against the temptation
to avarice, but orders them to sell their products at a price always

lower than that of seculars. In doing this, he had no intention, it goes without saying, of beating the businessmen at their own game with the minimum price of the monastery—that would be dishonest competition—but he wanted the monastery to prove itself worthy of its Master, the Lord, in all its common dealings with the people of the world—of that Lord who never allows himself to be outdone in generosity.

This is the rule that unifies and orders everything for the best: 'That in all things God may be glorified'. Intentions which cannot be reconciled with this cannot be retained. The only orientation for everything practised and done in the monastery is that God be glorified. It is the orientation imprinted on all creation by the Holy Spirit. The human person endowed with reason and will should enter with complete willingness into this current, which leads back to God everything that came from Him.

Could a monk depart even an inch from this way of acting— someone who proposes to live according to wisdom? If all unconscious nature sings the glory of God, this motto is for him a law, a rule of life—for him, the disciple of Christ who on the eve of his earthly life said: 'Father…I have glorified you on earth' (Jn 17:4) and whose whole life was a revelation to the glory of the Father. The monk, therefore, should give to his own life this same unity. Let it be in all things, in absolutely all things, a glorification of God. Then he will be truly a monk, *monachus*, a person of only one idea and only one line of conduct: 'That in all things God may be glorified'.

TOWARD THE EXPERIENCE OF GOD

EVERY PERSON DESIRES ardently, at one time or other in his life, to have 'his heart enlarged' by the Spirit (RB prol. 49). St Benedict teaches us that this experience takes place to the extent that the monk progresses in the *conversatio*, in faith, in the journey on the pathways of God's commandments. He tries, therefore, throughout the Rule to lead us by these pathways by showing us how, by means of courageous progress, we can arrive at this desirable enlargement of heart. Let us examine some of these steps.

THE INSTRUMENTS OF GOOD WORKS

St Benedict first of all enumerates the seventy-four instruments of the spiritual art (cf. RB 4) which are placed at the Christian's and very especially the monk's disposal, and he makes a promise: 'If we use them night and day without ceasing, then, on the day of judgement when we return them, the Lord will give us the reward which He himself has promised: what eye has not seen nor ear heard, that God has prepared for those who love him' (RB 4:76f, 1 Co 2:9). Now, that unfailing perseverance would be inconceivable unless the final recompense the text speaks of is preceded by experiences of deep union with the Lord, a union wholly immersed in the joy of His service and His friendship. The sure hope of ineffable munificence is already the dawn of happiness to come, a distant on-set of beatitude.

THE LADDER OF HUMILITY, THE LADDER TO JOY

'The ways of God's commandments' (RB prol. 49)—what are they if not the very pathways of Christ and His teaching, His journey from His birth to His glorification, passing through the events of His earthly life, His Passion, and His death? The monk's itinerary (cf. RB prol. 21) is nothing else but following Christ,

157

imitating Him, living in intimacy with Him. Like the apostles, the monk has linked his destiny entirely to Christ's, living, therefore, in the words of the Fathers, the 'apostolic life', growing little by little like them, according to his own pace, in the knowledge and love of Jesus. Like them, he has the promise of the Spirit to enlighten and comfort him.

In the second degree of humility he learns to imitate Jesus who says: 'I have not come to do my own will, but the will of Him who sent me' (RB 7:32 quoting Jn 6:38) and, intimately united to him, he begins to experience the happiness of doing the Father's will. On his way he meets suffering and the cross and learns to unite them to the Passion and Cross of Jesus. He knows that Jesus has said, 'Whoever does not carry his cross and come after me cannot be my disciple' (Lk 14:27), and in obedience he accepts 'his cross each day' (Lk 9:23) to follow his Master who 'became obedient even unto death' (RB 7:34 quoting Ph 2:8). Suffering accepted in obedience and obedience accepted even if it is the cause of suffering, become for the monk a source of joy—not a natural joy, which is doubtlessly legitimate, but the joy of having accomplished, in profound union with Jesus and in imitation of Him, the most lovable of all wills—that of the Father of heaven.

In the fourth degree of humility, St Benedict makes us grasp the deep satisfaction of the disciple who, subjected to injuries, in spite of the irksome orders or arbitrary demands by which he is overwhelmed, keeps his patience and declares with the Psalmist (Ps 65:10f): 'You have tried us, O Lord; you have made us pass through the fire like silver in the crucible. You have caught us in the net; you have heaped tribulations upon our shoulders' (RB 7:40), but in order to add 'with joy: in all these trials we are victorious because of Him who has loved us' (RB 7:39 quoting Rm 8:37). It is the joy of the saints who have passed through a thousand tribulations. Far from being oppressed by the cross, they have entered into the joy of their Master already in this life, for He has proclaimed them blessed. The monk counts on the help of the Holy Spirit, the Comforter, and trembling, accepts these provisions from the hands of St Benedict. He hopes to be able to respond as well in the joy of the Spirit in awaiting Jesus, with the assurance that neither tribulation nor anguish nor persecutions (cf. Rm 8:35) nor adversities nor injustice nor suffering can take from him the certitude and the joy of the love of Christ, according to the words: 'Your sorrow will be turned into joy' (Jn 16:20). He thanks the Lord and remains content with the by no means sublime occupations which he is given to do (cf. RB 7:49) while rejoicing in the good which this is doing him by humiliating him (cf. RB 7:54); for sincere humility creates a complete emptiness in the soul, he knows, and leaves free space for receiving 'all the fullness of God' (Eph 3:19).

The monk who has arrived at the top of the ladder of humility experiences a complete joy from which love casts out every sort of fear, hesitation, and retrogression, because love is the fullness of joy. 'Thanks to this charity, he accomplishes without labor, as it were naturally and by habit, what he formerly performed only with dread.' From here on he acts 'through love for Christ under the influence of a good habit and of delight in virtue. This is the grace which the Lord deigns to manifest by the Holy Spirit in his servant now purified of his faults and sins' (cf. RB 7:67-70). Thus in climbing the steps of the ladder of humility courageously and perseveringly, he tastes more and more the joy of finding himself at Jesus' side and of running the way of His commandments, His counsels, and His example in His company. Tempered by the Holy Spirit, he joyfully obeys the calls of grace and discovers that the redemption and great liberty of the children of God is found at the bottom of the chalice of suffering. Thus, with heart enlarged, he tastes the ineffable sweetness promised by St Benedict at the dawn of his monastic life (cf. RB prol. 49).

PRAYER

If one considers the Divine Office only from the standpoint of a 'duty of service' (RB 50:4), it is difficult to imagine that it could lead to mystical states. And nevertheless, the great offices, especially the Night Office, can stir up deep spiritual feelings in the attentive soul of the monk. Then, too, St Benedict seems to see (cf. RB 52:5) in common prayer, as it were, a logical introduction to personal prayer (cf. RB 52:3) which, under the Spirit's guidance (cf. RB 20:4) can lead to a state of great simplicity and purity. Through the expressions used here by St Benedict and inherited from the great masters of prayer, it is not hard to perceive the jubilant joy of the contrite and humbled heart (Ps 50:19) moved even to tears (cf. RB 20:3, 49:4) which experiences the limitless bounty of the Lord and His Providence and withdraws, even if the prayer was short, comforted (cf. RB 20:4) and enlarged to run again the pathways of the divine will.

THE SPIRITUAL DYNAMICS OF LENT

If works of penance are done under the influence of the Holy Spirit and in perfect submission to the abbot's judgement (cf. RB 49:8, 10), not only do they provoke no sadness in the soul, for sadness 'opens the door to the Evil One' (cf. RB 54:4) but, on the contrary, they produce a spontaneous feeling of freedom and openness and leave to the Holy Spirit the initiative of suggesting more sublime thoughts and desires to the purified soul: the renewal of the mystery of the redemption, the feast of Easter, the personal encounter with the Lord giving His life for us and by His resurrection taking the sting out of death (cf. 1 Co 15:55). The spiritual dynamics of Lent also make us give up what is superfluous—considered indispensable at other times—to cut short our talkativeness and to abstain from certain foods. Far from making us grumpy or disagreeable, it expands the religious soul and disposes it to offer its little sacrifices 'in the joy of the Holy Spirit to God' (RB 49:6). It teaches the soul to enter into itself and to enjoy real peace while awaiting 'with the joy of spiritual desire, the blessed Easter' (RB 49:7).

THE HOPE OF THE MONK

'What is sweeter, my dear brethren, than this voice of the Lord which invites us!' (RB prol. 19). The immense love of the Holy Spirit causes His chosen one (cf. RB prol. 14) to pass the shoals of hesitations and 'shows him the way of salvation' (RB prol. 20). He will travel it by following Christ 'under the guidance of the Gospel' (RB prol. 21). What indeed was the monk's purpose in entering the monastery if not to seek God, to learn to know Him better, to meet Him, to love Him more and more, and thus to arrive at the fulfillment of his own life (cf. RB 73:2)? The Holy Spirit and no other inscribes into his heart the 'good zeal which is able to separate from evil and lead to God and eternal life' (cf. RB 72:2). He teaches him that 'someone who does not love [his neighbor] has not known God, for God is love' (1 Jn 4:8). Likewise, someone who pretends to know

God but does not love his brother, is a liar (cf. 1 Jn 2:4). Good zeal is ardent charity manifested in respectful consideration for the brethren, by unalterable patience for their weaknesses of heart and body, by generous obedience and openness toward them, always preferring what is useful to them to one's personal interest (cf. RB 72:3-8). The monk has before his eyes the zeal of God leading Jesus even to the folly of the cross, not sparing His own Son, but delivering him up for us all (cf. Rm 8:32).

Thus impelled by divine inspiration, after having responded generously to pressing appeals to fraternal charity, he will not fail to experience, according to the measure of his generosity, how great is the Lord and generous is His love. The person who has comforted his brother in the name of Christ, even by a small gesture, will be gladdened and comforted by Christ. Indeed, the ways the Spirit acts remain His secret. There are a thousand ways to make a man experience His kindnesses and favors, and His comings and goings are mysterious. He can leave us yearning for Him; He can come upon the soul suddenly. Only one thing is certain: flesh and blood are powerless to obtain the Spirit's graces.

On the day of his monastic profession, the monk asks God three times in front of his brethren: *Suscipe me Domine*—'Receive me, O Lord, according to your word and I will live, and do not disappoint me in my expectation' (RB 58:21, Ps 118:116).

No, the Lord will not disappoint him in his expectation. St Benedict assures his disciples that if they remain faithful, they will arrive, with heart enlarged, at 'the highest summits of doctrine and virtue' (RB 73:9) and will experience the ineffable sweetness of His love (cf. RB prol. 49). The perspectives of the monastic life lose themselves on the Mount of Transfiguration. Certainly, the climb is always rugged, but the Spirit intervenes with His choice favors.

CONCLUSION

Perhaps some people regret the extreme reserve of St Benedict when he touches the gates of the mystical states, for clearly, he does touch them, to allow us to perceive what the Holy Spirit reserves for those who let themselves be attracted by him and who respond generously to his most intimate and most delicate appeals.

Let us understand St Benedict's intentions. He wishes to offer 'a very modest Rule written for beginners' (RB 73:8)—and we remain beginners even to the end of our days—so that in observing it we might 'show a certain moral uprightness and the beginnings of the monastic life' (RB 73:1). But at the same time, St Benedict promises without hesitation, as we have seen, that the faithful observer of his Rule will arrive at the highest summits of perfection (cf. RB 73:9).

His intention was to write a Rule where 'he tempers all things so that the strong might desire to do more and the weak might not flee' (RB 64:19). Those who want to go further in the ways of the Lord find themselves encouraged and informed, yet without discouraging others by perspectives that are too lofty. Basically, in writing the Rule, St Benedict wanted to teach the abbot 'to conform and adapt himself to the dispositions and the degree of intelligence of each' (RB 2:32) in accordance with the attitude of a good father who practices loving discretion. It is precisely this very wise trait that has given the Rule its universality, a trait which it has in common, in due proportion, with the Gospel.

SERENITY OF SOUL

THE WORD 'SERENITY' is not found in the Rule, but the attitude that the word indicates is. The expression is taken from nature. Is the sky serene? The human heart, at home in that nature from which humankind was drawn, experiences that serenity. If, on the other hand, the sky is somber, a certain natural impressionability moves him toward bad humor. Folk-wisdom teaches us that people tend to be affected by lunar cycles, to be in a good mood or a bad mood, or to react to his companions vexatiously according to changes in the weather.

Steadiness of soul is a requirement for human dignity. It is the virtue of equanimity. This obviously does not consist in a situation midway between clear and cloudy; rather it signifies the maintenance of serenity, the continuation of a state of soul which is sunny, bright, and peaceful. St Benedict requires this disposition of the cellarer: 'let him discharge his duty with a peaceful soul' (cf. RB 31:17). 'Equity' (RB prol. 47) is in some way a consequence of this. The *apatheia* of the Stoics denoted a proud indifference rather than a true serenity which is proper to the saints whose countenance—certain portraits or deathmasks bear witness to this—shone with a profound light, like a foretaste of blessed eternity.

Serenity of soul is nothing other than peace of soul, or if you prefer, has its origin in peace, a virtue which has always been considered characteristic of the monk faithful to the Rule. Does St Benedict not recommend, quoting the Psalms (Ps 33:15), seeking peace and cultivating it (RB prol. 17)? He does not take time to stress its importance with a special treatise, but one realizes that it underlies the common life.

This peace is one of the gifts of the Holy Spirit (cf. Ga 5:22). It is also a gift of Christ who has left us His peace (cf. Jn 14:27), the ineffable peace of His heart which surpasses all understanding (Ph 4:7). It is God Himself, the most serene and at the same time infinitely active tranquillity of divinity. This peace is offered us as the pledge of that eternal beatitude won by the monk with

163

the instruments of good works prepared by St Benedict. For God, peace is His very susbstance; for the monk it is a quality, a virtue of the soul.

Therefore peace, tranquillity, in us is a participation in the immutability of God. God reigns in His eternal calm and rules above all the vicissitudes and changes to which we are subject. But to the extent that our gaze remains fixed on the Lord, ever the same in His goodness, our heart experiences calm. If we succeed in living in God's presence and under His gaze, as the Rule recommends (cf. RB 7:13), and for Him it is a gaze that is always loving, always peaceful, then to that extent, a great serenity reigns in our soul. Certainly, we labor to progress in this effort, but faithful effort helps us lift ourselves little by little toward the Lord on the ladder of virtue above disturbing vicissitudes and become ever closer to Him. This nearness to God, although it is relative and fragile, does not fail to spread a certain evenness of feeling over the soul so that the labor of attaining it gives way to 'a holy habit and delight in virtue' (RB 7:69). The Spirit who in the beginning hovered over the chaos causes the monk who has arrived at relative maturity to rise above the pettiness with which life is filled. He has need of the divine absolute.

The human countenance is a mirror which reflects the sentiments of the soul. Let us go out into the street and observe passers-by. Very few give the impression of true serenity. Some are marked by hatred, insecurity, cares, sorrows, fear, disappointment, or indeed, by a sham and superficial joy, not to speak of countenances ravaged by vices and passions! Where is serenity? If the sky were as dark as the faces of many people today, what kind of weather would we be having?

The monk too, can let himself be troubled, like any other mortal. Did he not sleep well? The barometer of his humor goes down. Is there a delicate problem to resolve, a contact with an unsympathetic confrère, a little dissatisfaction? Look how our precarious serenity is threatened. Our calm, already put to the test by the prospect of this or that disagreeable task to be done, totters in agitation or discontent. The tone of our voice rises and bad humor invades our soul like a fog, darkening our countenance.

Yet the monk has at his disposal effective means for maintaining peace of soul, for reining-in the turbulent throngs of thoughts and passions by imposing a certain asceticism on them. How can someone be disposed for prayer and present himself to the Lord if he cannot rise above the coming and going of his thoughts? How can he be obedient to the Holy Spirit, open to His suggestions and to the commands of those who speak in his name if he cannot master his personal desires? Is peace not order in the soul?

To maintain evenness of soul, the monk is greatly helped by monastic observances, indispensable factors of order and discipline. In a busy and exacting life, they husband the regularity of the schedule, the serenity of the surroundings, the respect for silence, as well as the consideration and service of the brethren. His life does not run like a torrent or a waterfall, rushing from the heights of the mountain to seek its life violently. It should rather be like a peaceful river which knows its course.

And so the thought of the monk, even more than that of other Christians, is directed, and as it were diked, by firm principles freely accepted. It is not based on the shifting sands of a perpetual searching which never reaches the end of its uncertainty and leaves him out of breath.

Fleeing the world in the right sense, that is to say, fleeing what is not wholesome in the world and even everything in the world which diverts the monk from his profession of seeking God, assures him of a certain absence of alien troubles and helps him in his effort to remain in peace. It would, however, be false to imagine that we are dealing with a peace that lacks depth because it is not the result of struggle, but the monk of our day finds himself constantly confronted with the world which creeps into his life in a thousand ways; and he has to wage a constant battle to preserve his independence of spirit and the freedom to which Christ has introduced us (cf. Ga 4:31). This effort at renunciation, if it is done with regret, gives the monk a pessimistic or too natural turn of mind. If he accomplishes it in conformity with the divine will and in respect for the Rule accepted freely, he creates in his soul a zone of serenity, freed from the petty agitations of daily life.

Not only does the religious observance of the Rule establish a tranquil and serene conscience within us, but the Rule itself inspires serenity. At first glance, this might seem hardly convincing. How can we speak of serenity and evenness of soul when we read about severe and repeated measures of punishment, about regular discipline, to say nothing of the rod? Or again, when we read about certain prescriptions which are imposed straight out and apparently without mitigation? It is a fact—the person of today might feel shocked at reading things of this sort in a monastic rule. St Benedict, however, acts as a mother who, with all of her energy, goes to the defense of her child who is threatened by evil. It is the safeguarding of charity (cf. RB prol. 47, 65:11) which dictates the Rule to St Benedict and determines the measure. Serenity of soul has nothing to do with a passivity disposed to let the wolf enter the sheepfold. It is neither timid nor soft. Its allies are clairvoyance and the will to exclude, not only the fantasies of the capricious, but also weakness which would be an accomplice to irregularities.

When we look at it more closely, the entire Rule then breathes, serenity, and the spiritual atmosphere of the monastery is impregnated with it. It is the atmosphere of a family of which Christ is the *paterfamilias*, loved by all, considered universally present in the person of the brethren, the abbot, the sick, the poor with whom He chose to identify himself. Jesus leads His family to the Father, to the heavenly homeland (cf. RB 73:8) and unites all its members in the Spirit. In the community there reigns a delightful atmosphere composed of prevenient charity (cf. RB 72), common prayer, obedience, and mutual service; the whole Rule is penetrated with it. It is the fraternal race on the way of salvation (cf. RB prol. 48) which unites the monks. Together they accompany Christ in His Passion; together they travel toward eternal life (cf. RB prol. 50). The Rule wants to make the spirit of solidarity reign among the brethren who are often so different by origin, by temperament, by formation, but united in one same effort at the good of each and every person. St Benedict, it is true, speaks only exceptionally in an explicit way of this mutual affection (e.g. RB 27:4, 28:4); yet the common life recommended by the Rule closely links the brethren to one another and leads to this mutual corresponsibility. In fact, it would be difficult to admit that prayer offered in common every day by brethren side by side would not lead to a more exacting consciousness of the close union in life and in death which exists among them.

Now this ambiance of profound union which is ordinarily disturbed only superficially by minor discords, misunderstandings, or discomforts—let no one accuse us of too much optimism, for we believe in divine charity, an infused virtue poured into our hearts by the Holy Spirit—creates an atmosphere of serenity in everyone's soul, an atmosphere of confidence, promptness to forgive, peace, forgetfulness of offenses; it creates a magnanimous heart when one is confronted with ill-chosen words or lack of tact or charity. It is the serenity of deep joy, a fruit of the Holy Spirit (cf. Ga 5:22) which establishes itself in all receptive souls and thus in the community to the extent that it is careful to put the counsels of the Rule into practice.

Yes, serenity emanates from the Rule like dew which sparkles, not of itself, but beneath the light of the divine Sun. Its literal wording does not necessarily give serenity, but the spirit which is expressed by its text is a spirit of commitment and generous ardor, a spirit of confidence and openness, of strength and courage in the face of the suffering of the cross, sustained by a solid faith, an absolute hope, and the love of a child for his heavenly Father. This way of living can come only from the Holy Spirit, a torrent at once of love and of absolute repose in which resides the Most Blessed Trinity. St Gregory speaks of the vision of God with which St Benedict was favored. Is it not thus that the face of St Benedict became a mirror of God's splendor, transformed into His image by the Spirit's action (cf. 2 Co 3:18)? And why be surprised to see this serenity of countenance pass into the Rule as a reflection of eternal Wisdom?

It would, therefore, be impossible that the serenity of the Rule would not penetrate to the heart of the monk who is full of its spirit! People have always rightly spoken of benedictine peace, the characteristic of the perfect disciple of St Benedict. This serenity is contagious. A brother who has a tranquil heart becomes a catalyst of serenity for the community. Indeed, who would block out the sun, its light, its warmth, and its beauty with which it illuminates everything by its beneficent rays?

A brother of truly tranquil heart is like the sunlight for his brothers in distress. There is no better remedy for healing spirits, for overcoming moods of disheartenment or melancholy, or for chasing away the noonday devil than the serenity of a brother merry with the joy of the Holy Spirit. Is this not the monk of whom St Benedict speaks in the sixth degree of humility (cf. RB 7:49f), the monk who is always satisfied, that is to say, able to maintain evenness of soul with a sense of humor, even when it costs him something? Even when he is underestimated or overburdened with unenviable obediences? Is this the brother whose obedience is well pleasing to the Lord and agreeable to men (cf. RB 5:14) because he has learned to obey with a joyful heart (RB 5:16)? As a matter of fact, this is a marvelous formula for the monk desirous of maintaining evenness of soul: to obey, sincerely and with a supernatural spirit, one's superiors, one's brethren, one's community, one's Rule. This obedience keeps the monk's eyes clear and his heart content.

Thus serenity opens souls, forms faces into a smile, unties mute thoughts and tongues and creates an atmosphere of confidence, sincerity, and charity. A community which lives under the guidance of the Rule cannot escape these happy effects. Only then is it possible to grasp the truth of what the Rule affirms concerning the inevitable difficulties of the common life: this yoke is easy to bear. To see a brother constrained to walk a mile walking two joyfully, or asked to give his tunic leaving his mantle at the same time (cf. RB 7:42, Mt 5:40f) while still maintaining an absolute serenity: this no longer comes from the arena of ordinary holiness.

To learn serenity of soul it is necessary to contemplate Jesus. If we do not become penetrated by this Model of virtue, we will easily slip into error. He has taught us not to let ourselves be troubled (cf. Jn 14:1, 27), and yet He himself seems to have been troubled (cf. Lk 22:44, Jn 11:33, 35,38). But it is precisely by His example that we learn not to confuse evenness of soul with insensitivity, which, far from being a virtue, is rather a lack of charity or of delicacy of soul.

It is in His obedience to the Father that the serenity of Christ takes it origin. Jesus never loses evenness of soul or confidence in His Father, even if He feels Himself abandoned by Him (cf. Mt 27:46). He lives in perfect union with the will of His Father; it is like a light in His human soul and permeates it even to the point of death with profound certitude and a serene acceptance of His mission.

This, then, is the ultimate root of serenity of soul. Without obedience we could possess only a deceptive serenity, and our monastic heart will not truly experience it until the day when it will have fulfilled to the very end its *Fiat*.

IN THE PRESENCE OF
THE GODHEAD

FAITH IN THE PRESENCE OF GOD

TO SET A LADDER in place is at the same time to prevent it from slipping and to ward off a possible fall. On the spiritual level, St Benedict establishes the first degree of humility here, and Cassian makes it the base of his ladder.

Faith in God and in His presence is the foundation of the monastic life. Faith tells us God is everywhere present, and reason itself affirms this since the universe could not exist by itself. God is, and it is He who calls it into existence and maintains it, giving it its reality through Him and in Him.

God is therefore present to me. He is my Creator and keeps me in being. He is more present to me than I am present to myself, because he is the cause and is anterior to that which I am. Everything I am already existed in Him in infinite measure. He is not present to me as an impersonal being. He is all intelligence, light, vision, free will. He is a being open to personal relationships. He looks at me and loves me. St Benedict quotes the Scriptures (RB 7:14–18) in order to explain this to us: 'God scrutinizes the heart and the mind'. God is present to me in my heart, in the depths of my being; He is infinitely close to me. 'The Lord knows the thoughts of men'. He knows everything about me. Let us realize this: the desires and preoccupations which jostle and follow each other in me, good and judicious ones, perhaps holy ones, but also senseless, contemptible, and even evil thoughts, those I carefully hide from my neighbor—God knows them all. He scruitinizes my thoughts. 'You have understood my thoughts from afar', continues the Psalmist. A thought—what is it anyway? A little breeze that is soon past.

From all eternity God knew my thoughts and their entire development. He was and is present: 'The thoughts of a man lie open to you'. Nothing is hidden from the Lord; everything is bare before Him, because He is light and penetrates everything. 'Let a man remember that God sees him at every moment from the heights of heaven, that in every place the gaze of the divinity extends to his action' (RB 7:13). If he has sufficient understanding of the meaning of his life, he will become more and more conscious of this presence of God. Am I, then, inattentive to this staggering truth: God, the ineffable, the inconceivably great Being, is present to me, and cares for me in an altogether personal way? Do I not have the duty to understand ever better my dependence on Him at every instant? I owe Him my existence, my ability to think, to will, and to move myself.

To be conscious of God's omnipresence translates itself necessarily into an act of religion, of humble and profound adoration, of reverential fear, of praise. And since all human beings and all creatures find themselves in the same situation, a hymn of jubilation arises from the human heart in the name of all creation: 'Holy, Holy, Holy Lord God, Master of all. He was, He is, and is to come' (Rv 4:8). 'You are worthy, O Our Lord and Our God, to receive glory, honor, and power, for it is You who created the universe' (Rv 4:11). Like the beings of the Apocalypse who stand before the throne of God, we should remain in His presence. Of course, we should acquit ourselves of this duty, not as would angels, but according to our own condition.

Now our condition is that of a sinner. The basic sin is to forget God (cf. RB 7:10), not to take His presence into account, to allow the fear of the Lord in our heart to become dim. The monastic life is essentially a life under the eye of God, with this effect: 'to keep oneself at all times from the sins and vices of thought, of the tongue, of the hands, of the feet, and of self-will, as well as from the desires of the flesh' (RB 7:12), to keep oneself also from all the illusions familiar to our corrupt and impressionable nature, to be wary of the devil's deceptions, knowing that 'there are ways which seem right to men, but their end leads to the depths of hell' (cf. RB 7:21 quoting Pr 16:25). The greater our faith in the presence of the Lord, the more sin repels us.

Let us add that to live in the presence of God does not mean to belabor our imagination to, in some way, localize Him, but it is to believe in Him with a living, practical faith. It is to bear witness to this consciousness of His presence by all of our behavior. It is also to think of Him and to speak of Him with deep reverence and to cultivate in our heart the continual remembrance of God as a sort of subconscious habit.

With this first step of the climb toward perfection, St Benedict sets before us a teaching as simple as it is obvious—I might say, naive: God is watching us. Therefore, let us not fall into sin, because if He 'prolongs the days of our life as a respite for the amendment of our sins' (RB prol. 36), He might also 'as an offended Father, deprive His children of their inheritance', or 'as a fearsome master...deliver us up to eternal punishment' (RB prol. 6f). He therefore appeals to fear, mixing filial and servile fear in order to reach rude temperaments as well as well-developed sensibilities. This picturesque presentation is clear and effective for everyone. It is only the foundation of faith, but a solid, real, and effective foundation. Without this living and working faith, there is no spiritual life.

THE PRESENCE OF
FATHER, SON, AND HOLY SPIRIT

God is a personal Being. In Him there is an interpersonal life. 'The only begotten Son who is in the bosom of the Father—He has made him known' (Jn 1:18). God is therefore present as Trinity: Father, Son, and Holy Spirit.

The Father is present to us—He who, humanly speaking, seems the farthest from us. 'No one knows the Father except the Son and he to whom the Son wishes to reveal Him' (Mt 11:27). In a certain way, He has manifested himself visibly in the Son: 'Someone who has seen me, has seen the Father' (Jn 14:9). The Father is present; he is the origin of all things, the fountain from which life and everything that exists unceasingly spring forth. He is the *ONE WHO IS*. Where there is being, He is there, for everything is through Him and in Him, and nothing exists outside of Him. He is therefore present, or rather, we are present in Him. He is the Person of the Father, the Absolute of the Father, the Father creating, operating, loving. All of this concerns us existentially. 'It is in Him that we have life, movement, and being' (Ac 17:28). If He is not, then I am not. If He does not think of me from all eternity, if He does not love me, then I am not. If He does not choose me by predestining me, what would I be? If He is my Father, then, my desire is to live with Him in His presence.

The Son is present to us, but in parting He declared to the apostles: 'I am going to Him who has sent me' (Jn 16:5), while at the same time assuring them: 'I am with you always, even to the end of the world' (Mt 28:20). He remains, therefore, present with the Church for all time, and much more present with each one of us. Let us listen to what He says to His disciples: 'If anyone loves me, he will keep my word, and my Father will love him, and we will come to him and we will make our dwelling in him' (Jn 14:23).

This presence is full of mystery, as it is full of promises. For the presence of the Son in us is not inoperative; it is our whole joy. Let us contemplate Jesus and all that He was to the apostles: to Peter, John, Andrew, and all the others, with His teachings, His counsels, His considerateness, His friendship, His glance, and the warmth of His presence. He is present to me! He has come to me. 'Remain in me as I am in you' (Jn 15:4), He told us. And since He is in me, He would, without any doubt, want to reveal His Father to me and make me live as a true child of the Father.

In order to make us His brothers, did He not invent the sacrament of eucharistic nourishment, giving us His own Body and Blood, so uniting Himself to us in a profound intimacy as to dwell with us in a manner perceptible to our nature for which the senses are at once a screen and a vehicle of understanding? The extreme condescendence of love without measure! It is true: the eucharistic presence is a kind of trial for us. In the eucharist Jesus becomes visible under the form of bread, but all of our faith is needed to believe in that lovable presence. On the Lord's part, it is an approach to us—toward those who wish to accept Him and who say to Him with Peter: 'Yes, we believe, and we know that you are the Holy One of God' (Jn 6:69). The 'real' presence of Jesus on the altar in the tabernacle solicits our presence; the memory of His sacrifice, our readiness and loving generosity; the offer of His communion, our full communion.

The presence of the Holy Spirit is at once the most elusive and most penetrating. He is the Architect of creation, who forms the universe even to the last electrons of the atoms, according to the image which is the Word of whom He is the divine finger, *Digitus Dei* (from the hymn, *Veni Creator*). He is the Breath that gives life to all. Nothing moves in heaven or on earth without His strength, nothing is beautiful unless it is a reflection of His beauty, nothing is good except because He is Goodness. He is not satisfied with hovering over us (cf. Gn 1:2), He dwells within us (cf. 1 Co 3:16). Our feeble breath is an emanation of that which He is. Our body is His temple (cf. 1 Co 6:19). Does it not surpass in perfection the beauty of all the cathedrals and all the palaces on earth? Our body is the work of the Spirit; our heart still more. He forms it continually! Unceasingly at work, He is, at the same time, the sweet guest of the soul (from the sequence, *Veni Sancte Spiritus*) and baptizes it by fire (cf. Mt 3:11), burning the chaff of useless preoccupations in it, if indeed we allow Him to work. Yes, if by our narrow spirit we do not erect an obstacle to the immensity of the Spirit of God, would He not flood us with his ineffable joy? He is there, the 'divinizing' light of which St Benedict speaks (RB prol. 9), all ready to light the little lamp of our intellect and to make it share, by his gift of understanding, in His deiform intuition of the great truths. Through the gift of knowledge, we have from Him an ever sharper perception of God and the meaning of our life. But above all, we desire wisdom, not human wisdom, however attractive it may be, but that wisdom with which the Spirit enlightens everything with His own light and makes us understand that everything came forth from divine love. His touch is sweet, mysterious, without constraint; it produces a perfect liberty within us. We would never attain to this through our own powers and to this same degree of perfection. The more a man finds himself under the action of the gifts of the Spirit, surrendering himself to Him in everything that concerns him, the more the Holy Spirit sees to it that all things work together for his good. The man who is guided in this way is transformed. He accomplishes in himself that mysterious substitution which St Paul expressed in these words: 'If I live, it is no longer I, but Christ who lives in me' (Ga 2:20), the Spirit of Christ. The saints arrive at this state, but at the price of a total obedience to the most intimate and sweetest calls of the Spirit.

Happy shall we be if we know how to respond generously to the most loving of all advances—but which make us pass by way of the heroism of the saints.

Let us stop here! Let us assure ourselves by a deep act of faith in the blessed presence of the Spirit in us. The Father has willed to give Him to us so that we might be His children. 'Allow yourselves, therefore, to be led by the Spirit' (Ga 5:16), 'so that the inner man may be strengthened in you' (Eph 3:16). Not only 'do not sadden the Holy Spirit of God' (Eph 4:30), but seek your fulfilment in Him (cf. Eph 5:18).

Here is the meaning of the monastic life: a man allows himself to be seduced by the Spirit, by His calls. Thus the soul blooms in every situation, on happy days and in difficult times, under the touch of this Master, and nothing can separate him from the love of God (cf. Rm 8:39) present and working in us in the Holy Spirit.

GOD PRESENT TO THOSE
WHO CALL UPON HIM

'We believe that God is present everywhere and that His eyes are in every place upon the good and the evil. But it is especially necessary to be firmly assured of this when we are present at the Divine Office' (RB 19:1f); St Benedict adds in the Lord's name: 'My eyes will watch over you, and my ears will be attentive to your prayers, and even before you call upon me, I will say to you: "Here I am"' (RB prol. 18 quoting Is 58:9).

We are not first when we call on God. 'In your prayers, do not keep repeating yourselves like the pagans; they imagine that by speaking much they will make themselves heard better' (Mt 6:7). *Non in multiloquio*—'not in much speaking', St Benedict advises us (RB 20:3). God seeks us so that we might seek him. Therefore when we speak to the Lord, He is already there. We are not first when we knock at his door to ask him to enter. It is he who is knocking at ours (cf. 3:20).

God is always present, even more when we call on him and especially during the celebration of the Divine Office. The *Opus Dei* is, as a matter of fact, our official duty. The entire Church prays with and through the Divine Office of the monks. The Church entrusts us with this task, and God has a right to this homage rendered in common. It is an immense task and a great responsibility for the monk. St Benedict, it is true, tells us nothing of the social, ecclesial dimension of our liturgy; not that he had not thought of it—the dogma of the Communion of Saints, of the unity of the Mystical Body of which St Paul speaks (cf. Rm 12:5) were known to him just as they are to us, and he knew not only that if one member of this body suffers, all suffer; if one member is honored, it is a joy for all (cf. 1 Co 12:26), but also that if one member prays, everyone participates, according to his proper measure, in that prayer. We stand before the Lord through our liturgy, our psalmody and our chant, with the entire Church behind us, and we find him to be so much more present and so much the more inclined to hear us inasmuch as we represent the Church, that is to say, Christ his Son praying with us.

All these truths cause us to reflect on the manner in which 'we ought to stand in the presence of the divinity and of the angels' (RB 19:6) and in what spirit we ought to draw near the Lord.

First of all, St Benedict exhorts us to the fear of God: 'Serve the Lord in fear' (RB 19:3 quoting Ps 2:11). Why fear God, the God of love? Modern man refuses this feeling of the fear of God as a vestige of bygone days when man was at the mercy of the violent forces of nature, expressions of the divine anger; or indeed, he sees in this a sort of psychological compensation capable of reassuring a man held in check by his personal problems. Likewise, this modern philosophy supposes that, once this mechanism is unmasked, a person will affirm himself and assume his responsibilities, conscious of his dignity as a member of humanity arrived at the age of adulthood. But without going that far, the fear of God has, for many good Christians, the flavor of the Old Testament against which St Paul already put the Romans on guard: You have not received a spirit of slavery so as to fall back into fear (Rm 8:15).

And for us, how is it necessary to understand this fear of God and the insistence of St Benedict, not only in speaking of it, but in wishing to teach it: 'I will teach you the fear of God' (RB prol. 12 quoting Ps 33:12), up to the day when charity, become perfect, 'casts it out' (cf. RB 7:69)?

Faith tells us that the fear of God is a gift of the Spirit. Therefore, far from being a regrettable attitude, it is profoundly fitting for a person in the presence of God, not because he would be sometimes a kind Father and sometimes a fearsome and angry Master (cf. RB prol. 7), but because man has reasons for considering himself always as a sinner, for fearing eternal punishment and offending even in the smallest way this infinitely loving Father. The Spirit inspires us with this fear, and very especially during the time of prayer when we ask for graces and when our conscience accuses us. He inspires this fear to permit us to praise the Lord not only with our lips (cf. Mt 15:8) but, finding ourselves in His presence, to make our minds harmonize with our voices (cf. RB 19:7).

The Church introduces us to the liturgy of the eucharistic celebration through an act of contrition: we are sinners. We have very objective reasons for fearing to draw near God, because He sees the smallest stain, the least imperfection in our soul. The Holy Spirit guides us. At our humble request, He arouses filial fear in us to purify our soul and to open its inner eyes to our real condition; this attitude of deep contrition makes us melt into tears (cf. RB 20:3), and then, the Divine Office, with the Psalms, offers us the whole range of feelings which a deep faith in the presence of the Divinity is able to awaken in the soul.

It is necessary, therefore, to 'sing wisely' (cf. RB 19:4, Ps 46:8). Certainly, the presence of God arouses in us, first of all, the recognition of our unworthiness and fear; but wisdom does not remain there. It makes us see His admirable goodness which is inseparable from His glory and holiness. With the Psalms, we bow down in profound adoration and exult with all creatures in singing the grandeur of the Lord, His goodness, His mercy, His justice, and His power. The Holy Spirit, indeed, intervenes and gives birth to filial piety in our souls. Thanks to this gift, we experience the full dimensions of the relationship of children with their Father.

See, therefore, 'how we ought to stand in the presence of the Divinity' (RB 19:6), before this God who has chosen us for this priestly service, sanctifies us in it, and looks upon us unceasingly with an ineffable love.

He listens to us. Do we present our requests to Him? Those of the people of God? He is there. He listens to what we ask of Him 'with humility and respect' (RB 20:1) in the name of His Son. He will grant them to us (cf. Jn 15:16), because this hope is founded on the word of Jesus. It is trustworthy.

GOD PRESENT IN OUR BRETHREN

The monk lives in the presence of God. St Benedict recalls this: his whole existence is filled with God; God is his vital element. God is especially present in the brethren who surround him and who fight under the same Rule.

Let us put forward first of all, one important truth: God manifests Himself through the ministry of the abbot. He represents Christ, that is to say, he makes Him present. His person recalls the presence of Christ because he is the visible vicar of Christ who is invisible but present. We should not, therefore, see in him simply a personality in the natural order, the head of a line, the head of a group of monks. To consider him only that way would falsify our own situation, because our obedience and respect would be by that very fact deprived of their religious reason. The abbot would become a person vested with human authority, nothing more, despoiled of his sacramentality. In hearing the abbot, we hear Christ. This is the doctrine of St Benedict (cf. RB 5:61, Lk 10:16). By obeying him, we obey Christ (cf. RB 5:15). By honoring him, we honor Christ (cf. RB 63:13). From this it follows that a monk who would honor the abbot simply because of his natural dignity, or who would obey him because he agrees with him or because he loves him, would run the risk of secularizing his attitude toward the abbot and even of falling into the fault of flattery. On the other hand, anyone who would have 'the audacity to contend with his abbot insolently, or outside the monastery' (RB 3:9) would be guilty of a lack of faith through a want of respect for the abbot in whom Christ has chosen to be present.

In the abbot, Christ is made present as Father, Shepherd, and Master; in the person of our brother, he is our Brother, and he identifies himself especially with those who are suffering. In the Rule, St Benedict reminds us of two categories of sufferers: 'Caring for the sick must come above and before all else, so that they are cared for as if they were Christ in person, for He has said: "I was sick and you visited me" and "What you have done to one of these little ones, you have done to me"' (RB 36:1:3). Then St Benedict makes a similar statement regarding strangers: 'All the guests coming to the monestery shall be received as Christ, for he himself will say one day: "I was a stranger and you welcomed me"' (RB 53:1). And notice with what consideration, honor, and care guests are received at the monastery.

The same substitution of the Lord's person for that of the guests he made even stronger regarding the poor and pilgrims 'who should be received with the greatest consideration, because it is principally in them that Christ is received' (RB 53:15).

St Benedict, therefore, applies the teaching of Christ: he wishes to be recognized and honored in his brethren. Surely, when he wrote the seventy-first and the seventy-second chapters of the Rule, he had this doctrine in mind. Patience, charity, mutual obedience, and fraternal considerateness, very demanding virtues, are made so much easier by this view of the omnipresence of Christ in our brethren!

A monk certainly needs a solid faith to put this truth into practice. But basically, it takes the same effort to believe in the presence of God whom we do not see, and to believe that Christ wills to be represented by our brethren and to manifest himself in them. This also is an article of faith.

Christ is therefore present, or let us rather say that everything reminds us that Christ is present: our brethren, the abbot, and thus, the community itself. 'No one has ever seen God', says St John. 'If we love one another, God dwells in us and his love is perfected in us' (1 Jn 4:12). Love makes God present, because Love is God; it is the Holy Spirit. If we do not love each other, God is not made present because love does not exist.

Love, therefore, as it were, draws the Holy Spirit. The more love there is among us, the more we love each other, the more God is present. Thus mutual love makes God present. This is a beautiful and serious truth.

It follows that we must see one another in faith. 'God is light; in Him there is no darkness'. 'If we walk in the light...we are in communion with one another' (1 Jn 1:5,7). Now, to walk in the darkness is to walk without the light of faith where God is not present. Without faith we see each other simply in our poor nature without relationship to God. Whereas if we walk in the light of God we discover in others a creature of God, His child—God Himself transparent through a thin veil. And then we are truly in communion with one another. It is such a simple truth. Let us make a comparison. If we are gathered in a hall and someone turns off the light, we no longer see; we cannot enter into mutual communication. In the same way, if we lack the light of God, that is to say, faith, we are in the dark; we cannot enter into real communion with one another. Certainly, we might be able to live together like the employees or the workers of a business or a company in that peace which is based on a certain mutual mistrust which the world, by means of conferences and treaties, manages to control through non-aggression pacts, armed peace, peaceful co-existence—but nothing better. Christ has given us a peace which is based on communion with Him; through Him we are united with one another. This communion of love is the sign and the effect of His presence, of the operating presence of the Spirit who is the Communion of the Father and the Son and who leads us into this communion.

Our communion among brothers or sisters of a monastic community is, therefore, a witness to the work of the Spirit. 'You shall be my witnesses' (Ac 1:8), Christ commanded His apostles. The *raison d'être* of such a community is to give itself over to a common occupation so as to procure from the work its daily bread while also being useful to humankind, their brethren. Its very essence is to be communion in the Spirit, and thus witness to His blessed presence.

Did Christ not solemnly declare: 'Where two or three are gathered in my name, there I am in the midst of them' (Mt 18:20)? Let us therefore realize: when we are gathered for the Divine Office, Christ is with us, interceding on our behalf (cf. Heb 7:25) with the Father. He is present.

THE SACRED IN THE MONK'S LIFE

The world of today applies itself to delimiting neatly the arena of the sacred from the profane. Moreover, a great process of secularization is in progress. Science is discovering in countless natural phenomena the secondary, immediate causes where the Old Testament, in its picturesque language, mentions only God the primary Cause. Alas! Scholars often go too far in this work of discernment, and some presume to submit what is authentically supernatural to a process of 'demythologizing'. Thus the supernatural and the sacred find themselves reduced to the minimum or even suppressed to leave the whole business in the arena of the profane. God is left in His heaven, at least if He is not declared dead.

Benedict, on the contrary, opens a very different perspective to us: in the monastery, there is no division between the profane and the sacred. Everything is sacred—no laicization of what comes from nature in life. Obviously, St Benedict is not proposing that we go back to the cosmological faith of the pagans, and the teaching of science concerning the place of secondary causes in natural life is in no way contradicted; but by the consecration of His life to the Lord, the monk makes everything that constitutes the necessary framework of His life participate in that consecration. The profane itself becomes sacred, that is to say, finds itself ordained to the service of God and set apart for Him. All the objects of the monastery thus become religious objects.

Here is a new aspect of the omnipresence of God. Everything which the monk needs to carry out His task of adoring God, even in a remote way, and which helps Him in the task, becomes a religious object. Is this an abusive and naive sacralization? Certainly not, for the monastery is the house of God (cf. RB 31:19, 53:22, 64:5) not only inasmuch as it is the dwelling place of a religious community, but even in its material things—*locus sacer*—and everything that constitutes it participates in this quality. In a monastery, the very stones, all the things that contribute to the service of God, are sacred and thus recalls His presence, the supreme end of his reason for being.

That is why the cellarer should 'regard all the utensils and all of the goods of the monastery as if they were the sacred vessels of the altar' (RB 31:10). This is obviously a matter of a general norm. The abbot, therefore, should watch over the good use of the tools and objects of the monastery and reprimand severely those monks who fail to keep them clean or who use them carelessly (cf. RB 32). A similar remark is made concerning the linens and the utensils used in the kitchen (cf. RB 35:7-11). Do we not very appropriately have the custom of blessing all objects of some importance? Everything should be related to the Lord and consecrated to Him as being henceforth His property in the strictest sense of the word.

One immediate consequence of this frame of mind obliges us to treat the matter of buying and selling and regulating the salaries or wages of employees according to principles different from those of the world. The community should support itself from its work; that is a fact, and it cannot renounce fair remuneration; nevertheless, it should take St Benedict's admonition into account not only so that no kind of fraud may appear in the sale of its products, but so that the selling price is removed from the spirit of avarice to show clearly that the monastic community observes, even in its material transactions, its fundamental principle: that everything should work together to the glorification of God (cf. RB 57:4-9). The cellarer is told to act according to this norm (cf. RB 31:12). If a spirit of accumulating wealth, of profit, or of calculation were to rule the monastery's administration, nothing could be more contrary to this fundamentally religious attitude, because all this patrimony is vowed to the service of God, is the property of God, and should be administered according to the mind of the Lord: 'Do not trouble yourself about tomorrow' (Mt 6:34). 'Do not heap up for yourselves treasures on earth' (Mt 6:19). 'All these are things which the pagans seek after' (Mt 6:32), that is to say, those who do not realize that God is a Father and that he is present to those who love him.

The whole life of monks is entirely given up to the worship of the Lord. They dwell in the house of their Father and live with Him under the same roof. The refectory where they take their food is a counterpart of the Church where they receive the bread of Christ. The monks await it from their heavenly Father: 'The eyes of all are upon you; they trust you to give them their food in due time' (Ps 144:15). The monks of the Middle Ages gave their refectories the form of a church. Later on, refectories were often 'humanized' to give them the character of a dining room. The concept of life had slipped toward a profane style, and the end of monasteries was not long in coming. Even the good ones were swept away in the squall.

The refectory is one of the most meaningful of the regular places of the monastery and derives its sacralization from the consecrated community which it serves. Participation in common meals, prefigured by the non-eucharistic part of the Last Supper and by the agapé of the first Christians, is sacred for the monk. He should not, therefore, eat outside the set times for community meals (cf. RB 43:18), and even if he finds himself far from the monastery, he should not eat except with the abbot's permission (cf. RB 51:1-3). The monk arrives punctually at the hour of common meals (cf. RB 43:13) because sharing in these is at once an honor and a sacred duty. The punishment of excommunication from the table clearly emphasizes this principle, and the guilty monk (cf. RB 24:3-7; 25:1, 5f; 51:3) makes satisfaction (cf. RB 44:1,9) by being deprived of participation in the common meal. This corporal and spiritual privation shows beyond question the value that St Benedict attached to the sacred character of common meals.

The dormitory is also a sacred place. The role of sleep is to make the monk disposed for the state of vigilance. The Lord takes care of us (cf. RB prol. 18) and 'awaits day after day for our response to His holy ordinances' (RB prol. 35). He is waiting for us; it is therefore up to us to hurry to Him. Vigilance is, therefore, a basic attitude of the monk. With the whole Church he awaits 'the blessed hope and the coming of Our Lord Jesus Christ' (the Mass). He anticipates the dawn and hastens to Vigils to present himself to the Lord with the wise virgins. The monk's cell is not a comfortable place where everything is arranged for a long, easy life, but it is a place of waiting for the Lord. 'The monks should always be ready', St Benedict demands. 'When the signal is given, they should rise at once and hasten to arrive at the Divine Office before the others, although with all gravity and modesty' (RB 22:6).

The chapter room is the 'auditorium of the Holy Spirit' (St Bernard). Whereas the abbot or the readings speak to the monk's mind, the Spirit speaks to his heart. Likewise, the cloister contributes to the monk's recollection while also being a crossroads of communication. All of the regular places exist to recall the omnipresence of God and to lead the soul to the 'reverence of prayer' (RB 20).

Silence is another expression of faith in the presence of God. Since the monastery is His house, it is fitting to let Him speak and for the monks to listen to the Spirit of the Lord. 'At all times the monks should apply themselves to silence' (RB 42:1). For as it appertains to the Master to speak and to teach, it 'befits the disciple to be silent and to listen' (RB 6:6). The absolute Master is the Spirit. That does not mean to say that He speaks to us continually, but recollection is like a persevering expectation and a cry of, 'Speak, for your servant is listening' (cf. 1 S 3:10). And then, most of the time the Lord speaks to us through the circumstances of each moment, through the way of life of our brethren, through our readings, through nature. Silence leads us to reflection and gives us room for creative thoughts on our life in and with Christ.

Communication, recreation, time for useful and necessary relaxation likewise do not escape the law of the love of the Lord. Even there the monks find themselves gathered in His name, and He is in the midst of them (cf. Mt 18:20). It is not a matter of making secularized hours out of those inserted between the ones consecrated directly to the religious life. The house of God is always 'a house of prayer' (Lk 19:46), and the monk, everywhere and always, remains a man of God, a sign and a reminder of the divine presence.

THE MONK,
A WITNESS
OF HOPE

THE CHRISTIAN VISION of death far surpasses earthly limits. It is not a matter of an end, but of a door, the threshold of a shadow opening up into light, for without death there is no resurrection. Now 'Christ is risen from the dead, the first fruits of those who have fallen asleep' (1 Co 15:20). He has promised eternal life to all who believe in Him (cf. Jn 6:40). The Christian has the promise of the resurrection after death and the promise of eternal life. This hope gives his life its character, its features. It assures him, even under the greatest adversities, of joy and security through the certainty of a happy outcome. His life should have a positive, optimistic, and constructive stamp. A Christian, in every circumstance, always and everywhere, is a person of the future. No disappointment is definitive; no failure, no loss lacks the perspective of a victorious ending on a level that is beyond the reach of misfortune and death.

On the contrary, Christians, and monks in particular, 'having become stable and unshakeable by the hope of the Gospel' (cf. Col 1:23), receive the firmness of tranquil conviction, and having thus been made strong, they joyfully undertake the arduous course of life in the footsteps of Christ.

Entirely different is the condition of those 'who have no hope' (1 Th 4:13). For them, everything is terminal and a dark night with no tomorrow—no glimmer of an eternal dawn. Their work, their labor, their most extraordinary conquests for the good of humanity gain them only an earthly glory that is powerless to snatch them from the tomb. They have no future; it does not belong to them.

One danger, it is true, lies in wait for those who hope, as also for those who have no hope—in other words, the temptation to refuse a serious commitment to work for the betterment of the present world and for an ever better earthly future—some because they are content with the hope of a blessed life in the next world, others, on the contrary, because they are interested exclusively in the profit they can draw from this present life, without any concern for the future. The Christian, however, finds motives in his faith, especially motives of charity, for committing himself with all his might to the service of others, whether spiritually or materially. But the commitment of the Christian to the good of the world, being motivated by divine charity whose ultimate reason is in God, is not able to stop with earthly immanentism of well-being and progress in material ascendancy with its roots in unbelief. The relationship of a Christian to the world is that of a pilgrim travelling toward the city of the Kingdom. Now the city has its roots here below in truth and justice, in freedom, love, and security which, far from being obstacles, are able to help people to find the pathways to the future and definitive city.

THE MONK, MAN OF HOPE

The word 'hope' is found only twice in the Rule. 'To place one's hope in God' (RB 4:41) is, indeed, one of the instruments of good works, for to put all one's confidence in God is to turn away, little by little, from the illusions which our nature flaunts before us. It is to refuse false hopes which leave in the depths of the soul only bitterness, desolation, and failure. From the moment we expect the things from men that they in the last analysis cannot give us, we will be disappointed, and we will fall into the injustice of holding it against them, whereas it was our mistake in the first place! A too-human affection for a creature can become a veritable booby-trap at the moment of disillusionment and can cast us into an exaggerated distress to the point of leading us to decisions out of all proportion to the motive. It is only God who can entirely fulfil what He promises, and He promises everything, that is to say, Himself, infinite Fullness. Confidence in God is, therefore, a true instrument for pacifying the soul. It preserves us from false certitude and disillusionment. The monk who leaves the world by renouncing its false hopes and passes through the school of God's service has already traded the mistrust of this world for confidence in God.

We meet the word 'hope' a second time in the Rule in a sense no less meaningful: 'the confident hope of divine recompense'

(RB 7:39). The Christian has the promise of eternal life which the Father will give to those who love His Son in the Holy Spirit. He will give it as a reward out of proportion to our love, which is itself a gift of His munificence—a reward which 'eye has not seen nor ear heard and which God has reserved for those who love Him' (cf. RB 4:77, 1 Co 2:9). 'The glory of eternal life' (RB 5:3, prol. 7) is a powerful motive for obedience to the monk, even during his whole life. He strives for it and consciously seeks it (cf. RB 4:46, 5:10, 72:2, 12).

As the goal of a work determines its character, its value, the degree of its importance, as well as the intensity of the application to accomplish it, so too the desire (cf. RB 4:46, 5:10), the hope of eternal life, and the certainty of obtaining it (cf. RB 7:39), covers the monk's life with a luster of eternity. Today one likes to say of his life that it has an 'eschatological' character. The 'glory of eternal life' (cf. RB 5:3) liberally anticipated in his life, makes him a witness for God who is himself eternal Life. The monk who, by his prayer and meditation, knocks unceasingly on the doors of eternity, may receive, as it were, a foretaste of the beatitude of the trinitarian life of God promised to those who love and believe in Him. That life cannot be explained except through hope. Hope is wholly bent toward the good things to come. The monk is a person of intense expectation, the watcher with his lamp lit before the Lord's door. If there were no resurrection, if there were not to be this reunion someday, this eternal union with God, his life would be nonsense, even more than the life of any other Christian. 'If it is for this life alone that we have put our hope in Christ, then we are of all people the most miserable' (1 Co 15:19). But God is not far from us. Hope does not concern only distant goods: 'The Lord is near' (Ph 4:5). For one part, we already perceive it; for the other part, we have a glimpse of it by hope (1 Co 13:9f).

THE LIFE OF THE MONK
SUPPORTED BY HOPE

It is worth the trouble of following the ascent of the monk, according to the Rule, to realize the strength which characterizes his spiritual life and prevents him from stopping or stagnating as it were, from resting on what he has already attained, and keeping him from believing that he has already 'arrived'.

From the beginning of his career, the young postulant has to show that he has a resistance that is out of the ordinary and based wholly on hope. St. Benedict's welcome at the monastery gate is by no means encouraging. To wait so patiently and hold firm already requires the possession of a good dose of conviction and strong will. During the time of probation, the novice is confronted with the Rule, and these contacts are not particularly agreeable. The tone of the Master is often harsh there and must needs call forth a determination that is firm and full of drive, resolved to submit itself to the yoke (cf. RB 58:16) of monastic life. St Benedict wants to forge in the soul of the novice a will determined for sanctification supported by an unshakeable faith in divine goodness. To pass victorious through these trials requires an extraordinary temperament; it requires above all, a strong hope in order to throw oneself into this adventure which will last one's entire life, whose co-ordinates are unknown, and—to borrow the image used in the seventh chapter of the Rule—whose rungs cannot be mounted without the hope of being sustained by the grace of God. How many young people hesitate to undertake the adventure of religious life because they are looking for a sense of natural security before committing themselves. But here, it will not be the anxious who will hit the mark, nor those whose movements are unconsciously too human. The whole chapter on the manner of receiving brethren (RB 58) is penetrated by this same spirit. St Benedict wants to turn the novice away from every false support so as to lead him to a solid detachment, even on the psychological plane, so that he will put his trust in God alone. In this sense, the monk as he makes his promise lays aside everything, including his own clothing, and asks the Lord to accept him completely: 'Accept me, O Lord, according to your word and I shall live, and do not disappoint me in my expectation' (RB 58:21, Ps 118:116). The Lord will be his hope, his recourse, his reward.

This hope accompanies the monk throughout his life and remains his heritage. He needs it, because his life, although exteriorly peaceful, is far from exempt from difficulties. The common life, however beautiful it may be, puts him into contact with brethren who are often very different in character, education, and culture, and indeed whose interests are not necessarily his. The abbot is not the only one who must 'accommodate himself to a great number of temperaments' (RB 2:31). Each person needs to adapt himself to the weaknesses of others (cf. RB 72:5) with a clear awareness of his own. St Benedict even makes an allusion to the possibility of false brethren (cf. RB 7:43). This would be a very rare case, but that certain people might be sincere only up to a certain point instead of being completely so, may indeed occur in monasteries. Someone who supports the weight of such situations can say in the joy of hope: 'In all these trials we are victorious, thanks to Him who loves us' (RB 7:39 quoting Rm 8:37).

The fourth degree of humility is a wholly joyful expression of suffering accepted in union with the Passion of Christ: 'Take courage and wait upon the Lord' (RB 7:37 quoting Ps 26:14).

It is sometimes said that the life of a monk is the life of a penitent. Certainly, there might be in a monastic community penitents who are expiating their former life. According to the classification of St Bernard, there are in the monastery, three types: *Martha*, active and militantly acquiring the virtues, *Mary*, the contemplative, but also *Lazarus*, the penitent. At any rate, the monk's gaze is turned toward the blessings which he now possesses only very imperfectly, the blessings which the Holy Spirit dwelling in his heart guarantees. It gives him the wings of hope and breaks the attachments which paralyze his flight toward freedom. The monk knows that in order to rise, it is necessary to die, but that a simply physical death is not enough to gain eternal life. That is why, relying on the passion and resurrection of Christ, he causes mortification of the flesh of concupiscence to precede his death, so as to be ready for the day of resurrection (cf. Ph 3:10f). Like every Christian life, the monastic life is not only a passive waiting. Only valorous fighters win the Kingdom of Heaven.

Striving to acquire perfection: this is the state of the monk: *status acquirendae perfectionis*. He is therefore on the road, he is a pilgrim toward the incomparable goal of the perfection of charity (cf. RB 7:67). Never would he be able to content himself with what he has won and settle down definitively. To undertake climbing the ladder of humility (cf. RB 7) means to refuse to stay midway. Someone who finds himself on a ladder ought to go up or down—progress or regress. Not to advance is to go backwards. The monk should therefore strive to achieve what he has set out to do, with the help of the Lord.

NEVER TO DESPAIR
OF THE MERCY OF THE LORD

In a certain sense, the monk is always becoming. His life unceasingly offers him occasions for self-criticism, and therefore for humility. Experience assures us that even the just man falls seven times a day. The Spirit does not prevent him from falling, so that, with St Paul, he may recognize his weaknesses and even glory in them so as to be a witness to the power of the grace of Christ (cf. 2 Co 12:9). Defects of character or of temperament, even lapses into sin, should not discourage the Christian. They are occasions for getting back up, renewing oneself, and thanking the Spirit who lets us see what we are capable of without grace. We will not be judged so much by our success in virtue as by the love with which we strive to be faithful to the Lord.

Nevertheless, the more the monk advances in his conversion, that is to say, in the descent by humility and the ascent by purity of heart, the more he suffers setbacks which set him face to face with his own reality. He might be able, so to speak, to touch with his finger the privilege of love with which the Lord has favored him, but he finds himself incapable of maintaining himself in the intensity of fervor with which the Holy Spirit sometimes embraces the ordinary events of his daily life.

And then, is that long list of instruments of good works in the fourth chapter of the Rule not discouraging for those whose 'novitiate fervor' still attaches itself too much to little successes in virtuous acts? Does divine love not include all these virtues in its ardor?

The monk who is given over to such reflections has great need to be instructed by the last of the instruments of good works: 'Never to despair of the mercy of God' (RB 4:74). There is, indeed, nothing more depressing and more subtly discouraging than to see our relapses into weaknesses, however small they may be, with all their humiliating regularity and the piercing suggestion to beat a retreat and settle ourselves in mediocrity. But no! Maybe we have forgotten for a moment that it is not our works that sanctify us but the grace of Christ, and that it is not our success in the spiritual life, or what seems to us to be our success, that makes us advance, but the mercy of God which is capable, in an instant of purifying love, of transforming the heart of a thief into that of a saint.

The first of the instruments of good works is to love God above all things. The last is to hope in His love limitlessly. The greater the demands of the absolute love of God, the greater His mercy on those who seek Him in truth. It is only God who can demand everything and can give everything. The monk makes use of means for seeking Him that are practically inaccessible to other men. Without any doubt, he has more need of the merciful bounty of God than any others. For He will demand more of the one to whom He has given more.

It is not rare that chosen souls be terribly tempted to despair. They have been able to taste the inebriating chalice of divine love. The abyss of their own indigence terrifies them that much more, and the fear of being stranded threatens to crush them. The devil, enemy of the Holy Spirit, suggests to them the uselessness of human effort which is disproportionate in the face of the immensity of God's love. This temptation is really diabolical because it presents man as a sort of partner of God, capable of speaking with the Lord as an equal. Despair begins with pride, which supposes that it can pay God the tithe of His own money. This temptation is reducible to the one in Paradise: 'You shall be like God' (cf. Gn 3:5). The false idea of God suggested by the devil, the father of lies, upsets the person who finds himself confronted with his fault and at the same time with his powerlessness to respond to God's justice, but God infinitely transcends these petty calculations. And His mercy is as great as Himself; it is God. The despair which calls His mercy into doubt is therefore a veritable blasphemy. Since divine mercy never fails, hope cannot ever fail. Where sin abounds, grace superabounds (cf. Rm 5:20).

THE SUMMITS OF BEGINNERS

The last chapter of the Rule places a paradox before us. St Benedict says that he has written his Rule for beginners (cf. RB 73:8) so that the monks who are bound to observe it might 'show that they have some degree of virtue and a start in the monastic life' (RB 73:1). There is no question here of an invitation to be content to remain in the state of beginners, but of a presentation of the Rule as a norm for them with the intention of making us understand that in a certain sense we will remain beginners until our last breath. Although they are beginners, monks should hasten toward the perfect life, and for this, they should consult 'the teaching of the holy Fathers whose practice leads a man to the heights of perfection' (RB 73:2). Is there not a lack of proportion between the modest beginnings and the heights to be attained? This is why St Benedict ends his Rule on a vision of hope: 'Whosoever you are, therefore, who hasten toward the heavenly homeland, with the help of Christ keep this little Rule that we have written for beginners. Then at last you will arrive, under the protection of God, at those sublime heights of doctrine and of virtue' (RB 73:8f).

The monk always remains a beginner. And yet achievement is his vocation. Hope has written the prologue of the Rule, offering and promising life to the person who commits himself. It is at the hope of the summits to be attained that the Rule ends. The whole life of the monk is stretched between these two poles: the courage of the beginner tackling the conquest of the holy mountain, and the certain hope, with the help of the Holy Spirit, who is the promoter of every holy work.

THE MONK,
PERSON OF THE FUTURE

The monk, by his vocation, is bent upon a distant and ideal goal. Is he not likely to forget humankind, which needs him and sometimes accuses him of thinking of nothing but his own sanctification without caring for the distress of others? It is true, the monk is vigorously bent toward other countries, different from those of this world. Nevertheless, he also knows that he is going there by small steps, little ordinary steps which unite him to his brethren who are laboring like him in different ways. He is like the watchman on the city walls; his gaze is on the horizon and does not stop at the present. The nature of his vocation is to scrutinize the future. Does he, then, despise what man has made? Is he too preoccupied with the future to appreciate the value of this earth?

The monks have known how to preserve the riches of the past while straining out the useless. They have preserved true values in order to make of them elements in constructing the future. The moral vigor of the Benedictine Rule, its dynamics, its aim toward perfection, its refusal of any kind of stagnation, explains the constructive force of the monastic life for human culture. Supple and capable of adaptation to new situations, this life has always been a stimulant to progress. Certainly, the danger of institutionalization threatens it as with any other institution, and wrongly-understood faithfulness to traditions and usages can lead to a death by suffocation, just as a misguided concern for modernizing can, on the other hand, lead to a loss of identity. The Rule has within itself dynamic values of genuine renewal, such as the ability to discern iconoclastic spirits. At all times, a healthy respect for the Rule has been a force for regeneration in the monastic order. It seems paradoxical that it is the ancient, age-old abbeys which can promote human culture. Indeed, they are not so in an aggressive way. Their contribution to human well-being is wholly spiritual, but as a result, that much more solid and profound. Their stability helps the monks to love the land and the country to which they are attached by their vows, and encourages them to make their own the destinies of the people who live there, by collaborating with them for the betterment of the quality of their life.

THE HOLY SPIRIT, INSTIGATOR OF RENEWAL

For nearly fifteen centuries, the Rule of St Benedict has never ceased to bear the fruits of eternal life. This is a sign: the Spirit of God is working in it. To Him alone belongs the secret of renewing the face of the earth while still remaining eternally Himself. He is at once stability and progress, firmness and openness, solidity and transcendence. In Him is found hope for the future, but at the same time, the guarantee that this future is open to God and true values. It is in Him that the monk, to be useful to his brethren, should seek the criteria for keeping a balanced judgment concerning things that happen. As long as his life will be guided by the light of the Spirit, that long by serving the Lord very simply in truth in the midst of this godless desert of the world, will he be for his brethren, the voice of the Spirit, the messenger of true happiness, and the guidepost on the way of hope.

WITH HEART ENLARGED

DILATATO CORDE, the monk progresses in his life 'with heart enlarged'. This is a key word in our Rule. Let us read the passage of the prologue in full: 'To the extent that one progresses in the religious life and in the faith, the heart becomes enlarged, and with an ineffable sweetness of love, he runs in the way of the command-ments' (RB prol. 49). The image is taken from the life of the body. Joy and love, feelings of freedom or of hope, enlarge the heart, but this image also reminds us that one might have a heart shrunken with anguish or pain or upset by the passions.

Every sort of immoderate expectation, desires, ambition, the hunger for power and success, disturb our heart. The passion of possessive love shrinks it in a feeling of frustration by envy, jeal-ousy, and the disappointments which it inflicts on us. Lack of understanding, avarice, and hardships dry it up and make it rigid.

In short, if something obsesses us or if an inordinate passion tries to impose itself, we feel our heart shrink, as it were physically, and in the depths of our soul there is a sort of distaste and dissatisfaction, along with a discontentment with ourselves. Everything gets diffi-cult: generous charity, obedience, our daily duties. This is what a shrunken heart is, and this makes us understand better the opposite expression *dilatato corde*, having a heart enlarged. It is indwelt by serenity, light, and peace and not weighed down by the reproaches of conscience. It experiences freedom and magnanimity. These happy inward dispositions let us see our neighbor in the best light, let us appreciate him, and teach us to turn the page and to pardon by knowing how to go beyond our own petty troubles. Charity, after having cost us something, becomes brilliant for us. This is the *dilatatio cordis*. The depths of our hearts aspire for this enlargement because it is made for freedom, joy, and blossoming forth.

Now, St Benedict presents the monastic life to us as an ascetic way of arriving at enlargement of heart.

Does the monastic life not offer us a magnificent perspective? Obviously, this transformation does not take place in a day, and there are dark hours in our life when our heart shrivels up, but there are also sunny days. We are affected by our physical condition. Our heart experiences fatigue, and our soul gets gloomy. At other times, if the sun is shining and if nature showing herself in all her beauty, singing the praise of the Creator, we feel ourselves freer, more serene. Then everything becomes bright. Our heart beats faster, and we can see in these strong and regular beatings a sort of remote predisposition to a more sublime enlargement independent of physical causes, that *dilatatio cordis* of which St Benedict speaks and which is of the supernatural order.

What does it consist in? Here we need only apply to it the norms noted about the movements of our physical heart when it is joyous and serene and when peace floods the entire person because he knows he is in harmony with God, himself, and his fellows. Then he feels ready for great undertakings. The courage and joy of living animate him. As the rising of the sun excites the human heart to become enlarged, in the same way, the rising of the eternal light, Jesus Christ, causes the monk's heart to blossom. The night is far spent; the day is at hand. Let us cast off the works of darkness (Rm 13:12): the works of concupiscence, quarrels, jealousy, inordinate attachment, everything that makes the heart disturbed, tense, restless; and let us let in the torrents of grace, light, spiritual joy, freedom, and love.

Whence comes this enlargement of heart to us? St Benedict tells us: 'To the extent that one progresses in the religious life and in faith, the heart becomes enlarged'. There is, therefore, a relationship between the progress of our life in God through faith and the enlarged heart. It is within a living faith penetrated by the mysteries of God that this enlargement takes place.

Let us not deceive ourselves by blaming our lack of charity and joy in the Lord on a bad mood. What we lack is not a good mood, but the solid virtue of the *conversatio* well-established in a working faith; to believe in Christ is to follow him. Those who, following Christ, advance faithfully, will remain in him and in his love (cf. Jn 15:4ff); they will experience enlargement of heart. St John, young and fervent, experienced it himself and invites us to this same communion with Jesus, to friendship with the God-man! This then, is the *conversatio* of the monastic life of which St Benedict speaks (RB prol. 49). We feel the enlarged heart of St John quiver, we hear him speak to us of the experience he enjoyed in heart to heart communion with Jesus, we penetrate the rapture of his profound joy, measure his sovereign freedom, and grasp the radical transcendence of all creatures which that friendship brought him. He was able to taste and see how good Jesus is (cf. Ps 33:9).

But notice that St Benedict expresses himself in the very same way when he speaks of the ineffable sweetness of love which the monk experiences when he advances in his life of communion with God: he enjoys the unlimited bounty of the Lord, tastes the love of Jesus, savors the merciful condescension which makes him dwell in us; and his heart becomes enlarged.

This experience of God does not arise from our own deepest being, for our heart is far too petty to perceive the coming and the settling of the Triune God in our soul. This comes from the Spirit who dwells in us (cf. Rm 8:9). He alone can make us recognize the truth (cf. Jn 16:13) and speak to us of Jesus in an adequate manner, make us love and taste him, and move us to run 'with enlarged heart, the way of the commandments of God' (RB prol. 49).

Let us not, therefore, allow ourselves to be discouraged by difficulties. Of course we can slip or fall back on this road, and the spiritual heights frighten us; experience tells us this, and certain upsets risk stifling the voice of the Holy Spirit in us. But little by little, real progress stimulates our hope, and we are assured of the presence and the love of the Spirit. He will never abandon us to our forces alone.

How does he help us? First of all, he sustains our faith by showing us the mystery of the God of love, infinitely lovable, preferable to everything else. On this account he gives us the light of his gift of understanding. Through him, the right is given us, as dearly beloved children, to enter into the mystery of God, because he alone is 'the Spirit that searches all things, even the deep things of God' (1 Co 2:10). Thanks to the clear vision he lends us, we penetrate the great truths which it is his mission to reveal to us (cf. Jn 16:13). But he does not stop there. He is the Spirit of love, the divine Wisdom. What he teaches us, he makes us see as lovable and desirable. He gives us a taste for truth and shows us its beauty and perfect harmony. Dwelling in our heart, he understands it and teaches us exactly what we can bear and what is profitable to and a joy for us. For this reason he gives us wisdom, that faculty which adapts our spirit and our heart to what he wants us to hear and love. Instructed in this divinely lovable manner, our heart grows supple and open to the touch of the 'sweet Guest of our soul' (sequence for Pentecost) and grasps not only intellectually the truths of the faith, but experiences, as it were from within, their vital and attractive contents. The person of Jesus especially becomes for someone touched this way by the Spirit, as it were his vital center whose beneficial contact enchants him.

The wisdom of the Spirit changes our life from top to bottom, even without our knowing it and in spite of the distractions and pettiness inherent in our human condition. It exercises a divine force of attraction on the person who seriously seeks the Lord and wants to follow him.

The monk experiences all this with the gift of wisdom. His heart becomes enlarged and strengthened little by little and this makes him not only hardier on the sometimes rough road of the monastic life, letting him renounce his petty daydreams and questing after pleasure or honors, but it makes him become ever happier. Jesus' example becomes for him ever more admirable, more lovable, and following him, he is more fulfilled each day. St Benedict even promises him that in advancing faithfully in the practice of the monastic life, he will one day arrive at running with an ineffable sweetness along the narrow way where Jesus has gone before.

Once again, let us not be surprised if these lofty perspectives are not realized from one day to the next, and even if we experience the bitter disappointment of feeling our heart shrink from the idea of the exertions that must be made, along with the temptation to settle down, discouraged, halfway through the journey.

And as a matter of fact, we should not hide from ourselves the seriousness of these efforts. Because God does not stint in giving us His Spirit, He in turn requires everything. There can be in us no coexistence between the spirit of covetousness and the Spirit of God. Each day of our life requires of us a decisive choice: choosing the Lord and the demands of our conversion lie specifically in this. Let us therefore not deceive ourselves: if we want to arrive one day at running the ways of the Lord without looking back and with heart enlarged with that ineffable sweetness of which the Rule speaks, we cannot at the same time covet on earth the consolation of an easy life. However, 'the Spirit comes to the aid of our weakness...and we know that for those who love him, God collaborates in all things for their good' (Rm 8:26, 28). He sends us the 'Comforter' (Jn 14:16), our Advocate and Friend. Although we are tired, He is never tired. It is He who has chosen us from the crowd; He has attracted us to the monastic life. He is ready to help us if we seek the Lord with ardor and perseverance. If we will do this, the Spirit will hear our prayer even before we call on Him (cf. RB prol. 14–18). If we ask Him to 'bend what is rigid' (sequence for Pentecost), He will renew the gift of wisdom in our heart and it will be enlarged.

'May the God of Our Lord Jesus Christ, the Father of glory, give you a spirit of wisdom and of revelation which will make you truly understand! May He enlighten the eyes of your heart and make you see what hope His call opens to you, what treasures of glory His inheritance contains' (Eph 1:17f).

PREFER NOTHING TO THE LOVE OF CHRIST

THE HOLY SPIRIT unites the Father and the Son in His person. He is divine Love. In His love he envelops and carries along the whole of creation: both angels and men. He who searches the deep things of God (cf. 1 Co 2:10) knows the hierarchy of values and inspires the creature endowed with reason to love God above all things. He is infinite lovableness. Now God the Father was pleased to make all His fullness dwell in Christ (Col 1:19) and 'the Father loves the Son' (Jn 5:20) because nothing is more lovable. The Holy Spirit is the zeal of God; He will cause a person to grasp the impact of this truth in his life and will reveal to him the eminent place of Christ in his destiny.

A Rule of life written for people concerned with giving each value its proper place cannot pass over in silence the urgent call to love Christ, the prime Mover in their life. The monk is by definition a seeker of God; therefore a seeker of the way of God, of Christ (cf. Jn 14:6) in whom has appeared to us all the fullness of the Godhead. To Christ, therefore, belongs first place in all our aspirations. If the Rule of St Benedict gives us the admonition, repeated several times, to 'prefer nothing to the love of Christ' (RB 4:21) as the fundamental principle of our life, we must see in this the work of the Holy Spirit guiding its author. The divine influence makes itself felt throughout the chapters of the Rule and particularly in the way of teaching unique to St Benedict, far removed from any dry or theoretical expressions. Like an intelligent, loving teacher, one who knows people, he leads the monk to recognize in Christ the fullness of his own life. This profoundly theological way of acting makes us understand why he knew how to give each value its place, why he is so discreet in the matter of attaining secondary goals, and finally, why he does not attach himself to this or that asceticism or virtue as if it were an end in itself, but instead discreetly orders all a

201

person's effort to the love of Christ: 'Prefer nothing to the love of Christ' (RB 4:21).

THE ABSOLUTENESS
OF THE LOVE OF CHRIST

The love of God does not exclude others. The second command-ment says that we must love our neighbor as ourselves. Now, we love ourselves with total commitment. The love of our neighbor therefore commits us just as totally. We ought to give even our life for our brethren (cf. 1 Jn 3:16). Besides the love of God, therefore, here is a love which involves our entire being. But the love of God is special. Nothing can be preferred to Him, but every other love should be subordinated to Him and obey this supreme love.

The love of God, more precisely our love for God, should reign in us, absorb and enrich us all at the same time, and it is a stimulant for the fulfilment of every other love, on the condition that it be on the way of perfection. As its object, God, is the Absolute, so our love for Him should be absolute, without compromise, without adultera-tion. It is the spark born of the love with which God loves us and which He kindles in our heart through His Spirit (cf. Rm 5:5). This ardor has no limits on the part of the Beloved, on the part of God. It is, alas, limited by the inconstancy of our mortal heart.

If our love for God, as an act of our will, is necessarily limited, there can be no hesitation or compromise where creatures demand of us a form of attachment which is compatible with the absolute love due the Lord. The Rule cites as the foundation and first principle of our religion the commandment of absolute love: 'Before all things, love the Lord God with all your heart, with all your soul, and with all your strength' (RB 4:1). There can be no place for attachments which would want to divert or withdraw a part of our heart, a part of our soul or of our strength from the love due the supreme God. St Benedict translates this commandment into a formula which is humanly closer to us: 'To prefer nothing to the love of Christ' (RB 4:21). Like the 'all things' in the first commandment, the 'nothing' in the Rule declares with an unmitigated force the absolute precedence of the love of Christ. This 'nothing' of the Rule reminds us of the *nada* of St John of the Cross, liberty without obstacle to the action of the Spirit.

...AND THE LOVE OF OUR FAMILY?

Is this 'nothing' opposed to every other love outside the love of Christ? Will it be possible to love Christ more than one's family? We can distinguish between affective love and effective love. The force of passion—and love is one of them—may be greater in us for those united to us by blood than for anyone else. But if we have to choose between that natural love and the love due Christ, then the decision rests with neither flesh nor blood, but with the will. Jesus said so, using a Hebraism of striking force: 'If anyone comes to me without hating his father, his mother, his wife, his children, his brothers, his sisters, and even his own life, he cannot be my disciple' (Lk 14:26).

...AND THE LOVE OF OURSELVES?

The absolute preference to be given to Christ, therefore, puts into second place not only love for our family, but even love for our own life (cf. Lk 14:26). To love is to decide between ourselves and Christ and to choose Christ. The fourth chapter of the Rule, where St Benedict enumerates in detail the virtues to be acquired, is basically just a list of obligations incumbent on a disciple of Jesus, beginning with 'to love the Lord God with all one's heart, with all one's soul, and with all one's strength' (RB 4:1): the foundation, the sum, and the bond of the virtues.

Among the 'instruments of good works' is found this formula: 'to renounce oneself in order to follow Christ' (RB 4:10). It implies a requirement for preferential love for Him. In following Him we cannot at the same time seek ourselves, satisfy our self-will, our tastes, and our preferences. To run to Christ means to leave oneself behind. Nothing is more difficult. It is necessary to know how to discern within ourselves the assets of our personality, our individuality with its good qualities, and to leave aside everything that does not fit in with the demanding love of Christ. On the very first page of the Rule, St Benedict warns his disciple about the struggle he will have to wage, and he invites him to enlist to 'fight under the standard of the Lord Christ, our true King' (RB prol. 3). We accomplish this task during our monastic life: separating out in ourselves what is Christ's and what belongs to our corrupt nature, while renouncing what cannot be submissive to His sovereignty. Thus we participate in the sufferings of Jesus with persevering patience (cf. RB prol. 50) while struggling against the cause of His sufferings: the corruption of sin. If we are freed from our sins, it is by our sharing in that cross which we laid upon Him. Human beings are afraid of this combat. Tired of struggling, they imagine that in order to save their mental equilibrium it is necessary to accommodate themselves to the good and the less good they bear within themselves, stopping at a middle ground, a sort of balance they believe to be natural. Their principal motivation is seeking good psychological health. God, the Creator of their nature and the best of Fathers, however, assures a good human balance in an altogether different way: love is the supreme law of being.

THE LOVE OF CHRIST
THROUGHOUT THE RULE

The whole Rule illustrates this desire for God. As much a model of discretion and moderation as St Benedict is when it comes to applying the precepts of monastic observances, he nevertheless admits no half-measures concerning the principles of that life. The 'nothing' concerning the preferential love of Christ re-echoes in many phrases of the Rule, impregnated with that same total and undivided spirit. Already the first chapter gives evidence of this: there he simply refuses to consider the aberrant forms of monasticism open to discussion (cf. RB 1:12). The qualities demanded by obedience leave no place for evasions; the obedient monk cannot allow delay in his action, just as if God Himself had given the order (cf. RB 5:4). So it is understandable why the legislator does not waste time when the prior (cf. RB 65) or the deans (cf. RB 21) show themselves disobedient or the artisans show themselves arrogant (cf RB 57:2f) or when the vice of murmuring appears (cf. RB 34:6f). He shows the same severity in the matter of the vice of proprietorship: 'Let no one have the audacity...to possess anything as his own... absolutely nothing! (RB 33:2f, cf. 54:1, 55:16–18, 59:3, 51:1). A special vigor is displayed in leading the novice to a clear knowledge of what he is about to undertake and to lead him to a firm mature decision (cf. RB 58; 60–62). Anyone who reads the Rule is struck by the very frequent use of such vigorous expressions as *omnino*, *summus*, to emphasize the seriousness of a requirement. The threat of punishment in the case of disobedience likewise shows the gravity of the matter.

Why such insistence? For St Benedict, infidelities in the basic virtues of the monastic life are infidelities to Christ to whose call one must prefer nothing else. What in this world can one allow to take precedence over the voice of the Lord as He calls us (cf. RB prol. 19)? It is necessary, then, to run with the greatest haste and to act: *Currendum et agendum est* (RB prol. 44), *summa cum festinatione* (RB 43:1). In these and other similar phrases in the Rule, dictated by the fervor of attachment to Christ, one rediscovers the ultimate recommendation of St Benedict, the summary and epitome of the entire Rule: 'Let them prefer absolutely nothing to Christ' (RB 72:11).

THE OBEDIENCE OF LOVE

Should the absolute demand of love as the Rule prescribes it cast us into scruples about choices to be made? Should we be contorted in searching for the preferential love due to Christ, the love without shadows and without delay?

Here again the Rule answers these psychological questions. St Benedict repeats the same thought in a form closer to action: 'Obedience befits those who hold nothing dearer than Christ' (RB 5:2). 'Someone who obeys does not err', it is said. If ever that saying retained its full meaning, it is here: to act in all simplicity through obedience is necessarily to act through love of Christ. The joy of the Holy Spirit is the reward for heroic actions and even for the ordinary procedures of obedience; thus the monk rediscovers serenity of soul. The day we begin to understand that the generous love of Christ, in the final analysis, provides a solution to all our personal problems, small and great, then we will realize the extent to which it is a desirable grace to be able to follow Him and to prefer nothing to His love.

To prefer nothing to Christ: this is a desire that does not remain in the abstract; it gives each moment of our existence a character of determining energy which impregnates 'our hearts and our bodies, our senses, our words, and our actions' (collect) and orientates them firmly toward Christ, the supreme Goal of our desire, in an attitude of never-failing obedience. Of our desires! For even if our will remains united to Christ at its root, on the surface it can momentarily give in, swept along by the weakness of the senses and passions.

This preferential love does not attain its entire purity on the first day of our conversion; there is nothing surprising about this. The monastic life is essentially a patient search for that purity, and it would lose its reason for being if *conversio* were to end on the day of profession. This is not an arrival; it is a decisive beginning, a turning point marked by the recognition of the duty to give special place to the love of God, and it is a departure toward this great goal. This goal is clear from now on: nothing is comparable to Christ — not even close. St Paul had strong words for expressing this realization: 'For Him I have been willing to lose everything; I regard everything as refuse so as to gain Christ' (Ph 3:8). This is what preferential love is.

THE EXAMPLE OF THE APOSTLES

The spirituality of the monastic life is modelled on that of the apostles. Let us look at them; they follow Christ. Jesus became their life from the moment they discovered, with great amazement, this man vested with divine powers. They followed Him never to leave Him again. On Jesus' lips it was a great tribute to say of them: 'You who have followed me...' (Mt 19:28). They were not part-time apostles, going with Him one week and returning home the next. They stayed with Him. Jesus emphasized this at the Last Supper: 'You have remained constantly with me in my trials' (Lk 22:28); you will remain with me forever. They abandoned everything for him. Listen to Peter, upset at the Lord's judgment of the rich and their difficulty in entering the Kingdom: 'We have left everything and have followed you. What shall we receive?' (Mt 19:27). We know the answer that strengthened their fidelity.

Notice that Jesus was not cross with Peter for having momentarily given in by denying Him, because He knew the depths of His love; and again, even though the apostles did not follow in his footsteps from Gethsemani to the tribunal, Jesus did not doubt their will to follow Him. They knew that He demanded of them a total obedience and that they could not be His disciples unless they accompanied Him to the very end.

They followed Him by sharing His life of poverty and fatigue, His itinerant life, His insecurity about the next day, His persecuted life. They were celibates with Him or had left their wives if they had one.

Peter, after having left his family (cf. Mt 8:14), could say in all truth: 'We have left everything' (Mt 19:27), and according to the apostolic tradition, the apostles remained celibates after their Master departed to heaven.

Is it necessary to seek an explanation for their unshakeable fidelity? The apostles loved their Master because they felt loved by Him. They experienced the love of Christ in its human reality. This love must have been extremely attractive and fascinating. Of course they had a human, nationalistic hope for the restoration of Israel, mixed with a certain amount of selfishness, in view, but the case of Judas shows that this hope would not have been enough to sustain them and to cause their growing and ever more generous love to mature. For Judas, buried deeper and deeper in his own selfishness, the love of Jesus became a condemnation. The other disciples followed Him all the way to martyrdom. They held nothing dearer than Jesus Christ. The experience of the love of the loving Christ—this is the explanation of the apostles' life, their devotedness, their profound change, and this encourages us and gives us a good hope.

TO LOVE, TO FOLLOW CHRIST

The aim of the Rule is to teach us to follow Christ and to follow Him through love. Sin, the sloth of disobedience, has separated us from Him; through obedience we return to Him and follow Him (RB prol. 2). It is in the humility of submission to the superior out of love for God that we imitate Christ who was obedient for us even unto death (cf. RB 7:34, Ph 2:8).

If we examine the process of our decision to follow Him and to embrace the monastic life, we will discover His love for us, a love strong enough to change our direction. 'Follow me', He suggests to us. 'Only I am able to fulfil your need in love' (cf. RB prol. 19f). Little by little and in faith we have come, like the apostles, to know and admire Him more, we have become enthusiastic about Him, loved Him, and discerned His call and the fact that our happiness is to follow Him wherever He leads us. Little by little we have entered into intimacy with Him, and have begun to run the way of His commandments (cf. RB prol. 49). The Rule, we discover, teaches us on every page to love Christ, to remain in His company in times of consolation and joy as well as in times of trial, in the way that He wills: in His humility by making Himself the servant of our salvation, in His obedience toward His Father, in the abjection of poverty, simplicity, and renunciation of that which pleases nature, and this even to the Passion and the Cross. We realize that He has gone before us on this road and that now He is at our side. He helps us and does not abandon us to our own forces as long as we remain united to Him by confidence and trust.

He invites us to follow Him in His love for human beings, his brethren, and especially for those who share our monastic life. He wants us to follow Him in His concern for sinners, for the weak, for those who have not understood His love, for the sick of every sort. He came to serve and not to be served, and He wants us to know this. And finally, He asks us to follow him on this royal road.

Jesus wants us to be convinced that we are obeying Him when we obey those whom He has given us as His representatives and that we disobey Him if we disobey them. To the extent that our faithfulness increases, He opens our mind to understand progressively better how much our obedience is unified in Him, and that these are not two different loves, but only the love of Christ to which nothing should be preferred.

Monastic life should be understood as a commitment of the monk's person without reserve. His orientation does not allow half-measures. At profession he makes the definitive decision to love Christ with a unique love, concentrating on him his whole capacity for loving, by means of obedience, for detachment from what is superfluous, for perfect chastity, and for an openness of soul which makes him accept adversities, contradictions, and the cross even to the point of heroism in union with Chirst.

St Benedict knew that the experience of Christ's love practised through the perfect *fiat* of obedience is the only guarantee of true happiness. Mary, mother of monks, becuase she is the mother of all those who want to follow her Son, was the first to pronounce it. Thus he has repeated three times in his Rule this admonition which issues from his paternal heart: 'To prefer nothing to the love of Christ' (RB 4:21, cf. 5:2), ending it (RB 72:11) with the supreme recommendation: 'Let them prefer absolutely nothing to Christ'. Is the monk, the person of God, not the person of absolute love?

Happy is the monk who has found in Christ the center of his life and who, by that very fact has 'unified his heart' (Ps 86:11, Hebrew text).

THE FRUITS
OF THE SPIRIT

THE SEVENTY-SECOND CHAPTER of the Rule is a final exhortation, a little summary of its doctrine, but at the same time a final conclusion for the monk who has humbly and faithfully obeyed its inspirations throughout his whole life. More and more he gathers the fruits of the obedience which he adopted as his guide at the first steps of his monastic life (RB prol. 2) and which he has made the guiding light of his days. To conform himself to the will of the Lord was his purpose from the beginning; thus he has arrived at perfect charity whose triumphant hymn this chapter is.

St Benedict, always practical, lays out in just a few words in this little chapter the whole collection of charity's manifestations in its daily, true-to-life realization: behavior toward the brethren, toward the father, and toward Christ. To give charity its full dimensions is to succeed in practicing it in the most perfect and the most pure way. To be able, in all humility, not only to yield all honor to another, but still more, to load him with it (cf. RB 72:4), to accept one's neighbor as he is without demanding anything of him (cf. RB 72:5), to prefer, with perfect self-effacement, another's interests to one's own needs (cf. RB 72:6f), is for the monk to attain the fullness of charity! And finally, a humble and sincere love for the father of the family, the abbot (cf. RB 72:10), sets him above all pettiness and bickering! In spite of the sufferings inherent in the human condition, he tastes peace and deep joy of heart. Of course, the monk attains these heights of virtue because he prefers nothing to the love of Christ (cf. RB 72:11) for whom he has become capable of an admirable self-forgetfulness to the profit of the brethren.

In progressing in the practices of the monastic life, he succeeds in progressively simplifying his own efforts. His many good works are based on a disposition of charity which has become the predominant note of his personality. This love expresses itself in various, very attractive ways. St Paul calls them the fruits of the spirit (Ga 5:22f), and the seventy-second chapter makes one think automatically of the terms used by him: 'charity, joy, peace, longanimity, helpfulness, goodness, confidence in others, gentleness, self-mastery'.

Of course, St Benedict presents these fruits of the Spirit according to his personal manner and with all the common sense that characterizes him. The monk is like that tree planted beside the waters whose leaves never wilt and which gives its fruit in due season (cf. Ps 1:2). Like the tree, the monk grows, and more and more draws the sap of the grace of the Spirit in order to bear ever more beautiful fruits of charity, joy, peace, and all the virtues.

Planted in the enclosed garden of the monastery, he allows himself to be summoned by the Rule and takes in hand the instruments of good works presented to him by it (RB 4). He experiences more each day that the Spirit alone takes it upon Himself to draw from the tree of his life fruits which no human fecundity could produce by itself. The Spirit, acting freely in and through the monk's soul, by His operation divinizes the fruits borne by the human heart. These are truly fruits of the Spirit and, for that reason, they are the more precious and delicious. The simple and faithful observance of the Rule leads the monk to a state where he is indeed, the master of his actions, but where, still more, the Spirit is the real master. This is the state of that good zeal effected by the Lord in the person who is wholly abandoned to His sanctifying will. For the Lord, there is nothing more beautiful in His creature than a soul entirely filled and guided by the Spirit.

All the acts of this monk will thus find themselves under His ever-delicate guidance because he knows how to lend the ear of his heart to His calls (cf. RB prol. 1). Likewise his prayer will be more and more 'in the name of Jesus', that is to say, inspired by his Spirit, obedient to his invitations, and consequently, sovereignly efficacious because 'What you ask of the Father, He will give you in my name' (Jn 16:23).

These are the summits of doctrine and virtues promised to the monk by St Benedict (cf. RB 73:9) if he runs the path of monastic observance with perseverance and without looking back.

Let us not think that these summits are out of our reach. Even if our fidelity experiences eclipse, if our fervor flags, and we become buried in distractions, as long as our 'desire for eternal life' (RB 4:46) remains, that is to say, our aspiration for the true life, the only one worthy of the human creature called to ineffable marvels, as long as the fear of displeasing God remains active in the soul, the Spirit will work in us and show in 'his workman' (cf. RB prol. 24, ch. 7:70) the power of the unfailing love of the Father, at least at the hours of the sovereign choice of His grace, and will renew in him the ardor of his youth (cf. Ps 102:5). The monk who has entered into the daily routine of the Rule with all the strength and faithfulness of his soul, will be attracted irresistibly to the very depths of the source of the love of the Spirit which goes forth from the Son to the Father and will never cease to bear, in its season, the fruits of life.

CISTERCIAN PUBLICATIONS INC.

Kalamazoo, Michigan

TITLES LISTING

THE CISTERCIAN FATHERS SERIES

Texts and Studies
in the
Monastic Tradition

* Temporarily out of print

† Forthcoming

THE CISTERCIAN STUDIES SERIES

MONASTIC TEXTS

CHRISTIAN SPIRITUALITY

MONASTIC STUDIES

CISTERCIAN STUDIES

* *Temporarily out of print*   † *Forthcoming*

Saint Gregory Nazianzen: Selected Poems

Eight Chapters on Perfection and Angel's Song
(Walter Hilton)

Creative Suffering (Iulia de Beausobre)

Bringing Forth Christ. Five Feasts of the Child
Jesus (St Bonaventure)

Gentleness in St John of the Cross

Distributed in North America only for Fairacres Press.

DISTRIBUTED BOOKS

St Benedict: Man with An Idea (Melbourne Studies)

The Spirit of Simplicity

Benedict's Disciples (David Hugh Farmer)

The Emperor's Monk: A Contemporary Life of
Benedict of Aniane

A Guide to Cistercian Scholarship (2nd ed.)

*North American customers may order
through booksellers or directly from
the publisher:*

Cistercian Publications
St Joseph's Abbey
Spencer, Massachusetts   01562
(508) 885–7011

*Cistercian Publications are available
in Britain, Europe and the Common-
wealth through A. R. Mowbray &
Co Ltd   St Thomas House   Oxford
OX1 1SJ.*
*For a sterling price list, please consult
Mowbray's General Catalogue.*

*A complete catalogue of texts-in-
translation and studies on early,
medieval, and modern Christian
monasticism is available at no
cost from Cistercian Publications.*

*Cistercian monks and nuns have been
living lives of prayer & praise, meditation
& manual labor since the twelfth century.
They are part of an unbroken tradition
which extends back to the fourth century
and which continues today in the Catholic
church, the Orthodox churches, the
Anglican communion, and most recently,
in the Protestant churches.*

*Share their way of life and their search for
God by reading Cistercian Publications.*

Cistercian Publications
Editorial Offices
WMU Station
Kalamazoo, Michigan   49008
(616) 387–5090